Energy, Politics and Public Policy

Politics and Public Policy Series

Advisory Editor

Robert L. Peabody

Johns Hopkins University

Congressional Procedures and the Policy Process
Walter J. Oleszek

Interest Groups, Lobbying and Policymaking
Norman J. Ornstein and Shirley Elder

Mass Media and American Politics
Doris A. Graber

Financing Politics: Money, Elections and Political Reform, 2nd Ed.
Herbert E. Alexander

Invitation to Struggle: Congress, the President and Foreign Policy
Cecil V. Crabb, Jr. and Pat M. Holt

Implementing Public Policy
George C. Edwards III

The Supreme Court
Lawrence Baum

Congress Reconsidered, 2nd Ed.
Lawrence C. Dodd and Bruce I. Oppenheimer

The Politics of Federal Grants
George E. Hale and Marian Lief Palley

Energy, Politics and Public Policy

Walter A. Rosenbaum
University of Florida

Congressional Quarterly Press
a division of
CONGRESSIONAL QUARTERLY INC.
1414 22nd Street N.W., Washington, D.C. 20037

Jean L. Woy   *Acquisitions Editor*
Diane C. Hill   *Project Editor*
Maceo Mayo   *Production Supervisor*

Robert O. Redding   *Cover Design*

Printed in the United States of America

Library of Congress Cataloging in Publication Data

Rosenbaum, Walter A.
  Energy, politics, and public policy.

  Bibliography: p.
  Includes index.
  1. Energy policy — United States.   2. Power
resources — United States.   I. Title.

HD9502.U52R64   333.79′0973   80-29273
ISBN 0-87187-166-1

For
Brian and Doug

Preface

This book addresses two principal questions: first, how the American political system handles energy issues, and second, why it responds to energy issues as it does. The book deals primarily with energy *policies* and *politics*, rather than with the history of energy policy or the technicalities of energy production. History and technology have, I hope, been given appropriate recognition. I have used historical examples to illuminate the style of U.S. energy policymaking. And I have given attention to current U.S. energy technologies, energy resources, and "technical fixes."

My discussion focuses primarily on nuclear energy, petroleum, natural gas, and coal—those conventional energy sources likely to be prominent in policy conflicts for the immediate future. I give considerable attention to synthetic fuels because they represent the nation's most expensive and ambitious energy gamble of the 1980s. There is less mention of solar technologies only because they have been far less important in current energy policy debates when compared to other energy sources. I discuss energy conservation as a policy because I believe such a strategy can make a significant contribution to meeting future U.S. energy needs. Throughout the book, I have tried to maintain a balance in describing the interaction among policy issues, government institutions, policymakers, and energy technologies in the political process.

I emphasize the political theme for two reasons. First, I have been teaching a university course on United States energy policy and needed a book with a clear political focus. Second, I am convinced that the nation's capacity to resolve its energy difficulties successfully will depend as much on the creativity and resiliency of U.S. political institutions as on its technological skills or past energy experiences.

The book's organization and content follow from this concern for the political aspects of energy management. The first chapter describes the essential character of the U.S. public policy process, providing the reader with basic concepts for interpreting energy policies and issues. This chapter also suggests why energy has become such a salient political issue, what broad policy options confront policymakers, and what new challenges energy poses to government. The second chapter describes, in some detail, one major constraint on energy policy decisions—the basic U.S. energy resources, including available energy technologies and possible energy fixes. In the third chapter, I discuss another broad limit on energy policymakers—the "U.S. political formula." Chapter 3 also emphasizes how the values and structures of political institutions shape the behavior of policymakers in energy and other policy areas.

The succeeding chapters discuss three issues likely to be important when energy problems are brought before the government: acceptable trade-offs between energy production and environmental protection; proper distribution of the socioeconomic costs and benefits derived from energy use; and appropriate roles of government and the private sector in future energy management. I have chosen these three issues especially because they know no season. The final chapter treats some of the energy issues that will become important in the 1980s and attempts to establish some standards for the evaluation of future energy technologies and policies.

I had intended to write a book. Before it finally appeared in print, it had become a journalistic melodrama. That this book is now published is a tribute to the tenacity, good will, prudent criticism, and confidence of many people. First, a warm thanks to my professional reviewers: Cynthia Enloe, Richard Ganzel, Donald R. Kelley, Michael E. Kraft, Mark Rushesky, and Robert C. Saar. Having prevented many errors of omission and commission, these reviewers are hereby absolved of responsibility for those I insisted upon making despite their good advice. Second, special appreciation to Jean L. Woy, my Congressional Quarterly editor, for her early and dependable support. To Jean and to my text editor, Diane C. Hill, an admission also: you made me write a better book. Ed Artinian and Richard Lamb both merit recognition for their part in writing this book. I wish it were possible to have given them their proper reward.

Walter A. Rosenbaum

Contents

1

Something Like War:
The New Energy Politics

This is a tale of three cities. It is a story of Portsmouth, Ohio, where citizens gathered in May 1977 to pray that President Jimmy Carter might "listen to the voice of God and do what is right" and where, to their delight, Providence responded with a new nuclear fuel reprocessing plant. It is a story of Oak Ridge, Tennessee, which expected the same facility and received nothing. It is a story of how great presidential intentions, to no one's surprise, are born in Washington and perish in the political thickets beyond the Potomac. It is a brief episode in the nation's struggle to manage its energy resources that lays bare much of the character of the energy crisis.

The story begins on April 18, 1977, when President Carter delivered to the nation an energy message that most neither welcomed nor understood. The president described the nation's energy crisis as "the greatest challenge our country will face during our lifetime." He predicted that sacrifice would be required to balance the nation's ravenous energy appetite with its apparently dwindling energy resources. Carter spoke of high moral purpose, of national discipline, of survival:

> The most important thing about these proposals is that the alternative may be a national catastrophe. Further delay can affect our strength and our power as a nation. Our decision about energy will test the character of the American people and the ability of the President and Congress to govern. This difficult effort will be 'the moral equivalent of war'. . . .[1]

The president somberly explained the nation's precarious energy condition, the mounting disparity between U.S. energy demand and domestic reserves, and the many difficult but urgent programs that he was offering to restore a balanced energy economy. It was, as the president's advisers well knew, a complicated and unattractive message. "The real challenge," explained a close presidential aide, "is to get the people to put the interest of the country ahead of their own interests or the interests of their regions. The question for the president is whether . . . the people will believe that he is proposing something equitable for all."[2]

Events soon bedeviled the president's search for credibility when he attempted to reconcile two principles of his energy message with political realities. The first principle was energy conservation:

> . . . The cornerstone of our policy is to reduce demand through conservation. Our emphasis on conservation is a clear difference between this plan and others which merely encourage crash production efforts. Conservation is the quickest, cheapest, most practical source of energy.[3]

The second principle was "fairness," a constant theme of the president's appeal for support:

> Our solutions must ask equal sacrifices from every region, every class of people, every interest group . . . the sacrifices will be gradual, realistic and necessary. Above all, they will be fair. No one will gain an unfair advantage. . . . No one will be asked to bear an unfair burden.[4]

Soon the president was swept into a fierce regional struggle that set him at odds with his principles of conservation and equity.

Following guidelines declared in the president's address, federal energy planners decided that same week to cancel plans to build a mammoth $4.4 billion advanced nuclear fuel enrichment facility in Portsmouth, Ohio, as an addition to nuclear enrichment facilities already there.[5] The Department of Energy proposed instead the construction of an alternative $4 billion enrichment plant, using a newer technology, in Oak Ridge, Tennessee. The proposal seemed economically and scientifically sensible: the newer Oak Ridge facility would be energy conserving (using only one-ninth the power required to operate the older technology), and most of the scientists who had developed the newer technology lived in Oak Ridge, a national center of nuclear research. Moving the new system to Portsmouth would require several hundred million dollars in additional expenditure and, in economic terms, would not be "cost efficient."

Both communities had a substantial economic stake in the issue. The new facility would translate into billions of dollars in fresh capital, at least 3,700 temporary construction jobs, and perhaps 2,000 full-time jobs when the new plant became operational—but only for one community. Portsmouth was mired in economic recession, with the region's unemployment rate soaring as high as 16 percent. Oak Ridge, while apparently more prosperous, was nonetheless deeply troubled by the prospect that its huge Clinch River breeder reactor facility might be canceled with severe loss of federal jobs and private income. In other words, the new facility meant security against a hovering recession.

Then there was that promise. Approaching the end of the vigorously contested 1976 presidential election campaign and acutely aware of Ohio's crucial electoral votes, candidate Jimmy Carter left that state with a pledge to Portsmouth: "You can depend on me to provide the leadership to insure full funding" for the planned Portsmouth facility. To the people of Portsmouth, the Ohio congressional delegation, the governor, and the legions of regional economic interests, Jimmy Carter's commitment was irrevocable—no matter what the "cost efficiencies." But Oak Ridge and its allies insisted that science and economics dictated otherwise. Turning the rhetoric of the president's energy message against him, the governor of Tennessee asserted that placing the new facility in Ohio was "the moral equivalent of surrender." "We are in deep trouble," he fumed, "if Washington is considering starting a public works program to build nuclear facilities." What if the president divided the new facility between the two communities? "I want the whole thing—half is not enough," retorted Oak Ridge's mayor.[6]

For two weeks in early May 1977, the battle continued. In Portsmouth, the governor joined 500 citizens in prayer that the president might do "what is right"—and everybody knew what that meant. Most of the Tennessee congressional delegation, including Republican Senator Howard Baker (at that time minority leader), urged the president to keep the plant in Oak Ridge. Newspapers and other media in both regions implored citizens to write Congress and the president on behalf of their areas. Finally, on May 25, the White House announced that the president would "keep his campaign promise to the people of Ohio." The most substantial portion of the enterprise, and probably all of it, would go to Portsmouth. "We are disappointed," said Senator Baker. "We're just happy to get a chunk of it," said Ohio Senator John Glenn. The president said nothing.[7]

As a minor episode in the national effort to manage energy resources, the president's decision belied the "fairness" he had promised to achieve. His decision could not be justified either economically or scientifically: it overrode a commitment to Oak Ridge made by the federal government's own energy experts, and it turned on considerations having little relevance to the need for conserving energy. This is hardly surprising, however. Few public policies ever reach the lofty heights of intention charted for them by their sponsors. Indeed, no solution could have seemed "fair" or energy conserving to each of the squabbling interests. More important is the logic by which the president's decision was made. The nuclear facility was delivered to Portsmouth because its political geography had served presidential ambition: Portsmouth was in the right state, during the right election, when a candidate needed help.

The relevance of this tale to the energy crisis is direct and crucial: energy technologies have been regionally allocated by subordinating economic and scientific criteria to political calculations. In effect, the nuclear breeder technology has become a commodity in the political marketplace, hostage to a multitude of forces generated within the political arena. Its location has been swayed by calculations of presidential electoral advantage, by the relative influence of regional political leaders, by balancing political risks and rewards against economic and scientific factors. The calculus has been distinctively "political" rather than largely economic or scientific. In understanding the character of the U.S. energy crisis, it is this pervasive intervention of the political system in the development of a national energy strategy that marks the most significant element in the story.

ENERGY IN THE GOVERNMENTAL SETTING

The United States is moving rapidly into an era of vastly enlarged public authority over energy production and utilization. In effect, the nation's energy future is becoming increasingly the creation of public management. Energy supply and consumption have never been free of governmental management. However, governmental authority over the energy sector expanded so greatly during the 1970s that practically no domain of energy management remained unaffected by 1980. This expansion was prompted especially by the growing recognition of a national need to conserve rapidly dwindling U.S. energy reserves while also developing (when feasible) conventional and new energy sources, as well as by the need to moderate the disruptive economic effects of sharp increases in crude oil prices. Public energy management has been achieved, in good measure, by congressional legislation that is likely to endure through the 1980s, regardless of which political party controls the White House. As energy policy becomes ever more captive to the bias and values inherent in U.S. governmental structures, the energy crisis becomes as much a crisis of institutional adaptability as one of resource availability. The nation's political leaders, its public institutions, and its political style and political imagination have all been powerfully inspired by the presumption of unlimited resource availability. Effective future energy management requires that political institutions and leaders now reject this historical assumption. Otherwise, it will become a seductive, and ultimately disastrous, myth.

The energy crisis also requires the creation of a new national opinion climate congenial to wise energy use. The nation has been slow to accept the reality of national energy limits. When Jimmy Carter delivered his first energy message in April 1977, Americans had already experienced the sudden economic shock of the 1973 Arab oil embargo (gas rationing was then discussed for the first time since World War II), national addresses by Presidents Nixon and Ford warning of shrinking energy reserves, and constant media attention focused on national energy problems. However, polls taken immediately following the president's austere message disclosed that half the public still refused to believe that the U.S. energy crisis was "as serious as the president describes."[8] After the president's fifth national energy message in September 1979, the portion of the public believing that "the oil shortage is real" increased by 9 percent to a total of 35 percent.[9] So long as this divergence persists between the public and its leaders over the perceived nature of the U.S. energy situation, a decisive governmental response is inhibited.

Even if the nation's public officials and citizens shared an understanding of the country's grave energy condition, an effective U.S. energy policy would nonetheless be difficult to achieve. A major reason is that all energy policies create, in different ways, major benefits and costs for social groups and individuals. When benefits and burdens are reckoned, policies will always produce winners and losers, richer and poorer, contented and aggrieved. So potent a source of conflict is this apportionment of gains and penalties from energy policies that it constitutes a major focus of this book. In particular, as government assumes greater responsibility for national energy policy, controversies over the benefits and costs involved in energy management will arise. These struggles raise three fundamental questions that will be examined in later chapters.

First, what should be the balance between public and private benefits from energy policies? Energy planning requires that public officials decide, in economic terms, the "mix" between public and private benefits that will result from a particular policy. A public benefit—often called a "public good"—is "indivisible and cannot be captured by any social grouping whose membership does not include the whole community."[10] Environmental protection is such a public good: if Washington requires national auto emission controls, everyone can enjoy cleaner air. In contrast, a "private good" from energy policy selectively benefits specific social or economic groups—not everyone will be able to share the reward. If the federal government builds new superhighways, the automobile industry and highway construction firms benefit, but the nuclear power industry does not. Controversy often arises because public benefits from an energy policy may limit private ones. For example, if Washington raises standards for auto emissions—in effect declaring clean air to be more of a public good—the cost of automobiles will increase, their sales will diminish, and income will be denied to private interests such as the automobile industry and its stockholders.

Second, how should the economic costs and benefits of a policy be distributed among those affected by it? This is the "distributive" aspect of energy policy. Controversy over energy policy is often rooted in conflict among social groups, states, regions, and economic sectors concerning the "fair" distribution of economic penalties or rewards. Policy struggles often boil down to efforts by each side to increase its own benefits or to shift the resulting costs largely, or entirely, to someone else—no matter how significantly the controversy may be dignified by other arguments. For example, the cost of petroleum increases and, with it, the price of electricity. Should all the customers of an electric utility be forced to share the rising costs? Should the poor, those least able to bear the increase, be permitted reduced rates? Should the most inefficient users of electricity pay more to encourage energy conservation? Or should the utility itself bear some of the cost rather than pass it entirely to its consumers? Such distributive issues are often the most difficult to resolve in energy planning.

Third, what should be the respective roles of government and private business in future energy development? As government plans the development of new energy sources, or the restructuring of existing energy production, a recurring debate focuses on how much of this development should be conducted by government and how much should be left to private industry. Will the United States create a more vigorous, economical, and efficient solar power industry if Washington itself largely organizes the research, builds the technology and production facilities, and markets the power? Or will private business do a better job even though the industry will require profit incentives from the government and demand considerable independence in its work? Would some mix of responsibilities between the two sectors be the best answer? Such issues will become more frequent as the United States increases its investment in solar energy, synthetic fuels, and other unconventional energy technologies.

Resolving these issues requires concern for several other matters. Public policies evolve by a process of decisionmaking, a *cycle* of public policy. The various phases of public policy are each important as a distinctive policymaking arena with a constellation of forces that shapes the eventual design of the policy. And the various policymaking phases are related. It is helpful, therefore, to think of energy issues as moving through this policy cycle and to observe how the phases of policymaking contribute to each issue outcome. In addition, those who make policy must do so within a set of *constraints*—elements in the setting of governmental action that shape and limit policy choices. We will emphasize two kinds of constraints: "situational constraints"—those imposed by the nature of the nation's energy reserves—and "the political formula"—the institutional characteristics of the U.S. government, the political style of public officials, and the nation's historical experience that influence policymaking. We will observe how these constraints constantly impose themselves upon governmental deliberations.

Scholars describe both the policy cycle and policy constraints in somewhat different, although roughly similar, terms. Borrowing from several approaches, we can describe usefully yet briefly the character of the policy cycle and its constraints before turning to the energy issues that are the focus of this book.

THE CYCLE OF PUBLIC POLICY

Regardless of where they originate, public policies usually move through five identifiable stages: *agenda-setting, policymaking, implementation, assessment,* and (sometimes) *termination.* "Public policy" is used in the sense that Robert Eyestone defines it: a decision by authoritative government officials that "continues, terminates, or modifies an existing program, or . . . responds to a specific and limited aspect of a broader social issue."[11] The emphasis is on "authoritative decisions"—the determinations of public officials that carry the sanction of law, custom, or broad public acceptance. Each stage has its distinctive political setting and its particular combination of participants and political strategies that shape the character of policy conflict at that point in the policy cycle.

Agenda-setting

The United States has always had energy policies but not an energy policy. This mosaic of energy policies means that at any given time federal participation in energy management varies among energy sectors and, consequently, energy issues are at different stages of policy development. Generally, energy management within the U.S. government has been highly sectoral: policy evolved in response to the economic and political peculiarities of different energy sectors, not by some broad design that was sensitive to the relationship among energy sectors. "Coal politics is independent of oil politics, which is independent of nuclear politics," writes David Davis of past energy policy development.[12] This segmentation has led to different, often inconsistent, approaches to energy utilization. The federal government has left the coal mines to prosper or perish in an unmanipulated market, but has protected the domestic petroleum industry from foreign competition (through oil import quotas) while encouraging maximum production (through oil depletion tax allowances). Nuclear energy has been heavily subsidized by the federal government; solar technologies have been largely ignored.[13] In the end, some policies, such as those affecting nuclear energy, are so firmly rooted in American political practice that proponents of alternative approaches must first move existing policies through the termination stage of the policy process before they can introduce a new proposal to the cycle. Others, like solar energy policy, are only now moving from the policy agenda through the policy formulation phase. No matter how far U.S. energy policies have progressed in the policy cycle, however, they all began at the crucial stage of agenda-setting.

The first task of policy proponents is to promote their concerns to the "official agenda" of the government. This agenda, suggest Roger Cobb and Charles Elder, is the "set of items explicitly up for the active and serious consideration of authoritative decision makers."[14] Destiny rarely delivers an issue to its place on the public agenda as did the Three Mile Island, Pennsylvania, nuclear facility accident of March 1979. That incident forced Congress into a thorough inquiry on public standards for U.S. nuclear plant safety. More commonly, issues find their place on the agenda as the result of organized, sustained, and skillful activism by issue publics—those segments of the general public that are organized to promote their interests to the government's attention. The issue must be given public visibility, invested with an aura of importance and urgency, and made to seem so salient that it is in the best interest of public officials (and not simply in the public's best interest) to act on the matter. The politics of agenda-setting is competitive. Hundreds of interests struggle simultaneously to advance their particular concerns to governmental attention; only a handful succeed. The struggle to promote issues to the governmental agenda is fiercely competitive, in good part because public officials have limited time and resources to invest in the hundreds of issues that routinely clamor for their attention. And only some of the important issues they might consider will seem relevant enough to them personally to merit their full attention. Thus, officials are necessarily selective in the energy issues they address.

Skill in the business of agenda-setting is crucial to the energy crisis because there is no such thing as an "energy issue," but instead *energy issues*. The president's legislative proposals following his first energy address in April 1977, for example, arrived in Congress as a blizzard of 113 different measures dealing with matters as diverse as taxes on "gas guzzling" cars, federal support for research on geothermal energy, improved safety standards for power plants, federal income tax incentives for home insulation, and stringent energy standards for federal buildings. In fact, managing the nation's energy resources now embraces so complex a breadth and diversity of policy matters that energy management may be unprecedented among all domestic policy areas.

The rigors of issue promotion are suggested by the years that solar power advocates wandered in the political wilderness. For at least a decade prior to 1970, proponents of solar technologies had urged Washington to give solar power a place, however modest, in the federal energy research budget. Only after the 1973 Arab oil boycott did the federal government specifically appropriate funds for solar research. In 1974, the initial fiscal year of the solar program, it commanded only $45 million (3 percent of the federal energy research budget) compared to $1 billion (80 percent) and $110 million (9 percent) for nuclear power and coal technologies respectively.[15] Not until the Solar Lobby organized in 1974 and the grave fuel shortages of winter 1976 occurred did significant appropriations begin to appear for solar research. It was the deftly managed political campaign culminating in Sun Day 1978—a national demonstration of support for solar research—that finally triggered major federal investments in solar technology. President Carter's budget for fiscal 1980 contained more than $690 million for new solar programs, an 84 percent increase over the 1978 budget and the first appreciable reward for two decades of political activism by a small cadre of committed solar activists.

Agenda-setting is also important because energy issues quite often are competitive. One issue's promotion to priority on the official agenda may effectively diminish, or erase, the prospects for another's success. Consider the controversy surrounding the disposal of radioactive wastes from nuclear power plants. Opponents of nuclear power plant expansion insist that the federal government must carefully assess the danger to public health and the environment from different disposal techniques and must set rigorous standards for approving any method of waste disposal. By 1980 no disposal techniques had been federally certified. In 1979, Washington confronted the task of deciding what standards should be used to approve disposal procedures—in effect, an attempt to define "acceptable risk" in waste management. The stricter the standards, the less likely that any disposal technique will be judged acceptable. The federal government cannot easily adopt rigorous standards of acceptable risk and simultaneously pursue a program of rapid expansion in the nuclear power industry. In short, the nuclear power industry's future may be hostage to resolution of the waste disposal issue.[16]

Agenda-setting is continuous. Every congressional session begins with a determination by the leadership of issues to be given priority in that Congress. The annual State of the Union message declares the president's personal policy agenda for Congress and the American people. Federal agencies regularly prepare their own agenda of "action items" for immediate attention. From the perspective of the nation's more than 100,000 politically active groups, getting an issue on the official agenda changes its political character. Official agendas, observes Robert Eyestone, are "commitments to action." He explains:

> When an issue has reached an official agenda, there is a good chance that it will be resolved because there is such a commitment and because politicians would not usually have allowed an issue onto an official agenda they controlled unless they felt they could respond satisfactorily.[17]

Moreover, an issue that reaches the official agenda is almost always guaranteed a major share of public attention. "Indeed," remarks Eyestone, "official agenda setting may in some cases precede public agenda setting." Getting a matter on the official agenda is the first and fundamental test of an issue public's effectiveness. Failing this, the group's work remains largely ritual sustained by hope.

Policymaking

In his first energy message in April 1977, President Carter proposed that the United States reduce its dependence on imported oil "by making the most of our abundant resources such as coal" and, especially, by increasing substantially domestic coal production by 1985. In an attempt to hasten conversion to coal, the White House sent to Congress a proposal to tax existing industrial and utility boilers that burn oil or natural gas. In May the proposal reached the House Ways and Means Committee. By mid-July, the committee reported a weakened version of the White House plan to a special Ad Hoc Select Committee on Energy that in turn further gutted the bill before reporting it to the full House. Together with other revised portions of the president's initial energy proposals, the House passed the tax scheme in early August.

Meanwhile, the tax plan was also struggling through the Senate. The Senate Energy and Natural Resources Committee pondered the bill and reported an even weaker version of the original proposal in late July. The full Senate then approved this measure, together with other portions of the energy proposal, in early September. Like many other aspects of the president's original energy package, the versions of the coal conversion tax produced by each congressional chamber differed from the White House proposal as well as from each other. A conference committee was not appointed to reconcile conflicts between the two chambers' existing measures until mid-1978. The White House liked neither bill. The conference committee, finding each bill unsatisfactory and able to compromise not at all, threw out both measures.

A year after the original White House proposal, the president was left with no legislatively authorized coal conversion tax. During the multiple committee deliberations, more than a dozen competing bills and hundreds of amendments had been pondered at the behest of coal lobbyists, environmentalists, electric utility and industry spokesmen, energy and environment bureaucrats, and White House aides. Thousands of pages of testimony had been given, weeks of congressional floor debate had taken place, and hundreds of hours had been invested in the proposed measures by policymakers. And it would all have to be done again.[18] It may not inspire an observer to learn that the coal bill's fate is a typical example of U.S. governmental policymaking, but this abbreviated narrative does capture some of the realities of the policy-creating phase of the policy cycle.

It is helpful in understanding energy policy to look more closely at several aspects of the complex business called governmental policymaking. First, as Hugh Heclo observes, policymaking should be regarded as a "course of action or inaction" rather than as a single, specific decision.[19] An official may declare policy, but the creation of that policy involves a constellation of activities—sprawling across the whole institutional structure of government and spilling over the formal boundaries separating governmental from non-governmental institutions—made in response to an issue. And that response might be inaction. All these activities may yield no formal legislation, presidential order, or agency regulation. As in the case of the coal conversion tax, the policy response of Congress was temporarily to do nothing and, consequently, to leave policy as it currently existed. Nevertheless, this is also a "policy."

Second, policymaking involves two kinds of associated activities which Charles O. Jones has labeled policy "formulation" and "legitimation."[20] Formulation, he suggests, includes the setting of goals for action (the desired objective of policy), the creation of specific plans and proposals to meet these goals (such as proposed legislation, presidential messages, and committee reports), and the selection of means for implementing these proposals (such as enforcement by federal agencies, federal grants or assistance to private interests, and new research on an issue). The making of federal policy for energy has included, as we have seen, a presidential proposal with a goal to increase domestic coal consumption, a plan to tax electric utilities and industries that burn oil and natural gas, and an implementation strategy that (in the White House version) includes enforcement by the Department of Energy. The formulation of policy may stretch over days or even years, involve few or many actors and institutions, and be relatively harmonious or controversial. In any case, it is usually complex:

> People in government discuss what has happened, they do research, they interpret the available data, they prepare proposals, they meet and discuss some, they check with people outside government, they determine what is possible, they make proposals, they develop strategies, they co-ordinate, they refine proposals, they seek support.[21]

Eventually, officials act or they do not. If they produce a program, it must be legitimated—invested with sufficient authority to evoke public acceptance, if not enthusiasm. Customarily, government programs are legitimated when written and declared according to whatever constitutional and statutory procedures are appropriate. The program has become legal: the president issues an executive order, or Congress passes a bill that is then signed by the president, or a federal agency issues regulations as required under its enabling legislation. Yet government policies may be so unpopular that they are widely ignored or deliberately flaunted despite their apparent legality. So public officials strive to rally support for programs by investing them with all kinds of symbolism intended to heighten public approval. It is ritualistic for sponsors of new programs to assure us that they will serve the "public interest" and that the "majority of Americans" support them. Thus, legitimation marks the progression of a governmental response to an issue from the formulation stage to formal "public policy."

Third, policymaking rarely hews to its design as prescribed by law, or dictated by organizational charts, or otherwise formally declared. There are "informal" structures of policy formulation—the pattern actually observed—as well as "formal" structures—those more or less officially prescribed and technically followed. Individuals with no officially designated role or authority may actively participate in and strongly influence policy deliberations. The flow of governmental decisions moves easily and routinely across institutions and political levels, crosses the boundaries between the public and private sectors, and assumes a character departing in many ways from norms dictated by law or myth. A Senate committee may formally deliberate, then write and report a measure to the full Senate chamber according to rules prescribed by the Senate. But the committee's own staff, interest group spokesmen, members of the White House staff, and federal agencies affected by the measure will certainly have participated in drafting the legislation.

It is essential to accord these informal procedures their due in explaining energy policy. A minor episode during the formulation of federal regulations for surface mining is illustrative.* In mid-1979, the president's Regulatory Analysis Review Group—a group of executive branch staff members responsible for reviewing the economic impact of new federal regulations—publically criticized the Office of Surface Mining Reclamation and Enforcement in the Interior Department for drafting regulations alleged to be excessively expensive to the coal mining industry. The White House group cited figures as support for its allegations. Several members from the Office of Surface Mining, the butt of this criticism, were then approached by an environmental group offering help. The environmentalists had obtained a recent log of White House telephone calls (routinely kept by virtually all White House staffers) that contained numerous conversations between the White House reviewers and the National Coal Association, an industry lobbying group. Figures used by the White House group turned out to be identical to controversial data published previously by the coal industry in its effort to discredit the new regulations.

Armed with this information, the Office of Surface Mining counter-attacked its White House critics. It appeared virtually certain that the White House group had borrowed the coal industry's data and was, in effect, its ally. The White House group, charged the Office of Surface Mining, had "no business" working in such intimate collaboration with a special interest group. The data should have been more critically examined and the White House more objective. Eventually, the White House dropped the issue. No one familiar with the episode, however, was surprised at the consultation between the coal lobby and the White House group or between the environmentalists and the Office of Surface Mining. Groups and individuals with no official role in policy formulation, including those with "no business" in the policy process, commonly make it their business to be involved.

Finally, national attention in governmental policy formulation and legitimation is focused primarily on the presidency and the Congress, where policymaking is the predominant activity. In reality, policy is often formulated and legitimated in the federal bureaucracy and sometimes in the judicial branch of government. Nonetheless, Congress and the presidency remain the preeminent national institutions for defining the broad issues and programs from which public policy is fashioned. The media constantly observe the activities of

---

* The author is indebted to several participants in this affair for sharing this story with him.

the White House and Congress, enlarge these activities into national prominence, and interpret and report them to the public. These institutions usually assume the leadership in setting the issue agenda, formulating the broad design of policy, and educating the public to the meaning and significance of policy issues. The public role of these institutions is extremely important. The public's understanding of energy issues, and especially the public's belief in the credibility of the energy crisis, will depend in large measure on how it reacts to the personalities, activities, and institutional images of these governmental entities.

This abbreviated description merely suggests the nature of policy-making. We will elaborate upon its character as we explore various energy issues in later chapters. In any event, the policy process reaches far beyond policy formulation or legitimation to policy implementation, where its character is affected by other crucial institutions, actors, and political forces.

Implementation

Congress or the president may officially declare public policy but, ultimately, they are only proclaiming their intentions for policy. What the government does about an issue depends largely on the manner in which a policy is translated from the language of law, presidential order, or judicial ruling into action. Another complex of government institutions and actions is required for action—what is called "implementation" and which Eugene Bardach has compared to an "assembly process." It is, he writes, "as if the original mandate . . . that set the policy or program in motion were a blueprint for a large machine that has to turn out rehabilitated psychotics or healthier old people or better educated children. . . . Putting the machine together and making it run is, at one level, what we mean by the 'implementation process.' "[22]

Several aspects of the implementation stage in the policy process are crucial in understanding energy policy. First of all, to speak of policy implementation is usually to discuss the bureaucracy. Indeed, the "government" doing something about an issue often means that the bureaucracy is working to solve the problem. "It is the bureaucrats who control the personnel, money, materials, and legal powers of government," write George Edwards and Ira Sharkansky, "and it is they who receive most of the implementation directives from executive, legislative, or judicial decision makers."[23] So pervasive is this bureaucratic presence during the policy implementation stage that it must be given sustained attention in energy policy, as in any other policy domain, in order to understand the forces shaping the policy's development and impact.

The federal bureaucracy exercises power in many ways during implementation. The bureaucracy can interpret, alter, delay, promote, reevaluate, and otherwise shape much of the substance of a policy while implementing it. In effect, bureaucracy is a force separate from Congress or the president that shapes the meaning of policy. This is why President John F. Kennedy frequently remarked that he knew what the president intended to do about an issue but he was not sure what the "government" would do. Administrative influence in shaping policy derives from several sources. Congress and the president routinely delegate to administrative agencies the responsibility for filling in the details of law, for translating general objectives into specific programs, and for making many necessary technical determinations that Congress, or the White House, is not competent to make.

A routine delegation of authority is found in Section 546 of the Energy Policy and Conservation Act (1978) that instructs the Department of Energy:

> The Secretary ... shall establish and publish energy performance targets for Federal buildings and shall take such actions as may be necessary or appropriate to promote to the maximum extent practicable achievement of such targets by Federal buildings.

To comply with this mandate, in March 1979 the department produced a draft ten-year plan that ran to several hundred pages and included within its detailed provisions almost all aspects of new federal facility construction. Authority delegated to administrators for elaborating the law frequently results in the writing and enforcement of regulations or guidelines that often become a voluminous library of new laws in and of themselves. The Department of Energy's (DOE) regulations for the "uniform and equitable" allocation of petroleum products alone ran to 3,000 pages of specifications, exceptions, and special provisions.[24] Congress and the president also bestow on bureaucrats considerable "discretionary authority" to implement law— that is, the right to make choices in applying a general law to specific instances. Federal law requires DOE to file an "environmental impact statement" for any program that will "significantly affect the quality of the human environment," yet DOE, like other agencies, is left with considerable discretion when deciding *which* activities will actually require such a statement.

Sometimes deliberately vague or confusing legislation is tossed into the laps of bureaucrats because legislators, or the White House, will not or cannot agree on how to settle an issue or implement a policy. In effect, all actors concerned about the interpretation of an issue are invited to fight the battle on another front. When faced with an apparently irreconcilable controversy in Congress or the White

House, policy formulators can often put together a broad program with vague details for its implementation that allows a crucial policy to keep its place on the public agenda. Yet this also leaves administrators with the critical, difficult, and often thankless task of resolving what the president or Congress cannot—or refuses to—decide.

The broad authority commonly given administrators to both shape and implement policy details illuminates yet another important aspect of energy policy implementation: the struggle among those affected by a policy often quickly shifts from the legislative or White House arena to the administrative structure where it continues unabated. Virtually all those concerned with a policy's formulation and legitimation will be found, as Eugene Bardach suggests, once again involved during the implementation phase:

> Die-hard opponents of the policy who lost out in the adoption stage seek, and find, means to continue their opposition when, say, administrative regulations and guidelines are being written. Many who supported the original policy proposal did so only because they expected to be able to twist it in the implementation phase to suit purposes never contemplated or desired by others who formed part of the original coalition. They, too, seek a role in the administrative process.[25]

A policy struggle may continue with undiminished ferocity within the administrative structure, but it nevertheless differs in one important respect from the earlier policy conflict within Congress or the White House. The administrative battle transpires behind the opaque exterior of the executive branch, usually unobserved and unknown to all but a relative handful of administrators, interest group activists, members of Congress, and possibly White House officials. The public is less likely to be a major force in shaping the outcome of conflict in this more cloistered arena.

Finally, the implementation process requires almost constant oversight by Congress or the president if policy is to be enforced with reasonable speed and effectiveness. Delay, confusion, unanticipated and inexplicable events, competing demands for the time and resources of public officials—all are typical in policy implementation. Issues compete not only for position on the public agenda or for legitimation, but also for priority in the policy implementation process. Inevitably, some issues are shoved to the periphery of attention. When policy formulators fail to give sustained attention to ostensibly important programs, the result is often bungled implementation. Consider the following examples as disclosed in a review of the White House Federal Energy Office in the early 1970s by a Senate subcommittee:

—Senior White House officials "never saw" a report by the office that revealed domestic oil production had peaked. The president should have increased imported oil quotas in response, but no quota increase was ordered.

—The office prepared a standby emergency rationing plan for gasoline in 1972 which then "disappeared." William E. Simon, the president's chief energy adviser, had claimed no such plan existed.

—The emergency gas rationing plan, when finally found, had been sent to the General Services Administration, which has no responsibility for energy mangement.[26]

In short, within the White House and executive agencies there are agendas for implementing policy as well as for formulating it. Policies die not only by deliberate extinction at the hands of opponents during policy formulation; they also expire from neglect or abandonment during the implementation process.

Policy Assessment

Policy is implemented. Its impact on society stretches across years, spans a multitude of different social groups, and triggers a complex process of policy assessment. Those affected by policy inevitably form opinions about the desirability of its ramifications. Many consequences are unexpected, others take years to surface, and some will seem more or less tolerable in reality when compared to expectations. Broadly speaking, policy assessment involves all those procedures and institutions involved in evaluating the social impact of government policies, judging the desirability of those impacts, and communicating this information to the public. One possible consequence of assessment is policy reformulation: government alters the substance of policy in response to demands resulting from those who have experienced the impact of a policy and find changes essential. In this perspective, the policy process often seems to move through a continuing cycle of adoption-implementation-assessment-reformulation. Reality is seldom so simple, but in most issue domains, including energy, these recurrent policy cycles are common.

Policy assessment is, in reality, a commonplace civic activity in which several public institutions play an especially important role. The federal courts are one of these institutions. Practically all major federal policies will be brought before the courts for review and interpretation at some time or another. Often the courts must interpret the law, decide when it applies in a particular case, or decide if it violates constitutional principles—all of which amounts to defining the law's meaning and significance. In the mid-1970s, for instance, opponents of the nuclear power industry asserted that Congress acted unconstitutionally in passing the Price-Anderson Act (1957) that limited the insurance liability of nuclear facilities to $540 million in any nuclear power plant accident. Had the federal court agreed, existing and future nuclear power plant operations would have been disrupted severely. But the court, rejecting this challenge to the law, declared that the act did not violate constitutional "due process." In effect, the act had been further clarified and expanded; its constitutional status, especially, had been assessed.[27] Judges are important in the policy assessment process because major laws are often ambiguous in detail, seemingly contradictory in intent, or incompatible with constitutional principles—all legitimate reasons for requiring judicial interpretation. Administrators also may appear to misinterpret or mis-apply the law; a judicial review is often the essential remedy.

Federal judges often go to elaborate lengths to minimize their role in the policymaking process. But intervention is often unavoidable and, consequently, the federal bench contributes much to defining the impact and significance of energy policies through its interpretation and application of the law. Consider the following Supreme Court decisions that have substantially defined the meaning of energy laws in the last several decades:

—In 1954 the U.S. Supreme Court decided, against the argument of the Federal Power Commission (now the Federal Energy Regulatory Commission), that the Natural Gas Act invested the commission with the authority to regulate the price of natural gas from all com-panies selling to interstate pipelines. The effect was to make the Natural Gas Act an instrument of federal control over most domestic natural gas production.[28]

—In 1975 the Supreme Court declared that the federal government's legislation setting conditions for the leasing, exploration, and production of petroleum on the Outer Continental Shelf prevented coastal states from asserting control over such matters. In effect, the federal laws were interpreted to give Washington sovereignty over the Outer Con-tinental Shelf.[29]

—In 1972 the Supreme Court affirmed that the Atomic Energy Commission (now the Nuclear Regulatory Commission) was required by the National Environmental Policy Act (1969) to consider fully the environmental impact of a nuclear power plant before permitting its construction. The "spectre of a national power crisis," it concluded, did not permit a "black-out of environmental consideration."[30]

So predictably are judges involved in defining the impact of policy that, as a practical matter, policy assessment should always include careful review of judicial responses to policy after administrative im-plementation.

The mass media are equally strategic in policy assessment. They can publicize policy impacts, translate impacts into relevant, understandable terms for citizens, and make judgments about impacts and publicize them—all of which amounts to a civic education in the consequences of public policy. Eventually, opinion climates may emerge that are congenial or hostile to policy reassessment. The media seldom deliberately fabricate or otherwise distort information about policy impacts (although public officials constantly assail them for it). Yet the media, in an important sense, often do "create" impacts and issues from impacts.

It is often not the actual consequences of policy that lead to public assessments and, perhaps, demands for policy reformulation, but only those impacts identified and amplified through the media. The media's selectivity in defining what is "news" means that consumers of any particular medium are likely to have, at best, an incomplete view of policy impacts in any policy arena. Air pollution was a life style in large eastern industrial cities and smog wreathed Los Angeles for decades before the severity of national air pollution was "discovered" by the media in the early 1970s. The feeble impact of existing federal air pollution policy during the 1960s, in effect, was not a general public concern until the media—one of the most salient among public institutions—made the matter public property.

Organized interests also play a crucial role in the dynamics of policy assessment. Indeed, it is often only through the specialized channels of communication created by organized interest groups that many Americans learn about the impact of public policies most relevant to them. Of course, this is what organized interests are, in large measure, created to accomplish. Collectively, these organized groups—numbering in excess of 100,000—constitute an elaborate system of social intelligence. Gathering information from specialized staff, organized interests regularly monitor policy impacts in their own policy domains, constantly inform members about these impacts, and persistently seek to mobilize members to respond in ways deemed beneficial to the group. Consider a recent pamphlet sent to its members by the National Wildlife Federation, a large and influential environmental interest lobby. The pamphlet explains how the Resource Conservation and Recovery Act (1976) helps communities control toxic wastes. It also includes advice on how the act could affect members' local communities and what role citizens might play in the act's enforcement:

> Citizen opposition to the siting of facilities in their communities is another problem. In fact, a facility in Illinois, with valid State permits, was closed down by court order in September 1978, as a result of local opposition. The citizens' role in the new regulatory program is of ultimate importance, not only from the environmental viewpoint but for the continued prosperity of their communities. Without support by citizens to site new waste treatment, storage, and disposal facilities conveniently located for industry, some in-

dustries generating hazardous waste may choose to locate elsewhere. Lack of citizen involvement and support for effective hazardous waste management can thus have an adverse economic impact upon communities.[31]

This information, an informal policy assessment, translates what might otherwise seem to be a complicated and unfamiliar law into terms immediately relevant to citizens and their local communities. Thousands of such information networks exist within and among the organized interest groups that monitor and assess government programs and policies. Such communication, influencing millions of Americans daily, is often the most important factor in mobilizing groups to support exising policy or to demand policy reformulation.

Other institutions are, in different degrees, active in policy assessment. Public officials themselves are constantly attempting to persuade citizens as to whether or not various public policies are working or are desirable. Academic institutions and private research groups provide a perpetual flow of policy assessment information to consumers. In short, policy assessment is a continuing social process.

Policy Termination

Public policies, like government agencies, only seem immortal. The oil depletion allowance and federally regulated natural gas prices perished within the last decade. The congressional Joint Committee on Atomic Energy, once the unsleeping evangelist for nuclear power, was abolished by Congress in 1977. While it is more common for policies to be reformulated through incremental tinkering by public officials, the direct termination of energy policies, like any policy, does sometimes occur. Policies may be terminated because they are judged to have failed, because they have outlived their successes, or simply because they are no longer deemed necessary. Advocates of policy change often face a fierce struggle to terminate existing policies or programs. In the energy domain, it is an essential battle because often new energy issues can claim position on the policy agenda only if old policies are terminated.

Policy termination, suggests Peter deLeon, is the "deliberate conclusion or cessation of specific government functions, programs, policies or organizations."[32] The current effort to create a national energy strategy has spawned a host of termination efforts directed at various public policies deemed incompatible in some manner with the nation's energy interests. The petroleum industry has campaigned to remove all federal price controls on domestic oil production. Advocates of solar power and other "soft" technologies have assaulted federal subsidies for most nuclear and fossil fuel energy technologies. Many energy industry spokesmen seek to end so-called excessive federal environmental regulations on strip mining, coal and oil combustion, and other energy uses that involve possible risks to the environment.

Terminating any government policy is a forbidding affair because, as deLeon observes, "the coalition of internal and external elements that can be marshalled against an organization's or a policy's termination is formidable."[33] Groups seeking policy termination must assume heavy "start-up costs" in order to make their effort effective: they need the political resources sufficient to vanquish the coalitions already arrayed in support of a program. More specifically, opponents of a program must demonstrate convincingly that the policy has failed or, at least, has dubious merits. They must overcome the reluctance of policymakers and bureaucrats to admit a mistake. Advocates of change must formulate a plausible alternative program and then persuade strategic public officials, and perhaps large segments of the public, that their proposal is a better way.

Furthermore, agencies and their allies defending a program, almost always powerful agencies with influential friends in high places, can counterpunch. An agency can dispatch its own lobbyists to Congress where legislative friends of the agency or a particular program will rally to its defense. A bureaucracy also can turn for help to the multitude of organized groups with a vested interest in an endangered policy or program to counterattack critics. And agencies are able to unload a torrent of propaganda, often disguised as "public information," in defense of their own programs. Thus, the termination battle evolves into a campaign that can stretch across years or even decades.

Often the battle for policy termination succeeds only when some set of events, most often unexpected, forces both the public and federal officials to recognize the magnitude of a policy's failure or the risks of its continuation. For example, a major public opinion poll conducted immediately after the Three Mile Island nuclear power plant accident indicated that public support for further nuclear energy development dipped from a 1977 high of 69 percent to 46 percent in April 1979.[34] Opponents of nuclear power may not have actually wished for the accident, but they nevertheless welcomed its broader public consequences for the demise of nuclear technology development.

Termination politics are important in energy policy because, as we will observe, the success of one new policy often seems to require the elimination of another. A case in point is utility rate pricing. Conservation of electric power is inconsistent with "block rates," sliding rate schedules, and other practices that promote power demand by awarding preferential rates to large energy consumers. Generally, public utilities and state regulatory commissions that commonly set utility rates will have to abandon a multitude of traditional pricing policies if conservation is to replace promotion as an industry policy. Termination politics is likely to be evident in the energy policy cycle for many years, if not decades, as the nation slowly redefines the purpose of its energy programs.

Policy as a Process

To view policymaking as a set of different phases is useful, but to recognize it as a process is essential. The phases of policy are interactive: decisionmaking at one phase of a policy affects later policy decisions. Consider the conflict that erupted early in 1979 over which federal agency the Senate would designate to conduct research on the health effects of radiation. This minor dilemma appeared to be a matter of policymaking at the formulation stage, but the outcome would also shape, in critical respects, the character of policy implementation. Opponents of nuclear power development wanted to remove authority for this radiation research from the Department of Energy (DOE) and invest it in the Department of Health, Education and Welfare (HEW, now Health and Human Services, HHS), while friends of the nuclear industry preferred that DOE retain the program. Both sides recognized that DOE was more congenial to the nuclear power industry and was therefore less likely than HEW to promote vigorously research that would seriously impair the continued growth of that industry. In effect, the character of future federal research on the health effects of radiation would probably depend not only on how agencies carried out the law but on which agency inherited the implementation responsibility. The formulation of policy would directly affect the character of its implementation. We will observe many other linkages, or interactions, between policy phases in later chapters.

Policymaking is so continuous a process in government that it is almost never the case that any program, or set of programs, is completely finished or immutable. While federal regulation of natural gas prices is gradually terminating, federal policies to encourage utilities to switch their boilers from natural gas to coal are just being implemented, and programs to produce natural gas from coal are still being formulated—each a phase in the development of a national natural gas policy. Even confining attention to a single program suggests that, most often, it is likely to be moving through the policy process. Experience with the federal solar energy program proposed by President Carter in 1977 and passed by Congress in November 1978 was scarcely a year old when it became apparent that tax incentives for homeowners to switch to solar heating were inadequate. Proposals went before Congress to reformulate the policy almost before it had been implemented and assessed. The persistence of the policy cycle within any particular policy area indicates that policy battles are seldom settled, that change is virtually a constant in public policymaking, and that one should never say "never" when anticipating the future of existing government programs.

CONSTRAINTS ON THE POLICY CYCLE

To govern is to choose, but the choice is never free. Policymakers' freedom of action is bound by circumstance, by time and resources, by the rules and institutions through which they act, by inherited tradition, and by the attitudes, values, and assumptions (often unarticulated) that they bring to policy problems. Collectively, the factors commonly limiting governmental response to policy issues—and thereby limiting policy outcomes—are called "policy constraints."

Situational Constraints

In energy, as in other policy areas, there are certain "givens" about policy problems that must be accepted as practically unalterable. These "situational constraints" relate to the physical characteristics of the resource involved, the distribution of the resource, the existing technology for its utilization, the time frame in which solutions to various issues must be formulated, and other factors that are largely beyond the policymakers' ability to change. Situational constraints are arbitrary. Often unavoidable and undeniable, they force the direction of policy. It is possible, of course, for policymakers to disagree about the existence of a situational constraint—as in debates concerning the duration of adequate U.S. petroleum reserves—but the acceptance of situational limits on action is often essential to a determination of an appropriate policy response.

Situational constraints everywhere affect energy policy. Two "givens" in the energy policy formula that no one can deny—the relatively enormous abundance of domestic coal and the primitive state of U.S. technology for creating energy from unconventional sources like the wind or sun—make it almost imperative that national energy planning for the next 20 years rely heavily on coal, and fossil fuels generally, rather than on unconventional sources. These and other situational constraints on policymaking contribute so substantially to defining policy options in energy management that they will be given sustained attention in the next chapter.

The Political Formula

There are customary "rules of the game" by which public officials resolve policy issues. Policymakers also give significant recognition and weight in their decisions to commonly accepted "political elements" that reflect the nation's inherited cultural outlook on the notion of proper government and the role of public institutions in solving policy problems. We will call these elements the "political formula" by which policy problems are resolved. The political formula is, in effect, a constellation of factors that must somehow be combined in the process of defining public policy.

Much of the political formula is so common to government decision-making that it is considered normal, almost natural, in making public policy. The wary administrator in the Interior Department, who before writing a new coal leasing regulation telephones the National Coal Association to sound out its views, is practicing a common bureaucratic ritual: work with your agency's "clients" in the evaluation of new regulations. Yet this practice, endemic to bureaucracy, does help to define what policies will likely emerge from administrative deliberations because some of those groups whose views should be considered in the policy process are identified.

Political formulas are no less powerful for being inarticulate or unacknowledged. The senator who blandly assumes that the technological capabilities of the United States will sooner or later enable it to recapture its independence from imported petroleum is captive, whether he realizes it or not, to a seductive national assumption that shapes his energy policy preferences. The political formula, like situational constraints, is so essential to understanding the cycle of policymaking that we will examine these political elements more closely in Chapter 3.

CONCLUSIONS

This has been a chapter of themes. One is that the U.S. response to its own energy crisis will be shaped to a large extent by the character of its political institutions. A second is that the making of energy policy is a cycle of governmental decisions made within constraints imposed by the character of energy resources as well as by the nature of the political institutions and actors involved. A third theme—perhaps less obvious than the others—is that in policymaking the means shape the ends. To understand what government will do about energy problems, one must first examine the manner by which those decisions will be made.

What follows is variation, elaboration, and illustration of these themes in the context of different energy resources. It is an attempt to provide political depth and breadth to issues upon whose resolution the economic, social, and political stability of the United States is likely to depend. From one perspective, this is an introduction to public policymaking. In a different light, it is also an introduction to energy policy. Either way, it is an effort to make the governmental process more comprehensible.

NOTES

1. *New York Times,* April 20, 1977.
2. *New York Times,* April 19, 1977.
3. *New York Times,* April 20, 1977.
4. Ibid.
5. *New York Times,* May 2, 1977.
6. *New York Times,* May 3, 1977.
7. *New York Times,* May 26, 1977.
8. *New York Times,* April 29, 1977.
9. *New York Times,* September 18, 1979.
10. Matthew A. Crenson, *The Un-Politics of Air Pollution* (Baltimore: Johns Hopkins University Press, 1971), p. 137.
11. Robert Eyestone, *From Social Issue to Public Policy* (New York: John Wiley & Sons, 1978), p. 100.
12. David H. Davis, *Energy Politics,* 2nd ed. (New York: St. Martin's Press, 1978), p. 12.
13. Robert Stobaugh and Daniel Yergin, eds., *Energy Future: Report of the Energy Project at the Harvard Business School* (New York: Random House, 1979), chaps. 1, 7; Davis, *Energy Politics,* chaps. 3, 7.
14. Roger W. Cobb and Charles D. Elder, *Participation in American Politics* (Baltimore: Johns Hopkins University Press, 1972), p. 86.
15. U.S., General Accounting Office, *The Magnitude of the Federal Solar Energy Program and the Effects of Different Levels of Funding,* Report No. EMD-78-27 (Washington, D.C.: U.S. Government Printing Office, February 2, 1978); and Walter A. Rosenbaum, "Notes From No Man's Land," in *Energy and the Environment,* ed. Regina Axelrod (Lexington, Mass.: Lexington Books, 1980).
16. Ralph Nader and John Abbotts, *The Menace of Atomic Energy* (New York: W.W. Norton & Co., 1977), chap. 9; and Sam H. Schurr et al., *Energy in America's Future* (Baltimore: Johns Hopkins University Press, 1979), chaps. 12, 17.
17. Eyestone, *From Social Issue to Public Policy,* p. 88.
18. Congressional Quarterly, *Energy Policy* (Washington, D.C.: Congressional Quarterly Inc., 1979), pp. 5, 32, 89, 96.
19. Hugh Heclo, "Issue Networks and the Executive Establishment," in *The New American Political System,* ed. Anthony King (Washington, D.C.: American Enterprise Institute, 1979), p. 89.
20. Charles O. Jones, *An Introduction to the Study of Public Policy,* 2nd ed. (North Scituate, Mass.: Duxbury Press, 1978), chap. 4.
21. Ibid., p. 48.
22. Eugene Bardach, *The Implementation Game* (Cambridge, Mass.: The MIT Press, 1977), p. 36.
23. George C. Edwards III and Ira Sharkansky, *The Policy Predicament* (San Francisco: W. H. Freeman and Co., 1978), p. 293.
24. *New York Times,* June 24, 1979.
25. Bardach, *The Implementation Game,* p. 38.
26. *New York Times,* December 14, 1973.

27. Carolina Environmental Study Group v. Atomic Energy Commission, 431 F. Supp. 230 (W.D.N.C. 1977).
28. Phillips Petroleum Co. v. Wisconsin, 347 U.S. 622 (1954).
29. U.S. v. Maine, 420 U.S. 515 (1975).
30. Calvert Cliffs Coordinating Committee v. Atomic Energy Commission, 449 F.2d 1109, 1 ELR 20346 (D.C. Cir. 1971); certiorari denied, 404 U.S. 942 (1972).
31. U.S., Environmental Protection Agency, *Everybody's Problem: Hazardous Waste* (Washington, D.C.: U.S. Government Printing Office, 1979).
32. Peter deLeon, "A Theory of Termination in the Policy Process: Roles, Rhymes and Reasons" (Paper delivered at the annual meeting of the American Political Science Association, Washington, D.C., September 1-4, 1977), p. 2.
33. Ibid., p. 28.
34. *New York Times,* April 12, 1979.

2
Constraints:
Resources and Technology

In 1956 M. King Hubbert, a young petroleum geologist with Shell Oil Company, informed a meeting of petroleum experts in Texas that his calculations indicated U.S. domestic oil production would peak in 1971 and gradually decline thereafter. Later, these projections would be proven nearly correct. But in 1956, they created only disagreement and considerable argument. Shell Oil eventually deleted this prediction from Hubbert's paper; new graph curves were prepared that increased estimated oil reserves and postponed peak production until the turn of the century.

Apparently, uncertainty within the petroleum industry about the predictions did not prevent their general acceptance. This revised estimate subsequently was adopted by the National Academy of Sciences in its January 1963 report to the president on domestic petroleum resources. Almost from their inception, efforts to comprehend the magnitude of U.S. energy problems have been complicated by confusion, argument, disbelief, and suspicions of deliberate data manipulation.

The U.S. energy crisis is distinctive among the nation's serious domestic problems for the lack of a substantial national consensus on its very existence. Expert studies of the national energy economy usually describe an ominous derangement of energy supply and demand—"massive, dangerous, and growing" in the words of President Carter's third national energy address—while large segments of the public regard the energy problem as ambiguous, exaggerated, and certainly debatable. Nonetheless, this intractable reality eventually will demand full recognition. Moreover, its character imposes both immediate and long-term constraints upon the possible policy responses.

Current energy policy can be best understood by first examining U.S. energy production and consumption levels, the status of various energy production sectors, and the character of available energy technologies. These constraints define the limits and options that confront energy policymakers.

A FORESEEABLE CATASTROPHE

Amid constant national debate over the authenticity of the energy crisis, a constant theme in virtually all expert analysis is the imperative for action. The U.S. Congressional Budget Office offers a restrained but urgent appraisal:

> The long-term problem is simply that the growth in oil and gas consumption exceeds the growth in proven reserves—both domestic and foreign. Before long, we will have to shift to new energy sources or face drastic reductions in our standard of living. . . . The fact that almost half of the oil consumed in the United States is now imported creates national security risks and makes our economy highly vulnerable to shocks from outside, especially because the supply and price of oil are to a great extent dictated by an international cartel.[1]

In fact, most of the western industrial nations find themselves facing a common energy destiny. "The free world must drastically curtail the growth of energy use and move massively out of oil into other fuels with wartime urgency," concludes a global energy analysis by the Massachusetts Institute of Technology. "Otherwise, we face foreseeable catastrophe."[2]

The language of crisis loses its bite in constant repetition. The problem is better illuminated by examining aggregate estimates of current U.S. energy use and the imported petroleum component. We will then examine the constraints this situation places upon policymakers and, paradoxically, why millions of Americans and many public officials fail to be persuaded by the data on U.S. energy production and consumption.

U.S. Aggregate Energy Use

In June 1979, Philip Reid, a salesman from California's San Fernando Valley, was reading a book in his car, waiting for gas at the end of a line that stretched for blocks. "Look at all those cars," he remarked to a newspaper reporter. "You know what's happening? We're witnessing the demise of the American way of life."

Table 2-1 U.S. Energy Demand, Domestic and Imported Supply, 1976 and 1985 Projections (In quadrillion Btu)*

	1976	1985
Demand		
Residential/Commercial	27.4	39.0
Industrial	27.0	33.1
Transportation	19.4	25.5
Total	73.8	97.6
Domestic Supply		
Oil	19.6	20.3
Natural Gas	19.2	14.4
Coal	13.7	18.8
Nuclear	2.0	6.8
Other	3.1	4.3
Total	57.6	64.6
Imported Supply		
Oil	15.4	32.5
Natural Gas	1.0	.5
Total	16.4	33.0

*An average rate of growth in energy demand is assumed to be 3 percent from 1976 to 1985.

SOURCE: Office of Technology Assessment, *Analysis of the Proposed National Energy Plan*, 1977.

A massive level of energy consumption is the foundation of contemporary U.S. society. Its magnitude sets Americans apart from all other industrialized nations. The United States consumed the equivalent of 1.8 billion tons of oil in 1978, more than the combined petroleum consumption of the next six industrialized western nations.[3] Globally, the United States consumes one-third of the world's total energy production with about 6 percent of the world's population.

The United States can no longer satiate its energy appetite without increasing its dependence on imported petroleum. This dependence, spawned by a widening gap between domestic energy demand and production, will increase progressively if countermeasures are not taken soon. The short-term growth of energy consumption and its consequences are suggested in Table 2-1. The table describes the projected growth of domestic energy demand from 1976 through 1985 based on national patterns since 1956, as estimated by the U.S. Office of Technology Assessment (OTA). By 1985 U.S. energy demand will have increased by 32 percent, domestic energy supplies by 12 percent, and dependence on foreign energy by 101 percent, according to OTA.

Table 2-2   Estimated U.S. Energy Production by Major Source, 1978

Source	Percentage of Total U.S. Production
Coal	24.8
Crude Oil	30.1
Natural Gas	35.3
Electricity*	9.8

* Energy sources for electric power generation: coal 44.4 percent, nuclear 12.5 percent, petroleum 16.5 percent, natural gas 13.8 percent, hydroelectric 12.7 percent.

SOURCE: U.S. Department of Commerce, Bureau of the Census, *Statistical Abstract of the United States, 1979.*

All sectors of U.S. society depend on the major conventional sources of energy. Table 2-2 indicates the relative share of domestic energy production contributed by these major energy sources in 1978. An enormous amount of energy is essential for the production of the basic goods and services required by Americans to maintain an adequate standard of living, but much of the nation's energy production has catered to America's household deity—consumer convenience. What most Americans consider an "adequate" standard of living in large part consists of consumer goods and services deemed luxuries throughout most of the world.

Energy use often serves convenience:

—In 1976, for example, most of the 156,000 tractors sold in the United States had enclosed cabs with standard air conditioning and heating units; other accessories such as installed music, television, and CB radios often were available.[4]

—Between 1946 and 1968, the U.S. population increased by 43 percent and the gross national product by 59 percent. During the same period, however, production of electric household items increased by 1,040 percent, air conditioner units by 2,850 percent, synthetic fibres by 5,980 percent, and nonreturnable bottles by 53,000 percent.[5]

The automobile is the ultimate energy convenience. In 1980 there were approximately 119 million automobiles in the United States, or one car for every two citizens. The auto birthrate, at approximately five million per year, far exceeds that of the population. One-half million Americans commuted more than 50 miles daily one way in 1977. In 1975, more than 9 out of 10 heads of U.S. households drove to work. (In sprawling Los Angeles, the average commuter drove 20 miles each way.) Not surprisingly, the transportation sector uses 26 percent of all U.S. energy and accounts for half its annual petroleum consumption.[6]

Some Implications

The growing disparity between U.S. energy supply and demand creates several constraints that will affect future energy policy:

—*First, an energy supply adequate for all future domestic needs is unpredictable for the first time in U.S. history.* For two centuries, Americans have conducted their cultural, economic, and political life secure in the assumption that energy would always be there, in the abundant American earth, when national need demanded it. The truth is brutal and may banish forever the national confidence in energy resources that equal national intentions. It is a shaking of one foundation to American society.

—*Second, the national energy condition requires immediate remedial action within the next decade.* Many estimates suggest a global petroleum shortage by the late 1980s if world petroleum demand continues to increase at present rates. Even with maximum output by the Organization of Petroleum Exporting Countries (OPEC), world petroleum reserves are not expected to remain adequate beyond the first decades of the year 2000, well within the lifetime of children born in the 1960s and 1970s. The United States cannot assume there will be an adequate global petroleum reserve while the nation slowly struggles toward energy conservation. Rather, the United States has perhaps a decade at most to reorient its energy economy before circumstances will demand progressively more drastic, difficult, and disruptive policy choices and governmental responses.

—*Third, energy management will affect all sectors of U.S. society and will require national energy planning on an unprecedented scale.* Energy policy can no longer be regarded as sectoral, an approach that isolates one energy sector from another and often produces inconsistent, if not contradictory, policies and programs. Furthermore, the energy implications of policies, such as environmental programs, that were previously considered to be outside an energy context will have to be weighed for their energy implications. And federal welfare payments to the elderly, indigent, unemployed, and other dependent social groups will have to take account of rising energy costs. Washington will feel impelled to move increasingly into new areas of public management—such as the regulation of household construction—where consumer values and preferences will be challenged, and sometimes opposed, by energy planners.

—*Finally, government will be forced, for the first time, to impose deliberate and sustained energy conservation measures.* Americans have had no prolonged national experience with mandatory energy conservation. Fuel rationing during World War II was relatively brief and was accepted with a public confidence that it would be nothing but a temporary sacrifice. Even so, the rationing policy was a mixed success at best. Obligatory conservation as a life style may be as difficult for government to achieve as it is essential to the nation's survival.

Why Can't the Experts Agree?

The public and its officials might find these grave policy constraints easier to accept if there were less argument over the actual magnitude of current or projected U.S. energy resources and demand. The national energy debate abounds with disputes concerning the severity of the nation's energy problem. This disagreement only breeds delay and suspicion among policymakers. It erodes the credibility of public officials seeking to rally public support for essential policy decisions. The dispute over energy data is an energy issue itself, intruding upon all discussion of specific energy programs.

One reason experts disagree about the precise character of national energy supplies is the difficulty of estimating the amount of an energy resource that is physically present in the earth and how much can be technically and economically recovered. Furthermore, participants in policy disputes often fail to clarify whether they are talking about the total amount of the energy source (the "reserve") or the amount thought recoverable (the "resource").[7] Neither of these quantities is easy to estimate. The Office of Technology Assessment (OTA), for instance, suggested that U.S. uranium supplies in 1977 might vary between 250,000 tons and 740,000 tons at a price of $10 per ton. If the price increased to $30 a ton, the recoverable supplies might be as low as 680,000 tons or perhaps as high as 3,370,000 tons— but OTA could not predict the actual future price of uranium.[8]

Disagreements also arise over the size of the U.S. energy supply because, until recently, the federal government and most states have relied heavily on the oil and natural gas industries for such data. As the oil sector's credibility with the public has decreased, so has that of the public agencies using their data. When the government has attempted independent assessments, the resulting data often have been grossly inconsistent with industry figures. In 1977, for example, the Interior Department compared its figures for undiscovered petroleum with those estimated by the petroleum industry and concluded that actual reserves might lie somewhere between 48 and 130 billion barrels—an enormous range of uncertainty.[9]

The nation's energy future is further beclouded by the use of different forecasting models that attempt to predict energy supply and demand. These econometric models, especially beloved by economists, create different energy futures, or scenarios, as a way of understanding how present policies might affect future energy conditions. To create these scenarios, the economist or other expert makes assumptions about the future rate of energy demand, the price of energy, population growth, industrial expansion, and a multitude of other factors that influence energy utilization and consumption. Computers then manipulate these variables in different combinations, producing many permutations for an outcome—in effect, casting alternative energy futures for different hypothetical circumstances.

Such modeling permits the analyst to estimate how changes in present policies might affect future energy resources. Nonetheless, the data always can be bent to fit the shape of one's prejudice— the models are no better than the quality of the assumptions underlying them. Most experts attempt to make assumptions responsibly, but the models nevertheless are subject to misinformation, implausible assumptions, and deliberate errors. Ultimately, the scenarios conjured up by the computers—the visions of future energy conditions—are only a fabric of suppositions held together with the glue and paper clips of "if" and "assuming."

One consequence of econometric modeling is that predictions of future energy conditions almost always err. In April 1979, for instance, President Carter predicted that his proposal to decontrol domestic petroleum prices might raise the average cost of domestic gasoline by a moderate seven cents per gallon; and in September he assured the nation that his total energy program would cost $142.2 billion. But world petroleum prices increased at a more rapid rate than expected. By late 1979, the White House admitted domestic gasoline would increase at least 15 cents per gallon, and the total energy package might cost $10 billion more than originally predicted.[10]

Another consequence of modeling energy futures is that partisans of different policies and political parties almost never resist the temptation to manipulate some element in the models to their advantage. In 1974, for example, the Nixon administration, anxious to construct the Clinch River breeder reactor facility, used an econometric model that predicted that the project's benefits would exceed costs by an impressive $14.7 billion. In 1978 the Carter administration, committed to terminating the project, performed its own analysis. By altering the model's estimate of future energy demand as well as other factors in the original calculation, the Carter analysts demonstrated that *no* economic benefits would result from the project.[11] Similarly, in 1977 the Republican Caucus in the House of Representatives countered

President Carter's National Energy Plan with its own version asserting, among other things, that the nation's actual energy resources far exceeded the administration's estimate. The nation was left to decide whether it had Democratic or Republican energy resources—a situation explicable only because the "facts" of future energy conditions inherently are subject to different interpretations.

Controversy over energy data will continue, but essentially it is a dispute over the magnitude of the U.S. energy problem and not its actual existence. Constraints on policymakers flow not only from the general character of the energy problem, but also from the particular physical qualities and conditions of the individual energy sectors.

CONVENTIONAL ENERGY SOURCES

The United States primarily depends on crude oil, natural gas, coal, and nuclear power for its energy production. Petroleum remains the most important of these sectors, but derangements of supply and demand, triggered by the petroleum shortage, have occurred in every energy sector. Thus, the U.S. energy crisis actually turns out to be a set of energy crises. Petroleum remains the most critical sector, however, due to its dominance in both U.S. energy production and consumption.

Petroleum

America's energy problems were real long before they became apparent. They began in the 1950s when, for the first time in its history, the U.S. demand for petroleum began to exceed domestic production by significant amounts. The United States has depended increasingly on imported oil as domestic production has fallen further behind soaring domestic demand. The nation's crude oil production peaked at approximately 3.5 billion barrels in 1970 and thereafter has declined steadily. (One barrel of crude oil contains approximately 42 gallons of petroleum.) The 1973 Arab oil embargo merely signaled the dangerous implications of a situation that had existed for nearly two decades.

The extent of the domestic petroleum deficit can be appreciated by comparing U.S. petroleum data for the period 1970 to 1980. In 1970, the United States imported approximately 24 percent of its total petroleum consumption; by 1980, this figure had doubled to almost one-half of total petroleum consumption. Although energy demand moderated somewhat in the late 1970s, the nation's addiction to imported crude oil grew at an annual average of 20 percent between 1970 and 1980.

Faced with the need to reduce domestic demand for petroleum and with mounting dependence on foreign oil, the strategies available to policymakers are limited. The United States can consider four alternatives in various combinations. First, the nation can attempt to increase domestic petroleum production. The most attractive new sources are the Outer Continental Shelf (OCS) and Alaskan petroleum reserves, both part of the U.S. public domain. Estimates suggest that OCS—the border of submerged coastal lands stretching from 3 to 200 miles off U.S. shores—may contain 200 billion barrels of oil, approximately twice the total amount of petroleum produced in the United States since the 1960s.[12] Major OCS reserves are located in the Beaufort Sea off Alaska's North Slope, the Gulf of Alaska, the northeastern edge of the Gulf of Mexico, and the Baltimore Canyon and Georges Bank off the Atlantic Coast. Total Alaskan petroleum reserves may exceed 15 billion barrels; the Alaskan North Slope alone contains the continent's largest oil field with 9.6 billion barrels of proven reserves, approximately 29 percent of total proven U.S. petroleum reserves.[13]

Moderate additional petroleum also may be squeezed from existing or new fields in the continental United States. The petroleum industry has urged Washington to provide financial incentives, such as a generous federal income tax deduction, for investment in new oil exploration. The industry also wants similar incentives to recover "old" oil, reserves left in now abandoned oil fields because a company's cost for obtaining the reserves is prohibitive.

Second, the United States may attempt to replace crude oil consumption with increased use of currently available alternative fuels. Since 1973, all comprehensive federal proposals for energy management have called for the replacement of significant crude oil consumption by other domestic energy sources in various combinations. President Carter's 1977 National Energy Plan (NEP) promised to achieve a 66 percent increase in domestic coal production by 1985, as well as substantial (although lesser) increases in natural gas production and nuclear power generation. By supplementing these alternative sources with mandatory conversion of most electric utility and industrial boilers to coal, the NEP expected to reduce the rate of domestic crude oil consumption by approximately 20 percent by 1985. In mid-1979, the Carter administration proposed governmental incentives for increased synthetic gas and oil production from coal and for new production from heavy oil, shale oil, and natural gas.

Energy planners almost inevitably see some glimmer of salvation from dwindling petroleum stocks in coal and natural gas because

these energy reserves are the nation's most abundant remaining resources. Although nuclear energy accounted for a modest yet significant
portion of U.S. energy production in 1980, its future looks increasingly
bleak. Governmental strategies for energy management do not rely
solely on increased production, however. Indeed, no reasonable assessments of short-term energy demand suggest that the United States
can reduce dependence on imported oil unless extensive energy conservation also is initiated.

Energy conservation, especially petroleum conservation, is the
third strategy that is proposed consistently as an essential component
of national energy planning. Estimates suggest that perhaps 30 to
40 percent of present U.S. energy consumption could be saved by
requiring increased auto engine efficiency, improved home and office
insulation, conservation of waste heat in industrial processes, and
energy-efficient residential construction.[14] A recent study at the Harvard Business School suggests widespread opportunities for impressive
energy savings:

—Residential buildings account for 20 percent of total national
energy consumption. Standard insulation of older houses (more than
one-third of all U.S. dwellings contain practically no insulation) could
reduce residential energy requirements by 20 percent of current consumption.

—Perhaps 20 percent of total U.S. industrial energy consumption
could be eliminated by the use of cogeneration, a technology that
simultaneously produces electric power and steam heat.

—Recently enacted federal mileage standards for new automobiles
could result in cumulative fuel savings of as much as 20 billion
barrels of oil by the year 2000, twice the total Alaskan North Slope
oil reserves.[15]

What is more, most conservation methods do not require advanced
technologies, but can utilize readily available technical and governmental approaches for increased energy savings.

Energy conservation may be proposed consistently as an essential
component of national energy management, but its enthusiasts considerably outnumber its practitioners both in and outside the government. Two formidable obstacles are responsible. First, conservation
lacks political glamor. Results are undramatic, slow, often invisible,
and even unpopular because conservation policies attack the sacred
private consumption sector, where politicians are loathe to chant
sacrificial admonitions to their constituents. Second, many economists
and business, labor, and government leaders believe there exists "a
direct, even inevitable, one-to-one correlation between economic growth
and consumption of energy, and accordingly, that encouraging conservation could easily plunge the nation into serious economic straits."[16]

Significant conservation can probably be achieved without severe consumer or economic impacts, yet Washington, like most state and local governments, has been slow to enact such measures. Congress has attacked the wastefulness of automobile fuel by imposing a national 55 mph speed limit on highways and by requiring new car manufacturers to improve engine efficiency gradually to 27.5 miles per gallon by 1985. But recent administrations have achieved no comprehensive conservation programs. As the U.S. energy situtation becomes more critical and the argument for conservation more persuasive, citizens and government likely will accept more ambitious conservation programs. In the near future, however, conservation probably will remain a stepchild in the family of national energy policy.

Finally, various "technical fixes" can be promoted to produce energy from untapped or underexploited sources. A technical fix generally involves the creation of expensive new, experimental energy production systems. The most commonly promoted new technologies are solar, synthetic fuels (from coal, oil, oil shale, and tar sand), geothermal, and nuclear fission and fusion. In response to studies that suggested solar energy might provide as much as 20 percent of the nation's energy by the year 2000, President Carter increased federal solar energy research expenditures to $650 million in the fiscal 1980 budget. This amount is minuscule, however, compared to the $88 billion ($20 billion of which was actually appropriated by Congress in 1980) earmarked for a massive national program to develop commercial facilities for the synthesis of petroleum and natural gas— "synfuels technologies"—by the mid-1990s. Compared to these programs, federal expenditures on other experimental alternative technologies have been modest. Among existing technologies, nuclear facilities have plummeted in official favor, and most experts concluded in the early 1980s that the nuclear power industry's future looked increasingly dismal.

Despite their many liabilities, soon to be examined in detail, technical fixes seem irresistible to the American public and government officials. The summoning of technology during crisis appeals to America's national pride in its scientific achievements, to its tradition of technological innovation, and to its apparent success in avoiding past disasters through technological imagination. Indeed, Presidents Nixon and Carter, who shared little else, both rallied public support for energy programs by comparing the nation's energy problems to the challenge once posed by World War II—a conflict Americans commonly cite as the most dramatic vindication of the nation's technical genius.[17] Technical fixes are also appealing because they appear to boost the economy and produce other tangible benefits coveted by politicians.

Table 2-3   U.S. Natural Gas Consumption by Economic Sector, 1978

Sector	Consumption*	Percentage of Total Domestic Consumption
Commercial	2.60	13.2
Electric Utilities	3.19	16.3
Industrial	8.40	42.8
Residential	4.90	25.0
Transportation	0.53	2.7
Total	19.63	

* Trillion cubic feet.

SOURCE: U.S. Department of Energy, Energy Information Administration, 1979.

Natural Gas

Whatever combination of new oil production, energy substitution, conservation, or technical fix is utilized to meet energy problems depends, in good measure, on the availability of the nation's other energy resources. The United States did not draw heavily upon its natural gas resources until after World War II, when pipeline technology permitted the economical transport of natural gas across the country. Natural gas production gradually increased from 13 percent of domestic energy output in the late 1940s to a high of 40.2 percent in 1971. The United States produced in the late 1970s all but 5 percent of its natural gas consumption. In many respects, natural gas is an ideal fuel: clean burning, easily transported, and efficient.

Table 2-3 indicates U.S. natural gas consumption by economic sector in 1978. The industrial sector currently consumes about half of natural gas production, but all sectors of U.S. society depend on energy from this source. Natural gas often can substitute directly for fuel oil in industrial, commercial, and residential facilities; in the short term, it appears to be the premier petroleum substitute. Unfortunately, the nation's natural gas stocks appear to be declining to an extent that forces energy planners to look elsewhere for long-range petroleum substitutes.

U.S. natural gas production peaked in 1971. Proven gas reserves, at their highest in 1967, apparently had decreased by 25 percent by the late 1970s. The declining curves of gas production and proven reserves are described in Table 2-4, which summarizes estimates of gas supply for the period 1972 to 1978. A perverse aspect of the national gas situation is the inability of experts to agree on the extent of future natural gas reserves or the severity of the natural gas problem. Economists cannot reach a consensus about the magnitude of remaining reserves because they disagree about the "elasticity" of natural gas production—the extent to which natural gas production is sensitive to changing market prices. Some argue that higher gas prices will spur new exploration with the resulting new wells, while others assert there exists a limited supply of new gas that cannot be enlarged by higher market prices for the product.

Geologists can neither estimate easily the physical volume of underground gas reserves nor agree on the conditions required for the profitable exploitation of marginal reserves. In light of these circumstances, it is understandable that the Office of Technology Assessment would recently suggest, with no real precision, that known reserves of domestic natural gas range anywhere between 688 and 1,128 trillion cubic feet—or enough to last the United States as few as 35 years or as many as 59 years.[18] A further complication is the recent "gas bubble"—the sudden appearance in 1978 and 1979 of three trillion cubic feet more gas supply than Washington had predicted. As a unique, short-term increase due to unanticipated market factors, the bubble apparently did not signal any major increase in known U.S. reserves, but it did emphasize how precarious are current predictions of gas availability.

Regardless of estimation errors, the situational constraints presented by gradually dwindling natural gas reserves are reasonably straightforward. First, natural gas is an unlikely long-term substitute for petroleum, despite its admirable combustion qualities. Indeed, most federal proposals for long-term energy management contemplate the replacement of both petroleum and natural gas by coal or other fuels in crucial sectors such as industry and electrical utilities. Furthermore, imported natural gas from Canada and Mexico, while available and increasing in supply, is likely to provide no more than

Table 2-4 U.S. Natural Gas Production and Consumption, 1972 to 1978

Year	Production*	Percentage of Total U.S. Energy Consumption	Proven Reserves†
1972	22,532	31.7	266
1973	22,647	30.2	250
1974	21,601	30.0	237
1975	20,109	28.3	228
1976	19,952	27.5	216
1977	20,025	26.0	209
1978	19,661	25.4	200

* Billion cubic feet.
† Trillion cubic feet.

SOURCE: U.S. Department of Commerce, Bureau of the Census, *Statistical Abstract of the United States, 1979.*

10 percent of current domestic demand; consequently, the United States cannot depend on imports to relieve gas shortages for much longer. Finally, the most critical supply problems in the next decade probably will occur among industrial and commercial gas consumers. This vulnerability exists because gas producers and transporters are required by federal regulations to give residential consumers highest priority, and industrial boilers and electric utilities lowest priority, in supplying natural gas.

Coal

The relatively limited policy options imposed on public officials by diminishing gas reserves is one compelling reason why many have turned to coal as the Black Hope for future energy management. Providence was merely lavish in endowing the United States with its original oil and natural gas reserves—with coal it was extravagant. Estimates suggest that the United States may possess one-third of the world's total coal reserves. Coal currently provides only 18 percent of the nation's energy consumption, yet represents perhaps 90 percent of the remaining U.S. hydrocarbon reserves.[19]

America's coal reserves are located primarily in three geographic concentrations: Appalachia's wooded hills and hollows, sprawling across seven southeastern states; the midwestern coal pocket, embracing seven additional states; and—richest of all—the western deserts and grasslands. The extent of present coal production in these regions is suggested in Figure 2-1. Electric utilities alone consume approximately 85 percent of current coal production; industrial (13 percent) and residential and commercial use (2 percent) account for the rest of consumption.

Despite the grave environmental risks inherent in coal utilization, the resource is attractive to federal energy planners for several reasons. First, coal is a wholly domestic resource, immune to external supply interruptions. In addition, more than half the western region's coal reserves are located on federal lands, and the technology for producing coal is relatively simple and readily available. Since coal can be substituted for petroleum or natural gas in industrial or utility boilers, it might also diminish dependence on these more scarce fuels. Studies suggest that a stepped-up coal utilization program could reduce national dependence on imported oil by perhaps 2.5 million barrels daily by 1985.[20] Finally, an increase in coal production and coal car loadings could revive the nation's moribund railroad system.

Against all these attractions are balanced potentially severe constraints that limit coal policy choices. The formidable problems of increased coal utilization relate to protection of the environment and transportation of the resource. Unless the environmental pollution

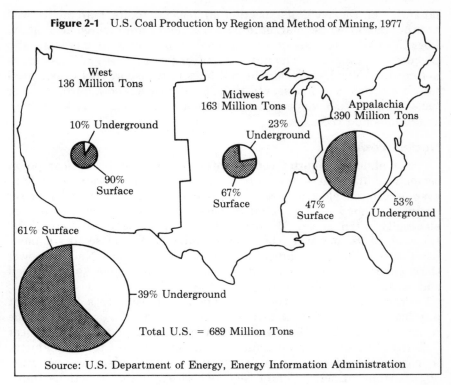

Figure 2-1 U.S. Coal Production by Region and Method of Mining, 1977

West
136 Million Tons

10% Underground

90% Surface

Midwest
163 Million Tons

23% Underground

67% Surface

Appalachia
390 Million Tons

47% Surface

53% Underground

61% Surface

39% Underground

Total U.S. = 689 Million Tons

Source: U.S. Department of Energy, Energy Information Administration

from coal combustion is regulated stringently, increased coal utilization could become an ecological catastrophe. Whether the environmental risks can be controlled acceptably remains uncertain. A recent comprehensive federal survey tersely described the issue:

> The very real deficiency in our knowledge of environmental processes makes it difficult to determine whether current plans for coal development could cause unacceptable environmental impacts. Some of the more spectacular impacts that have been attributed to coal development . . . represent risks rather than certainties.[21]

Unfortunately, some of these risks may involve practically irreversible environmental degradation and thus cannot responsibly be relegated to "further research" while the nation embarks on a new raid on its coal resources. So crucial is the environmental issue to coal combustion that it constitutes a major theme of Chapter 4.

Two other potential constraints on coal utilization are costs and logistics. Coal's future attraction will depend to a large extent on its economic competitiveness with other energy sources. The market price of coal is determined by several factors, including the cost of environmental controls imposed on coal suppliers, the actual heat potential of the coal, its location in respect to its market, as well as other factors whose market impacts cannot be anticipated accurately. Logistics—the business of getting coal from mines to markets—also plagues coal planning. The nation's railroad system currently possesses neither the rolling stock nor the rail lines to transport coal to potential future customers (such as utilities and industries now burning other fuels). Thus, coal remains in ambiguous abundance, rich in both attractions and risks.

Nuclear Power

For almost a quarter century after World War II, nuclear power seemed to illuminate the nation's march toward cheap, abundant, even unlimited electric power. In its early years, the nuclear power program seemed invincibly attractive—partisans of nuclear-generated electricity often spoke of power almost "too cheap to meter." By the late 1970s, however, the nuclear industry was close to stagnant, beset with crippling technical and economic problems. Nuclear power threatened to become a paradigm for technology gone awry, a dead end rather than a high road.

From its inception, the nuclear power industry to a large extent has been subsidized and regulated by the federal government. The Atomic Energy Act (1946) gave Washington a monopoly over nuclear facilities. In 1954, Congress amended the act to permit private industry to construct and operate nuclear power plants under the regulation of the Atomic Energy Commission (whose regulatory functions transferred to the Nuclear Regulatory Commission in 1974). A major share of research, development, and demonstration programs leading to commercial nuclear power plants has been underwritten by the government. Nuclear fuels also have been mined and processed with generous federal assistance. By 1979, federal investment in nuclear power development exceeded $12.1 billion.[22]

Seventy-one nuclear power plants had been licensed to operate by government authorities in 1980. These facilities, whose location is represented in Figure 2-2, produced about 13 percent of the nation's electric power. In addition, 92 more plants were expected to be operational by 1985, at which time nuclear power might generate one-fifth of U.S. electricity production. Nuclear facilities currently operating or under construction use "light water reactors" whose core (where the nuclear fission actually occurs) is cooled by ordinary water. The Department of Energy estimates that proven domestic uranium reserves are capable of powering approximately 375 such reactors for at least 30 years.[23] If spent fuel from the light water reactors were reprocessed, the anticipated uranium stocks might be extended to permit additional power of perhaps 20 to 40 percent.

Figure 2-2 Status of Nuclear Power Plants, December 31, 1979

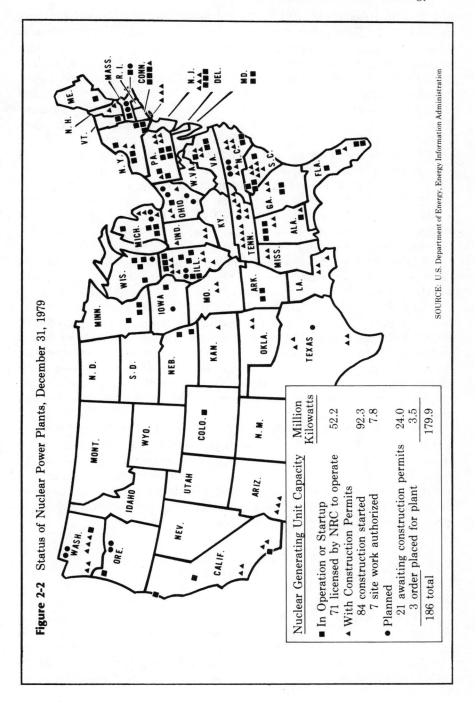

Nuclear Generating Unit Capacity	Million Kilowatts
■ In Operation or Startup	
71 licensed by NRC to operate	52.2
▲ With Construction Permits	
84 construction started	92.3
7 site work authorized	7.8
● Planned	
21 awaiting construction permits	24.0
3 order placed for plant	3.5
186 total	179.9

SOURCE: U.S. Department of Energy, Energy Information Administration

The nuclear power industry's fortune began to plummet in the mid-1970s. In September 1974, the industry consisted of 239 reactors with more than 237 megawatts of capacity either under construction, on order, or already operating. By late 1978, these figures had shrunk to 219 reactors and 215 megawatts. And by 1980, utilities had stopped ordering reactors for delivery after 1985. The industry's malaise has been an amalgam of environmental, economic, and technical problems. The risk of nuclear facility accidents—no longer considered mere speculation after Pennsylvania's Three Mile Island accident of March 1979—has fostered reservations about reactor safety among the public, the scientific community, and government officials. Furthermore, by 1980 the nation still lacked a satisfactory method for disposing of the 15,000 spent fuel assemblies that had been accumulating from existing reactors since the early 1950s. The health of nuclear plant workers and the international security risks of nuclear fuel reprocessing also have been worrisome.

Further complicating these problems—and sometimes because of them—the industry also has suffered economic and regulatory ills. As the average time for plant completion has approached 12 years, the material costs have increased, and the capital expense of facilities has mounted. Faced with these escalating costs, utilities gradually began replacing nuclear facilities with coal-fired plants in their future planning. The nuclear power industry attributed much of its economic ills to the protracted, complex regulatory procedures necessary for plant licensing and to "ratcheting," the federal government's habit of unexpectedly ordering more stringent safety standards effective retroactively.

But the industry has had its own technical problems as well. Generally, nuclear facilities have been notoriously poor performers: the output of operating nuclear facilities averaged only about 63 percent of rated capacity in the late 1970s.[24] By 1980, whether any additional nuclear facilities would be built after the mid-1980s seemed uncertain to an extent almost unimaginable during the industry's glory years scarcely two decades earlier.

UNCONVENTIONAL ENERGY SOURCES WITHOUT TECHNICAL FIXES

Unconventional energy sources can be divided into two categories—those that could become available commercially with a major technical fix and those available without one. As mentioned earlier, a technical fix commonly involves some sort of massive expansion of new or existing energy production technologies that requires large resource investment. In contrast, unconventional sources without fixes are either available presently or require only modest modification of existing technologies. Many Americans presume that unconventional energy resources inherently require technological fixes but several—including small solar, biomass, cogeneration, and wind systems—for the most part utilize available technologies.

Small Solar

The heat energy striking the earth's upper atmosphere in less than 30 minutes' time exceeds total U.S. annual energy consumption. Sunlight is an infinite energy source that is potentially available to anyone, anywhere. Responsible estimates suggest that solar energy, when collected and converted to residential, commercial, and industrial use, could provide with existing technologies between one-fifth and one-fourth of national energy requirements.[25] The President's Council on Environmental Quality concluded in a 1979 study that the prospects for solar energy were "brighter than most imagined."[26]

While debate continues over the relative cost and contribution of specific solar technologies, there is little doubt that solar energy production can, and eventually will, be a significant energy resource. Today, a major public issue concerns which kinds of solar technologies the federal government should promote vigorously, especially whether Washington should invest heavily in so-called big solar systems that require technical fixes. Less complex small solar systems are available with existing technologies and have their own significant attractions.

Small solar systems are primarily decentralized, technologically uncomplicated, and relatively inexpensive energy producers. One approach—actually not a technology at all—is a "passive system" requiring that structures be designed and sited so that in themselves they become solar energy collectors. For example, a house can be built deliberately facing south so that in winter, sun heat is captured through large double-glazed windows and retained in suitably insulated walls at night. Passive systems essentially require careful home and office design and make their impact primarily through new building construction. Consequently, passive systems are not expected to have a significant impact until after the 1980s, as more newly designed homes and offices gradually are built and put into use.

More immediately available and potentially important are "active systems" that utilize moving parts and relatively simple technologies for residential heating, hot water production, and sometimes air conditioning. These decentralized active solar systems usually depend on a collection of aluminum, glass, plastic, and copper materials that function as solar collectors to gather sunlight and then transfer its heat to some medium for distribution or conservation in residential and commercial structures. Active solar systems are especially promising because they can usually be retrofitted in older buildings. One-third of the existing dwellings in the United States are capable of using active solar systems. If they were all retrofitted, perhaps as much as three million barrels of oil in equivalent energy could be conserved every day.[27]

A limited but steadily growing small solar industry exists in the United States. In recent years, the federal government has taken some modest steps to encourage increased small solar utilization. The 1978 National Energy Act permitted homeowners a single tax credit (to a maximum of $2,200) for installing residential solar energy equipment; that same year, Congress also enacted a small loan program encouraging more firms to enter the solar energy field.

Problems remain, however. The cost of active solar systems is still relatively high, and pay-back periods too long, for the average homeowner. Workers skilled in the installation and maintenance of small solar systems are scarce. In most communities, building codes are more an obstacle than an encouragement to solar system installation. And public utilities, wary of a formidable new technological rival, remain ambivalent about increased solar energy use. A bank, for example, installed solar collectors for heating only to find that it no longer "qualified" for preferred lower rates from its utility because it had ceased to be an "all electric" business.[28] Despite such obstacles, small solar appears to be an energy sector with a vigorous, if still limited, potential for growth.

Biomass

Mankind's most ancient energy resources included the combustion of plant and animal materials, now dignified as "biomass conversion." The burning of organic materials liberates solar energy stored in plants and animals. Among the materials currently available in the United States for biomass utilization are wood, agricultural and forest wastes, municipal garbage, many grains such as corn, and animal manure. After the turn of the century, fossil fuels increasingly displaced these traditional energy resources, and biomass gradually shrank to insignificance in U.S. energy production.

Nonetheless, the potential energy available from biomass conversion remains impressive. It is estimated that the wood available in U.S. timberlands could yield 3 million barrels of oil per day in energy equivalent; municipal solid and liquid wastes could add an additional 1.5 million barrels to this figure. These fuels can be used directly, converted to fluids (such as alcohol), or in some cases decomposed into methane gas. The Harvard Business School study recently asserted that wood, when pelletized for utility boilers, could compete economically with coal in many fuel markets.[29] Presently, almost all U.S. wood fuel is consumed by the forest products industry and, to a much lesser extent, by home heating.

Cogeneration

The simultaneous production of heat and power in an industrial process, an electric utility, or a waste disposal system is called "cogeneration." In Europe, cogeneration is used widely to produce "district heating," whereby steam (or hot water) used for generating power is piped to homes and offices close to the power station. In industry, cogeneration means producing electricity and utilizing the resulting process steam that otherwise is wasted to obtain more efficient use of energy. It is the industrial possibilities of cogeneration that are particularly attractive to energy planners; estimates suggest that between 10 and 20 percent of domestic industrial energy use could be provided by cogeneration. In the early 1950s, in fact, about 15 percent of domestic electricity was so generated.

Like small solar and biomass energy systems, no technological fix must precede cogeneration. But industry does need incentives to return to an older technology it has largely abandoned, which is no simple matter. Utilities regard cogeneration as a potential competitor; industries appropriate for cogeneration, not concerned with producing electricity for consumers, often fail to explore the procedure's possible economic advantages. Municipalities that possibly could adopt cogeneration for garbage disposal often are not overly impressed with the technical and economic attractions of available municipal systems for its use.

Until recently, federal, state, and local governments failed to create economic incentives for municipal or industrial cogeneration. However, the relentless increase in the cost of crude oil and its byproducts, sure to continue through the 1980s, will also progressively add to the attractions of cogeneration. With a readily available technology and a large potential fuel supply, the United States is likely to move far more resolutely into the exploration of cogeneration within the next decade.

Wind

Like sunlight, mankind has harnessed the wind for its energy since antiquity. Why not turn again to the wind, as to the sun, in an energy crisis? The United States once possessed the world's largest windmill, in Rutland, Vermont, that generated 1.3 megawatts of electricity between 1941 and 1945. The World Meteorological Organization has estimated that perhaps 20 million megawatts of wind power is available globally.[30]

Only a small portion of this unfettered energy can be converted economically to electricity, however. Although the federal government is actively promoting the development of large experimental windmills using existing technologies, the contribution of wind-powered systems to the U.S. energy demand is expected to be relatively minuscule until at least the year 2000. Nevertheless, wind energy systems similar in design to windmills once typical in this country might be used at limited geographic sites as highly decentralized energy technologies capable of generating moderate electric power for residential or commercial use.

UNCONVENTIONAL ENERGY SOURCES FROM TECHNICAL FIXES

To move from small solar, biomass, or other uncomplicated energy systems to more sophisticated technologies such as nuclear fusion and synthetic fuels is to cross a threshold of social organization that requires a different magnitude of planning. High technology is complexity in the design, creation, and organization of energy sources— a world of huge, centralized energy systems with megabudgets of multibillion dollar investments promising extravagant benefits. It is the stuff of big social gambles where all considerations must be made on an appropriately enlarged scale. Many U.S. officials consider these fixes a test of whether the nation's technical competence is equal to its political intentions. Many Americans treat them simply as a challenge to American know-how that must be met.

Nuclear Fixes: Breeders and Fusion

The extensive risks and massive potential rewards of high technology affect proposals for national nuclear breeder and fusion programs. A nuclear breeder reactor creates fissionable material from nonfissionable sources. The raw element (U-238 and thorium-232) is converted to plutonium-239 or U-233, in the process generating energy that leaves new atomic fuel as a byproduct. A potential attraction is the breeder's virtually unlimited, relatively inexpensive fuel: 1 pound of common granite and shale might be refined to yield enough fissionable materials to produce the energy equivalent of 150 pounds of coal. A breeder reactor uses its fuels far more efficiently than does the light water reactor now employed at nuclear power plants. The breeder reactor thus could extend appreciably the nation's existing uranium stocks.

The federal government has invested heavily in programs to create a commercially viable breeder reactor.[31] Through fiscal 1979, more than $4.67 billion had been spent on the liquid metal fast breeder reactor (LMFBR). The most ambitious of the LMFBR programs is Tennessee's Clinch River reactor project intended "to demonstrate that the LMFBR can be licensed and operate reliably and safely in a utility setting, to develop data concerning the technological, environmental and economic characteristics of LMFBRs, and to confirm the value of LMFBRs in conserving nonrenewable uranium resources."[32] Originally scheduled to begin operation in 1982, the Clinch River project was entangled in an ongoing conflict between the Carter administration (that supported its termination) and Congress (that favored its continuation).

Breeder reactors are also freighted with considerable risks. The LMFBR is susceptible to technical breakdown and severe environmental hazards. The nation's first breeder reactor, the Enrico Fermi installation about 30 miles from Detroit, Michigan, malfunctioned in October 1966, when two fuel subassemblies partially melted (contrary to the Atomic Energy Commission's low estimate of the "maximum credible accident" possible there). Only slight radiation escaped from the plant, but the threat of major environmental contamination and extensive population exposure to radiation were plausible enough to result in a radical reassessment of the breeder technology.[33]

Another liability concerns the plutonium-239 produced in the breeder fuel cycle, which is amenable to use in constructing an atomic bomb. President Carter had opposed the federal government's current LMFBR program on the grounds that it could produce a global proliferation of nuclear materials. In short, the economic advantages of breeder-produced electricity remain tenuous.

Nuclear fusion is far more attractive than the breeder technology, but nevertheless more speculative. Energy produced through nuclear fusion—similar to that driving the sun's energy cycle—is released when the nuclei of two light elements are fused under appropriate conditions. The most suitable fusion fuels are considered to be the heavy isotopes of hydrogen (deuterium and tritium) and the light isotope of helium (helium-3). Theoretically, fusion reactors have compelling advantages. Fusion fuels can be extracted relatively easily from sea water (which can then be returned to the ocean unharmed) or can be created in the fusion reaction itself. Most fusion fuels and reaction products are nonradioactive. The reactors are generally secure from dangerous core accidents and other runaway events. However, there currently exists no fusion reactor at any stage of development, no proven technology capable of leading to a fusion reactor, and no reliable estimates of a reactor's commercial availability.[34]

Developing a fusion reactor requires conquering three formidable technical problems: (1) heating the fuel to temperatures ranging from ten to hundreds of millions of degrees; (2) creating sufficient density of fuel particles during the heating process in order to produce intense fusion reaction; and (3) confining the superheated fuel ("plasma") for sufficient time to obtain more energy than had been contributed originally to the reaction. Achieving all these conditions simultaneously thus far has been impossible. The physics of these procedures is itself complex. Scientists have experimented with magnetic fields ("magnetic bottles") to confine the plasma long enough to produce the desired intensity of fusion. But these bottles leak much faster than anticipated, leading one scientist to compare the procedure to an effort to hold watery jello in a cage of rubber bands.

While technological progress continues on reactor design, most experts expect no demonstration of the reactor's scientific feasibility before the late 1980s. Commercial reactors likely will not be available before the end of the century, and costs remain prohibitive. Fusion reactor technology, suggests the Congressional Research Service, is no short-term energy prospect:

> The Department of Energy predicts that, given funding labelled as "aggressive" in which levels of physics and engineering are expanded to meet programmatic needs and new projects are undertaken when scientifically justified, a complete demonstration fusion power plant of commercial size, 500 megawatts electric, could be operational by 1998.[35]

There are enough suppositions here to sober even a fervent apostle of technical fixes.

Synthetic Fuels From Coal

In June 1980, President Carter signed legislation that established the U.S. Synthetic Fuels Corporation to finance the rapid development of a viable domestic synfuels industry. The federal corporation will dispense up to $88 billion over the next 12 years to develop commercial synthetic fuels facilities with capacity to produce two million barrels of oil equivalent daily. Synfuels have always been among the most common technical fixes suggested by energy planners to relieve the U.S. dependence on imported petroleum. With the signing of the Energy Security Act, synfuels became the primary technical fix on which the United States would depend to reduce its energy imports. What is more, synfuels represent a technological gamble whose magnitude overshadows all other U.S. technological productions, anytime and anywhere.

Synthetic fuels are natural gas and oil derived from coal, oil shale, tar sands, or biomass. Typically, a commercial-scale synfuels plant is assumed capable of producing daily either 50,000 barrels of liquid fuel (a process called "coal liquefaction") or 250 million cubic feet of natural gas (through "coal gasification"). The recent national plan calls for even larger installations, however. Synfuels derived from coal—the most abundant domestic energy source—are particularly attractive. Furthermore, synthetic fuels technology has been proven on a small scale. The Republic of South Africa, with the world's most completely developed coal liquefaction facilities, produces a small portion (about 30,000 barrels daily) of its total petroleum demand with synthetic fuels; and Germany manufactured most of its natural gas by coal gasification during World War II.

Synthetic fuels facilities capable of the large yields required for commercial success require mammoth scale, analogous to that of nuclear power plants. U.S. energy planners often have been captivated by visions of gargantuan installations. A synfuels complex once considered for Montana's abandoned Glasgow Air Force Base, for example, would have cost about $2.6 billion to construct in the mid-1970s and $1.1 billion to operate over its lifetime. When finished, this plant would have employed about 7,400 workers and used 76.2 million tons of coal annually—more than three times the state's entire 1975 coal yield.[36] It would have produced daily 900 megawatts of electricity, 100,000 barrels of synthetic oil, and 1 billion cubic feet of synthetic gas. Most currently planned commercial synfuels facilities suffer only in comparison with these technological behemoths. Taken individually, however, they are huge installations in all respects.

Synfuels installations entail large, often uncertain, economic and environmental risks that will be examined more carefully in a later chapter. Suffice it to note here that the resource demands for synfuels plants and the environmental spillovers from their operation are both serious problems. And whether such plants can actually produce an economically attractive product remains to be seen. Enormous start-up costs together with cloudy economic prospects discourage private capital investment, and without government subsidization such installations are relegated to an uncertain future. "The overriding restraint facing this industry is short supply of venture capital," notes the Harvard Business School study.[37]

Big Solar

Among the solar energy systems currently proposed for government or private sector development, several may be classified as high technologies. One is solar thermal electric systems, which accounted for 20 percent of the federal government's solar budget in fiscal 1979 and whose funding is expected to increase. Thermal electric systems basically are highly centralized technologies for converting sunlight into large-scale electric power or heat output. These include microwave space power satellites, ocean thermal conversion systems, and "power towers" (similar in purpose to the giant 10-story parabolic mirror system currently operating near Font-Romeu, France).

The United States is exploring power towers with considerable interest. The favored American design is a concrete tower several stories high capped by a steam boiler. Several acres of remote-controlled mirrors ("heliostats") are arranged to concentrate sunlight on the boiler. While electricity produced by such a power tower would still exceed the average kilowatt cost of conventional electric power by 300 percent, the power would be available during peak sunlight hours in the West and Southwest when air conditioning creates heavy loads for electric power facilities.[38]

Another big solar fix is the photovoltaic cell. Such cells, made by procedures similar to the manufacture of transistors and integrated circuits, use silicon-base cells to generate electricity from sunlight. The cells were extremely expensive when first used in orbiting satellites, but further research has reduced their costs to 1 percent of the original expense. With further cost reduction, photovoltaic cells might be attractive for residential and utility use. Cells could be used in decentralized residential or commercial heating systems or in highly centralized voltaic "farms" creating large heat or electric output. In an effort to increase private sector development of big solar systems, Congress in 1979 passed a tax credit (varying between 20 and 30 percent) for businesses investing in the development of such technologies.

Oil Shale

The Interior Department estimates that oil shale deposits underlying the Rocky Mountains and northern Plains states constitute an enormous fuel reservoir. As much as 600 billion barrels of oil—about 15 times the nation's proven conventional oil deposits—may be locked up in the Green River rock formation underlying Idaho, Utah, Wyoming, and Colorado.[39] Perhaps 2 billion barrels of this deposit are recoverable, under an 11 million acre expanse of land. The most commonly proposed oil shale technology calls for bulldozing the shale from the ground, crushing the rock, and then heating it to 900°F. to liberate the captive oil and remove impurities.

Another proposed method, called *in situ* conversion, involves heating the rock underground and forcing out the petroleum: a chamber is blasted in the oil-bearing rock, then natural gas is injected and ignited to produce the necessary heat. Whatever its theoretical attractions, oil shale conversion poses such formidable practical problems that the few experimental efforts undertaken by industrial and federal collaboration largely have been abandoned.

FIXES IN PROPER PERSPECTIVE

This brief survey of available technical fixes highlights the substantial constraints involved in any national effort to alleviate U.S. energy ills with existing unconventional energy technologies. Most of the technologies examined impose constraints also applicable to newer technologies. Indeed, such constraints often are inherent in the development of *any* energy technology.

Some Inevitable Constraints

First, the time period required from the theoretical definition of a new high technology energy system to its possible commercial demonstration must be reckoned in terms of decades.[40] The Department of Energy estimates that the development cycle for a new fossil fuel technology consumes between 18 and 30 years; nuclear technology cycles may be even longer. Most currently discussed energy fixes are at relatively early stages in their development cycles. Estimates indicate that the United States is at least 10 years away from commercial-scale synfuels plants and perhaps 15 years from a commercial breeder reactor.

Second, estimates of the potential contribution to energy supply from new technical fixes—especially those prepared by advocates of advanced technologies—often disregard possibly disruptive political or economic events. Econometric models, like many other forecasting tools, are politically ignorant. Political factors are rarely taken into account in such forecasts, which usually makes sense. Analysts cannot predict how a future change in party control of the White House or Congress—if and when it occurs—may affect domestic crude oil prices or future funding of U.S. energy research, or if it does. Nor can analysts anticipate what, if any, events in the politically volatile Middle East might drastically affect oil shipments from that region to the United States. Nonetheless, unanticipated political events will bedevil any predictions from econometric models. Thus, the result can be economic or scientific tunnel vision.

In 1976, for example, the American Gas Association's vice-president for planning and analysis could confidently assert: "We have the technology to generate as much electricity as we want.... Scrubbers are getting better every day.... The Clinch River demonstration breeder reactor will be built by the early 1980s assuming no irreversible regulatory problem."[41] In February 1977, however, the Carter administration initiated plans to terminate the project. The resulting battle with Congress relegated the Clinch River facility to political limbo with no certain completion date. Or consider the crucial qualification dangling at the conclusion of the Ford Foundation's assessment concerning the impact of expensive new energy technologies on future economic growth:

> Any conceivable demand for energy could be met—at least during the next 50 years—from surface mining for coal and reclamation, nuclear facilities at remote locations, domestic oil from shale and OCS [the Outer Continental Shelf].... To be sure, this is only one way events could unfold and it makes optimistic assumptions about the solutions to technical, environmental and national-security problems.[42]

Third, almost all technical fixes involve enormous capital costs. These investments burden developers with the demanding task of attracting generous risk capital before the market attractions of a new fuel system even have been demonstrated. Recent capital estimates for various new fuel technologies suggest the magnitude of these speculative investments:

—*Synthetic Fuels.* Commercially acceptable coal gasification or liquefaction facilities may cost as much as $5 to $6 billion each. Conservative estimates suggest a minimum of $1.5 billion. Reducing U.S. crude oil imports by two million barrels per day through increased production and use of synthetic fuels might require a total national investment of $100 billion.[43]

—*Oil Shale.* To produce approximately one-half of 1 percent of U.S. domestic oil consumption (about 100,000 barrels per day) would require a total investment of at least $1 billion.[44]

—*Nuclear Fusion.* Department of Energy studies set the total funding for a commercial fusion reactor (with output capacity of approximately 500 megawatts of electricity) at between $15 and $20 billion.[45]

—*LMFBR.* The Clinch River facility itself will cost at least an estimated $2.2 billion to reach its commercial demonstration stage. Total program costs for the liquid metal fast breeder reactor will be at least $4.4 billion.[46]

It is often difficult to predict the total capital investment that will be required for any new energy system, however. Cost overruns are common, inflation is difficult to estimate, and interruptions in program development are frequent. The RAND Corporation has calculated, for instance, that actual costs for synthetic fuels plants now being planned by the Department of Energy likely will be 250 percent of estimated costs.[47]

Finally, many new fuel technologies create numerous potentially dangerous environmental impacts. These environmental spillovers—"externalities" in economic terms—are social costs that are difficult to calculate in any economic assessment of a project, yet they are of crucial importance to policymakers. The environmental risks in nuclear reactor technologies and synthetic fuels systems will be explored in Chapter 4. The pervasiveness of the environmental issue can be suggested, however, by considering the case of exotic technologies like oil shale combustion and geothermal facilities that use steam, hot water, or hot rocks from the earth to generate electricity or steam power.

Experts have suggested that geothermal facilities, although benign when compared to the environmental risks inherent in many other energy systems, might nonetheless exhaust the nation's underground steam reservoirs within a century. Oil shale combustion leaves environmental damage less to the imagination. For each barrel of oil produced from shale, 1.5 tons of rock must be crushed. Mountains of spoil must somehow be redistributed, while the environmental devastation to the mined lands is minimized. "The shale rock that remains expands to a greater volume than that previously occupied, which necessitates the filling in of some canyons," the Harvard Business School study recently warned in a singular understatement.[48]

Fixes Have A Place

The constraints inherent in energy fixes are more a caution against the mismanagement of energy technologies rather than an argument against further exploration and research on technical fixes. Considering the nation's creative scientific and technological community, its vast economic resources, and the imperative need to balance its energy budget, the United States inevitably must turn to its technological skills in resolving energy problems. Continued heavy investment in new energy technologies by both the public and private sectors not only stimulates necessary research in known (if unproven) energy technologies, but also encourages the discovery of unanticipated (and perhaps unimagined) new technologies. Indeed, crucial discoveries leading to the solution of major scientific problems often are the unexpected spinoff of research on other matters. The greater the national investment in energy research, the more fertile the scientific environment becomes for creative solutions to the nation's energy dilemma.

Yet the constraints involved in new technical fixes demand that such research be managed prudently, a point to be elaborated in later chapters. It should be clear that a national energy conservation program should be encouraged along with further exploration of new energy technologies—fixes are not a substitute for conservation or a rationalization for avoiding real energy conservation. This should be abundantly clear in light of the enormous time, economic uncertainty, and technical complexity required for the development of new technologies. To gamble solely on technical fixes in order to spare the nation the task of energy conservation is to ignore a proven and easily implemented form of energy saving in preference for what may be nothing more than a technological illusion.

The nation's energy technology development also must be balanced between investment in technical fixes and in less complex, existing forms of unconventional energy systems. Essentially, the risks of investment must be spread across a wide spectrum of technologies in order to maximize the probability of favorable returns.

Unfortunately, technical fixes that entail highly centralized energy systems, huge budgets, and massive potential rewards often tend to capture attention in the political marketplace more readily than less glamorous technologies; consequently, the more complicated high technologies are favored in government legislation and the budgeting process. This disproportionate interest in part results from the short-term economic and political glamour that such technologies hold for public officials. Considering the potential value of existing unconventional energy systems like solar heating, biomass, and cogeneration, a prudent national energy policy should seek to preserve a balance of investment and incentives for the development of both technical fixes and less complex energy systems, regardless of the apparent attractions of the former.

Finally, it seems important that new technical fixes be developed with sufficient deliberation to expose the true economic, environmental, and social costs of their utilization. This is a warning against crash programs or other steeply accelerated efforts to compress the time required for the proper development of new energy fixes. The danger of such crash programs, aside from the economic waste often involved, is that the environmental and social effects cannot be explored fully until after a major (often irreversible) national investment has been made in the technology.

The development of commercial nuclear reactors since 1945 serves as an example: the negative technical, economic, and environmental factors in the reactors' development were largely ignored, concealed, or rationalized away in their sponsors' desire to prove quickly the commercial viability of the industry. It is admittedly difficult to determine the proper pace at which a technology should evolve, but, as recent history suggests, it appears that new technologies can be assessed most fully only when their evolution is free of governmental pressure to produce "results" within a very few years.

CONCLUSION

It has been said that to govern is to choose, but this chapter emphasizes that the circumstances of the nation's energy condition limit the policy choices available to policymakers. There is now a genuine, enduring limit to the prime fossil fuels upon which the United States has recently depended. Both domestic crude oil and natural gas are unlikely ever again to be in the bountiful supply once sufficient to satisfy all national economic and political demands. The remaining energy resources, including especially coal and nuclear power, are freighted with serious economic and environmental liabilities that dictate careful, moderate future development.

Moreover, new technologies, despite America's undeniable skill in technical innovation, are unlikely in the immediate future to pluck the country from the difficulties of an energy shortage and its social risks. We have seen that the technical fixes that might eventually provide new, perhaps unlimited, energy resources to replace depleting crude oil and natural gas are not likely to become commercially available very soon. And these new technologies, such as synfuels and breeder reactors, may sometimes involve economic and environmental costs that limit their availability.

In short, the Golden Age of Fossil Fuels—the decades of cheap, abundant, environmentally acceptable energy production suitable to all U.S. demands—is dead. This means that energy planners must formulate new policies according to emerging realities. First, the United States should consider for the first time a serious, sustained national program of energy conservation, the economically least expensive strategy for increasing the available energy supply. A national conservation strategy could make an especially important contribution to U.S. energy needs during the next several decades by bridging the gap between present energy limits and the development of new technologies in the next century. Perhaps such a strategy will liberate the nation from its dependence on fossil fuels.

Second, energy planners should consider using solar, biomass, and other forms of renewable energy as a realistic option for future energy development. Third, planners need to free themselves from an obsession with technical fixes. We have observed the promise and liabilities of currently available fixes. These technologies must be developed with a prudent restraint that permits full exploration and debate of their economic and environmental drawbacks without denying their potential advantages.

This suggests that a key concept in future energy planning should be balance:

—A balance between aggressive new fossil fuel production *and* equally aggressive energy conservation.

—A balance between dependence on new energy technologies *and* restraint upon their hasty development.

—A balance between using exhaustible *and* renewable energy sources.

—A balance between U.S. determination to have all the energy it wants *and* a concern to keep energy demands within the limits of national needs.

—A balance between U.S. absorption with its own energy demands *and* a concern for the energy needs of other nations.

In effect, U.S. policymakers should seek a creative combination of policy stategies involving both old and new approaches to energy management.

NOTES

1. U.S., Congressional Budget Office, *President Carter's Energy Proposals: A Perspective* (Washington, D.C.: U.S. Government Printing Office, June 1977), p. xiv.
2. *New York Times,* May 17, 1977.
3. *New York Times,* January 18, 1979.
4. *New York Times,* June 28, 1977.
5. James O'Toole, *Energy and Social Change* (Cambridge, Mass.: The MIT Press, 1976), p. 31.
6. Robert Stobaugh and Daniel Yergin, eds., *Energy Future: Report of the Energy Project at the Harvard Business School* (New York: Random House, 1979), p. 147.
7. U.S., General Accounting Office, *Domestic Energy Resource and Reserve Estimates: Uses, Limitations and Needed Data,* Report No. EMD-77-6 (Washington, D.C.: U.S. Government Printing Office, March 17, 1977), p. i.
8. U.S., Congress, Office of Technology Assessment, *Analysis of the Proposed National Energy Plan* (Washington, D.C.: U.S. Government Printing Office, 1977), p. 62.
9. *New York Times,* May 8, 1977.
10. *New York Times,* July 17, 1979.
11. Library of Congress, Congressional Research Service, *Breeder Reactors: The Clinch River Project,* Issue Brief No. IB77088 (Washington, D.C.: U.S. Government Printing Office, December 1978), p. 9.
12. Congressional Quarterly, *Continuing Energy Crisis in America* (Washington, D.C.: Congressional Quarterly Inc., 1975), p. 43.
13. *New York Times,* April 17, 1977.
14. Stobaugh and Yergin, *Energy Future,* chap. 6.
15. Ibid., pp. 160, 166, 170.
16. Ibid., pp. 141-142.
17. For the World War II analogies, see *The National Energy Plan,* Energy Policy and Planning Staff, Executive Office of the President (Washington, D.C.: U.S. Government Printing Office, 1977). See also President Nixon's remarks as reported in I.C. Bupp, "Energy Planning in the United States: Ideological BTUs," in *Politics and the Future of Industrial Society,* ed. Leon N. Lindberg (New York: McKay, 1976), pp. 286-287.
18. U.S., Congress, Office of Technology Assessment, *Analysis of the Proposed Energy Plan,* p. 35.
19. Walter A. Rosenbaum, *Coal and Crisis* (New York: Praeger Publishers, 1978), chap. 1.

20. U.S., Congress, Office of Technology Assessment, *Analysis of the Proposed Energy Plan,* p. 157.
21. U.S., Congress, Office of Technology Assessment, *The Direct Use of Coal* (Washington, D.C.: U.S. Government Printing Office, 1979), p. 6.
22. U.S., General Accounting Office, *Nuclear Power Costs and Subsidies,* Report No. EMD-79-52 (Washington, D.C.: U.S. Government Printing Office, June 13, 1979), p. ii.
23. Congressional Quarterly, *Energy Policy* (Washington, D.C.: Congressional Quarterly Inc., 1979), p. 106.
24. Ibid., p. 108.
25. Stobaugh and Yergin, *Energy Future,* p. 183.
26. President's Council on Environmental Quality, *The Good News about Energy* (Washington, D.C.: U.S. Government Printing Office, 1979), p. ii.
27. Ibid., p. 188.
28. Stobaugh and Yergin, *Energy Future,* chaps. 4, 6.
29. Ibid., p. 199.
30. John Holdren and Philip Herrera, *Energy* (San Francisco: Sierra Club Books, 1971), p. 111.
31. Library of Congress, Congressional Research Service, *Breeder Reactors,* p. 5.
32. Ibid.
33. Holdren and Herrera, *Energy,* chap. 6.
34. Library of Congress, Congressional Research Service, *Fusion Power: Potential Energy Source,* Issue Brief No. IB76047 (Washington, D.C.: U.S. Government Printing Office, October 1978), p. 4.
35. Ibid., p. 5.
36. *New York Times,* December 15, 1975.
37. Stobaugh and Yergin, *Energy Future,* p. 205ff.
38. Ibid.
39. Library of Congress, Congressional Research Service, *Shale Development: Outlook, Current Activities and Constraints,* Issue Brief No. IB74060 (Washington, D.C.: U.S. Government Printing Office, November 1978), p. 1.
40. U.S., General Accounting Office, *Fossil Energy Research, Development, and Demonstration: Opportunities For Change,* Report No. EMD-78-57 (Washington, D.C.: U.S. Government Printing Office, September 18, 1978).
41. *New York Times,* December 5, 1976.
42. *New York Times,* April 4, 1977. See also conclusion of *A Time To Choose,* Energy Policy Project, The Ford Foundation (Cambridge, Mass.: Ballinger Publishers, 1974).
43. Library of Congress, Congressional Research Service, *Coal Gasification and Liquefaction,* Issue Brief No. IB77105 (Washington, D.C.: U.S. Government Printing Office, October 1978), p. 6. See also *New York Times,* July 5, 1979.
44. Stobaugh and Yergin, *Energy Future,* p. 44.
45. Library of Congress, Congressional Research Service, *Fusion Power,* p. 4.
46. U.S., General Accounting Office, *The Clinch River Breeder Reactor: Should the Congress Continue to Fund It?,* Report No. EMD-79-62 (Washington, D.C.: U.S. Government Printing Office, May 7, 1979), pp. i-vi.
47. *New York Times,* July 15, 1979.
48. Stobaugh and Yergin, *Energy Future,* p. 44.

3

Constraints:
The U.S. Political Formula

In July 1979, President Jimmy Carter addressed the nation for the fifth time concerning "its intolerable dependence on foreign oil." But the principal and undeclared issue was the president himself. The presentation was attended by spectres of impending electoral calamity, shadowed by the substantial defeat of Carter's 1977 National Energy Plan, and conceived in rising anxiety that the president's tenuous hold upon his congressional partisans was failing. Like all major presidential policies, this new energy program was inspired by the particular logic of the political marketplace. It was policy tailored to the form of the president's political need.

Trouble had been gathering about the White House for months. The president's standing in public opinion polls, never secure, was eroding. Following his successful negotiation of the Egyptian-Israeli Peace Treaty in 1978, approximately 59 percent of the American people had expressed approval of Carter's performance. But that changed with a series of national problems that culminated in the "energy crunch" of summer 1979. Long lines multiplied at service stations nationwide, and several states initiated limited gasoline rationing. By July the public distemper had turned on the White House: a week before his television address, three of every four Americans interviewed in one major poll disapproved of Carter's performance.[1]

Democratic party leaders warned presidential advisers that the president's energy policies seemed timid and ineffectual. Carter's National Energy Plan—the 100 related measures he had proposed to Congress in 1977—had been shredded almost to incoherence by the legislators. What remained, according to one expert, was at best "an empty shell with minimal negative impacts."[2] The administration's attack on energy problems did seem to be proceeding at a glacial pace. At the time of Carter's inauguration in 1977, the United States was importing 43 percent of its total petroleum consumption; the figure had risen to 48 percent on the eve of his July 1979 national energy address.

With the 1980 presidential campaign only months away, presidential advisers were convinced that President Carter had to take decisive measures to restore his public stature and to secure some semblance of a legislative victory for his energy program. In early July, the president was greeted by a cheerless memorandum from Stuart Eizenstat, his chief domestic policy adviser:

> Congress is growing more nervous by the day over the energy problem . . . members are literally afraid to go home over the recess, for fear of having to deal with very angry constituents. . . . I do not need to detail for you the political damage we are suffering from all this. . . . Nothing which has occurred in the Administration to date—not the Soviet agreement on the Middle East, not the Lance affair, not the Panama Canal treaties, not the defeat of several major domestic legislative proposals, not the sparring with Kennedy and not even double-digit inflation—have added so much water to our ship. Nothing else has so frustrated, confused, angered the American people—or so targeted their distress at you personally. . . .[3]

Eizenstat then prescribed a strategy calculated to transform energy policy into a vehicle for the president's political resurrection. The president, advised Eizenstat, should appear "dealing with—and publicly to be seen dealing with—the energy problems now facing us." The administration must announce "a new approach to energy" and convince the public that "we have a firmer grasp on the problem than they now perceive." And the president should be observed to "stay the course. . .demand answers. . .convince others of the need to act. . . ."

What emerged on Sunday, July 15, 1979, was a presidential energy message whose creation, substance, and delivery hewed closely to this prescription. For a week preceding the message, the president cloistered himself at Camp David from which he summoned national leaders in all fields to the energy mountaintop—a maneuver calculated to attract media attention, arouse public curiosity, and proclaim earnest deliberation. The message itself advertised Jimmy Carter's incisive leadership. Its substance was declared in the first person singular:

> I am tonight setting a clear goal for the energy policy of the United States. Beginning this moment, this nation will never use more foreign oil than we did in 1977. Never. To insure that we meet these targets, I will use my presidential authority to set import quotas. . . . I am asking for the most massive peacetime commitment of funds and resources in our nation's history to develop America's own alternative sources of fuel from coal, from oil shale, from plant

products ... from the sun.... I'm asking Congress to mandate— to require as a matter of law—that our nation's utility companies cut their massive use of oil by 50 percent.... I am proposing a bold conservation program to involve every state, county and city, and every average American in our energy battle.[4]

The conclusion was equally emphatic: "I will lead our fight, and I will enforce fairness in our struggle, and I will insure honesty. And above all, I will act."

The proposals were new in two ways that affected the president's reelection campaign: they were substantively different from the earlier unsuccessful energy plans, and they appeared far more palatable to both Congress and the public. The previous unpopular tax measures that placed heavy weight on energy conservation were largely replaced by ambitious new energy production schemes: a massive $88 billion synthetic fuels program, new petroleum exploration on the Outer Continental Shelf, mass transit, and new procedures to speed the licensing and construction of energy facilities—proposals that translated into stepped-up public spending, jobs, and economic activity. While energy conservation was not ignored (a major boost for solar energy research was included), the president's new energy approach clearly was more delicate in handling the issue of consumer convenience. It was as if the president had been meditating on presidential primaries as much as on petroleum imports.

Despite its unique aspects, the president's new energy proposal was nurtured in an institutional environment largely similar to that of any presidency. Calculations of political risk and advantage, careful attention to opinion polls and electoral impacts, sensitivity to the congressional temper—as well as other factors that entered into the political calculus shaping the Carter energy proposal—are to be expected in any governmental milieu.

The greater importance of these events is the clarity with which they illustrate that national energy policy is shaped by *political* as well as situational constraints. Indeed, the resolution of substantive issues by government—in this case, energy issues—is mediated by characteristic political styles, institutions, and rules to the extent that it is impossible to explain their outcome without appreciating the logic of U.S. political decisionmaking. In this chapter, we will carefully examine some of these political constraints, collectively called the American "political formula."

POLITICAL STYLE

Public officials responsible for energy policy decisions bring to the task a characteristic set of values, attitudes, and beliefs about how decisions should be made. This political style often is an unarticulated set of convictions (no less important because they are unspoken) so widely shared that they seldom require formal recognition. They become rules of the decisionmaking process that we identify as distinctively political.

Incrementalism

Charles Lindblom writes of the United States:

> Policy-making typically is part of a political process in which the only feasible political change is that which changes social states only by relatively small steps. Hence, decisionmakers typically consider, among all the alternative policies that might be imagined to consider, only those relatively few alternatives that represent small or incremental changes from existing policies.[5]

This political style, commonly called "incrementalism," relies heavily upon the past as a cue for making policy choices in the present.[6]

Incrementalism appeals powerfully to public officials. It enables them to draw upon their own experiences when confronting a possibly unprecedented problem and favors restraint by making relatively small policy adjustments "at the margins," thereby minimizing the risk of radical, and possibly irreversible, consequences. Policymakers can thus avoid upsetting the interest coalitions that support existing policy and causing a new political bloodletting. Incrementalism often reduces what otherwise might seem to be a bewilderingly complex and unmanageable array of policy options to a set of limited, comprehensible ones. Moreover, it is congenial to the fragmented political power common to American governmental structures: incrementalism accommodates bargaining and compromise among multiple political interests demanding a voice in policy decisions.

The disadvantages of incrementalism enlarge proportionately as new policy issues demand truly new solutions, however. Incrementalism often inhibits rapid policy innovation and frequently stifles imaginative solutions to issues. Public officials are very tempted to treat new issues as familiar ones that can be resolved in the usual way, even when new issues may depart so severely from past experience as to require fresh definition and novel solution. The Nixon and Ford administrations treated American energy problems largely as a problem of temporary resource scarcity to be remedied, as past U.S. energy shortages had been, by increasing energy production. Project Independence, the first national energy plan promoted by Presidents Nixon and Ford, did little but hurl ink at the maelstrom. The project, which promised to bring the United States by 1980 "to a point where we are no longer dependent to any significant extent upon potentially insecure foreign supplies of energy," depended almost exclusively on a rapid acceleration of new domestic energy production so unrealistic that it was largely abandoned by the end of President Ford's term.

The Carter administration abandoned any illusions of energy independence and accepted the reality of significant domestic energy scarcity until at least the turn of the century. Yet President Carter did continue to favor a rapid increase in domestic energy production—albeit in different guise—as a primary energy strategy in preference to a vigorous, and perhaps coercive, program of energy conservation. As the energy education of recent American presidents suggests, public officials may gradually abandon an incremental bias when it fails to yield a satisfactory solution to a new issue. Such education can be costly, however.

Finally, incrementalism favors prolonged deliberation even when decisive governmental response is essential. Incremental policy formulation assumes that cautious decisionmaking is both normal and desirable; frequently nothing short of severe crisis can or will disrupt such thinking. Current projections of U.S. and global energy demand generally imply critical world energy scarcities within the lifetime of the next generation unless countermeasures are initiated soon. In late 1979, the World Energy Conference, an international organization representing most nations, predicted that world petroleum production would decline by one-third during the 1980s and once-anticipated nuclear power generation by one-half before the end of the century.[7] Such predictions of imminently grave energy scarcity are so popular that the danger from incremental energy policies seems acute. And the longer the major energy-consuming nations require to impose appropriate conservation measures, the more severe will be the policy options.

Bargaining and Compromise

Most policy decisions result from bargaining and compromise among the institutions and actors involved in the political process. "What happens," remarks Graham Allison, "is not chosen as a solution to a problem but rather results from compromise, conflict and confusion among officials with diverse interests and unequal influence."[8] This style of decisionmaking transcends formal boundaries that separate the legislative and executive branches and confounds distinctions between "politics" and "administration." It is a process inherent in the making of almost any decision in Congress, the White House, or the federal bureaucracy:

> ... Sometimes one group committed to a course of action triumphs over other groups fighting for other alternatives. Equally often, however, different groups pulling in different directions produce a result ... a mixture of conflicting preferences and unequal power of various individuals—distinct from what any person or group intended.[9]

Policymakers, whatever their institutional or ideological loyalties, normally assume that they will have to accept bargaining and compromise as a style. Leadership in American political institutions gravitates toward those who most artfully and diligently display a skill for successful negotiation.

It could hardly be otherwise. The U.S. Constitution, inspired by the Madisonian notion that government is best conducted by setting "ambition against ambition," creates a structure of countervailing and competitive centers of political authority. Within the federal government, power is dispersed between legislative, executive, and judicial institutions. The principle of federalism fragments authority between the national and state governments. Constitutional protection for freedom of expression, petition, and assembly has nurtured a vigorous pluralism of organized private interests that pursue their own advantage within government at all levels. National policymaking requires the aggregation and reconciliation of the interests of these fragmented power centers in order to assure a broad coalition in support of policy. Under these circumstances, it is understandable that for most public officials to govern means to bargain and compromise on public policy.

This negotiating style shapes policy outcomes in profound ways. Policymakers usually seek not to optimize but to "satisfice" in making policy choices—to find the policy formula that best reconciles divergent interests in a major issue rather than the policy that may best resolve the problem. No matter what political rhetoric may insist, this negotiating style also means that few policy decisions are ever truly final. As coalitions weaken or new interests gain sufficient power to demand a voice in government, policymakers redesign policy formulas to accommodate these changing realities. Finally, it means that broad policies often are an amalgam of sometimes inconsistent and even contradictory measures that are patched together—often deliberately—because they can hold or create support among fragmented power centers.

Consider the 1946 Atomic Energy Act which, among its many provisions, created the Atomic Energy Commission (AEC). The commission represented Congress's attempt to reconcile widespread apprehension within the scientific community concerning the dangers of peaceful nuclear technologies with the Eisenhower administration's eagerness to develop electric power from nuclear reactors. The AEC was given concurrent and incompatible mandates to promote peaceful uses of atomic power while also regulating it. Abetted by powerful congressional and private proponents of the nuclear power industry, AEC so zealously subordinated regulation to industry promotion that Congress finally was convinced in 1974 that the two responsibilities had to be restructured to protect public safety. The independent Nuclear Regulatory Commission assumed responsibility for AEC's safety, licensing, and regulatory powers for the commercial use of nuclear power, while the Department of Energy currently protects the interests of the nuclear power industry.

Tyranny of the Electoral Cycle

The electoral cycle, and all the circumstances shaping election outcomes, claims an imperious hold on the mind of most public officials, especially presidents, members of Congress, and their staffs. For an elected official, the clock segmenting the time within which he or she must make decisions ticks away in two-, four-, and six-year intervals—the constitutionally ordained electoral cycles of the federal government. Within these time frames, separate policy decisions will be sifted continuously for their individual electoral implications. "Good" and "bad" policies often are defined in terms of their electoral acceptability.

Administrators, too, may respond to electoral pressures in a manner belying their apparent insulation from the electoral arena. Career civil servants customarily know quite well that their agencies, programs, and budgets will languish or prosper according to the electoral fortunes of those with authority over such matters in the White House or Congress. The middle- and upper-level bureaucrats responsible for setting broad agency policy learn that if they are to survive they must be alert to the public impact of their policy choices. The flow of policy decisions across the institutional lines of government is so saturated with electoral calculation that no area of government decisionmaking wholly escapes its influence.

Elections affect the style of policymakers in two ways particularly relevant to energy policy. First, the short term dominates the long run when elected officials evaluate new programs. Presidents and members of Congress may talk of programs for decades or defend the interests of unborn generations, but policies often are assessed according to their impact on the next primary or general election. Thomas Cronin observes:

> Presidents and their staffs arrive at the White House charged up to produce results, to make good on the pledges of their campaign. A President and his staff think in terms of two- and four-year frames, at the most. They strive to fulfill campaign pledges and related priorities with a sense of urgency, seeking ways to build a respectable image for the forthcoming electoral campaign.[10]

Representatives and senators are similarly bound by electoral circumstance. Explaining why many of his colleagues would not support President Carter's 1977 gasoline tax proposals, a Florida representative got down to essentials: "A lot of guys who have marginal districts can't vote for a gasoline tax."[11] This preoccupation with the short term often reduces the existence of a long-term White House or congressional policy to a public fiction. Efforts at long-range planning frequently degenerate into a succession of segmented programs responsive to the political pressures of the moment. Over time, episodic policies may be strung together and dignified as a "continuing policy," but they usually lack the continuity of purpose and consistency of substantive logic that are expected of broad-range policy planning and implementation. Thus, it often happens that there is no truly long-range policy in government; rather, the short-range policy becomes the long-range one.

Second, policymakers must constantly test their decisions in the public arena, which means that major technical decisions within government are usually politicized in varying degree. Administrators, technicians, scientists, and other professionals who daily make technical decisions about energy—deciding, for example, which method of creating synthetic coal gas is more efficient or which type of solar electric power system is most promising—can rarely make major energy decisions without weighing public reaction or the electoral impact of such decisions against the technical aspects. Along with the public officials whose authority turns technical recommendations into government policy, these professionals eventually will introduce standards of political feasibility in exploring options in technical planning.

Although inevitable, such politicizing of decisions can easily create pressures or expectations that are inconsistent with prudent technical planning. In federal funding of scientific research, development, and demonstration projects—federal RD&D—it has been impossible for public planners to draft research agendas without an eye to their public impact. Technologies with features attractive to the public often have been hastened to commercialization without sufficient evaluation. Conversely, other technologies have been neglected, or dispatched to the limbo of "further evaluation," when their public attractions failed to match their technical virtues.

The RAND Corporation has asserted that such was the case when the Atomic Energy Commission (AEC) decided in the early 1950s to rely on pressurized water reactors rather than on alternative technologies for the nation's nuclear power program. This decision apparently was shaped by a strong desire to demonstrate quickly to the public that peaceful nuclear power was both reliable and feasible.[12] Alternative technologies, brought to commercial development with less haste, probably would have produced greater long-term economic payoffs. In short, technical factors were weighed less heavily than public effects in the Atomic Energy Commission's desire to create a climate of opinion congenial to continued congressional support of the embryonic nuclear power program.

Public Power of Private Interests

In May 1978, Ralph Nader's Congress Watch organization protested what it described as "an extraordinary infiltration of the Department of Energy." Lobbyists for the American Petroleum Institute, the industry's principal spokesman, were allegedly receiving from senior DOE officials advance notice of many sensitive department actions. In one instance, the institute had been invited to comment on a letter to a U.S. senator before he himself had received it. The revelation of such "extraordinary infiltration" was greeted by its intended audience with profound disinterest. The *New York Times* relegated the story to a remote back page.[13] No congressional committee stirred. The Department of Energy did nothing more than issue its ritual promise to be more discreet in the future.

In American politics, group access to the inner citadels of public power is treated, at best, with public and official ambivalence. When group activity assumes unconstitutional or unethical proportions, penalties are sometimes imposed. But it is the excesses, not the existence, of group claims to public influence that invite censure. That privately organized interests should share in formulating public policy—often to the point that they capture a share of public power—excites almost no one.

A major reason why organized interests of all persuasions do penetrate the legislative and executive domains of government is, as Theodore Lowi remarks, that most American public officials assume it is "both necessary and good that the policy agenda and the public interest be defined in terms of the organized interests of society."[14] Indeed, many officials conduct their business "as if it were supposed to be the practice of dealing only with organized claims in formulating policy, and of dealing exclusively through organized claims in implementing programs."[15] This attitude leads to many formal and informal governmental arrangements for creating and sustaining group access to strategic policy arenas. In the legislative arena, lobbying is accepted as a normal, if not essential, arrangement for assuring organized interests a major role in the lawmaking process. In such a congenial environment, the already large number of organized groups exercising significant influence over congressional energy policy is constantly expanding. Indeed, any social, economic, or geographic group with ambitions to influence such policy realizes it must organize a lobby or risk political invisibility.

In the administrative branch, accommodation to organized interests assumes many forms. Administrators routinely consult, both formally and informally, with spokesmen of major private groups during deliberations on administrative policies affecting these groups. Moreover, Congress frequently mandates in legislation that the administrators responsible for implementing important programs create advisory committees whose memberships include representatives of the interests affected by those programs—a device that assures that such interests will be informed about and solicited for opinions during a program's administration. Should Congress fail to mandate advisory committees, administrative agencies often create them anyway. In the late 1970s, the Department of Energy (DOE) had formed 20 major advisory committees that collectively covered all the department's principal energy programs.[16] The care and feeding of these DOE committees cost about $1 million annually. However, when compared to older departments where the number of advisory committees often exceeds 100, DOE (created in 1977) is hardly in the advisory committee business.

Administrative agencies also collaborate with organized groups by "working the clientele." Agencies often turn to organized interests strongly sympathetic to their programs for support in legislative struggles, for aid in swaying public opinion (and especially the opinion of group members) to the agency's advantage, and for assistance in writing policy and implementing programs. Thus, in 1978 when the Environmental Protection Agency (EPA) and DOE were drawn into a struggle over a congressional proposal to relax air pollution controls on public utilities, both sides urged their clientele to bring pressure on Congress: EPA appealed to environmentalists to urge the measure's defeat, while DOE encouraged major energy producers to pressure Congress for its passage.

The membership of hundreds of large, quasi-public associations mingles legislators, administrators, White House personnel, and private group representatives that share policy concerns. These associations promote a community of concern among members and in effect dissolve the formal boundaries between public and private interests. A typical example in the domain of energy policy is the powerful Highway Users Federation for Safety and Mobility, whose accomplishments include the sprawling multibillion dollar interstate highway system. Its membership embraces representatives of almost all major public and private organizations concerned with the national highway program: National Crushed Stone Association, National Association of Motor Bus Owners, American Trucking Associations, American Automobile Association, the Teamster's union, many officials within the U.S. Department of Transportation, as well as executives of state and local government transportation agencies. The names of these associations are legion. Populating the boundary between public and private sectors of American political life, these private organizations represent constellations of quasi-public power.

The generous influence conceded to organized interests in the American political process affects energy policy in important ways. Public policy primarily responds to those interests with an organized expression. Moreover, officials tend to equate the "public interest" with whatever policy settlements are synthesized from the aggregate of particular interests claiming attention on an issue. Interests that lack organized representation during policy formation, in effect, do not exist in the political space of a particular policy discussion. Energy conservation was slow in being accepted in the United States because, as one federal agency official has suggested, it was until recently regarded as a good idea that lacked an organizational base:

> Outside of perhaps the insulation manufacturers, there is no organized conservation industry in this country. So we have nothing to compare to the energy producers in terms of marketing, distribution and lobbying. The oil companies and utilities are busy talking up how much they need to produce. But no one's out there wholesaling conservation by the ton and barrel.[17]

Finally, interest group activism favors the viewpoint of the socially advantaged: upper- and middle-class Americans, the affluent and educated citizens—the people with the time, information, and resources to support organized advocacy of their viewpoints. The socially disadvantaged are not wholly lacking in representation or official concern, but organizations speaking for the underprivileged often lack the technical and financial resources required to argue their case persuasively.

In energy-related matters, these groups often represent perspectives inconsistent with those of the more affluent. The poor, for instance, depend on public transportation to a greater extent than do more wealthy citizens. Low-cost public transportation and, more generally, policies promoting greater public support for public transportation systems have largely been neglected in the past, as public officials responded more readily to the numerous advocates of protection and promotion of the American automobile with all its social support systems.

CONGRESS: THE FRAGMENTATION OF POWER

As the official attitude toward interest groups suggests, the various elements constituting the American political style are so deeply and widely accepted that they are considered the norm for public management. But this political style is not alone in shaping American public policy. Another constant influence is the fragmentation of authority at all levels within American government institutions, a dispersion of public power deeply woven into the fabric of the American political system since its beginnings. This fragmentation of power within government institutions is displayed with particular clarity in the U.S. Congress, where the dispersion of power leaves its mark on all energy legislation.

In formulating national energy policy, Congress is not sovereign, but it is preeminent. The president may propose energy programs and sometimes, within bounds usually dictated by Congress, may mandate them. But only Congress can legislate energy policy, appropriate funds to underwrite energy programs, or mandate the tax structure to raise the necessary money. The president's freedom to act independently of Congress on energy matters is limited severely by law, custom, and political circumstance. Judges and administrators may formulate policy by interpreting or implementing a congressional enactment, but such policymaking is usually limited by congressional guidelines and oversight.

Yet Congress is a house divided, its authority dispersed and diffused between two chambers, with its members often torn by claims of conflicting local and national interests. For all its apparent authority, a close observation of the Congress often reveals not power exercised but power dissipated, not policy made but policy paralyzed.

The Committee Muddle

As in other legislative matters, congressional authority over energy legislation is broadly divided within each chamber. The congressional tradition of creating numerous committees with vague and overlapping jurisdictions has meant that energy proposals frequently are concurrently referred to several committees in each chamber. The existence of so many committees with claims to energy authority assures jealousy and competition between committees and their leaders for influence in policymaking.[18] In the House, more than 38 committees and subcommittees claimed jurisdiction over some domain of energy policy in the 96th Congress. The Senate traditionally has fewer committees, but nevertheless, at least 10 major committees and several dozen subcommittees exercise some authority over energy legislation. Table 3-1 lists and describes the jurisdictions of the principal energy committees and subcommittees in each congressional chamber during the 96th Congress.

Further swelling the list of legislative entities with influence in energy policy are congressional staff agencies that advise the Congress on matters including energy, like the General Accounting Office and the Office of Technology Assessment; joint House and Senate study groups, such as the Environmental Study Conference and the Joint Economic Committee; and a host of ad hoc groups formed by legislators to promote particular energy resources, such as the Solar Coalition, the Senate Coal Caucus, and the Congressional Fuels Caucus.

Congressional conflict over energy policy, vigorous enough with each chamber's own array of squabbling and ambitious energy committees, is further intensified by rivalries between energy committees in the House and those in the Senate. Such competition feeds on the traditional differences between the two chambers—their divergent constituencies, constitutional responsibilities, and institutional histories—and on conflicting personalities and committee aspirations. And the various energy committees, within the two chambers and between them, often are responsive to differing energy interests.

The results are predictable. Congressional responses to energy problems, more often than not, are sluggish. The complex, tedious (yet essential) bargaining and compromising process imposed by the diverse congressional interests with leverage in the policy process often yields extremely complicated, vague, and inconsistent legislation. So many congressional actors and interests may claim a voice in policymaking that no legislative reconciliation of these divergent viewpoints may be possible. In fact, preventing or stalling legislative action under such circumstances is much easier than achieving it. Almost no major energy policies are enacted, in any case, without many preceding years—even decades—of repeated failure in the Congress.

Recent congressional efforts to reform this disarray only reveal how tenaciously Congress clings to it. In early 1980, a special House committee headed by California Democrat Jerry M. Patterson recommended, after study requested by the House leadership, that the principal authority over energy affairs be drawn from six powerful existing committees and vested in a new House Energy Committee. The chairmen of the six committees scheduled to yield this power unanimously opposed the idea. Leading the opposition, not surprisingly, was West Virginia Democrat Harley O. Staggers, chairman of the House Commerce Committee and the biggest potential loser in the proposed committee realignment.

Groups influential with existing House energy committees generally fought the plan, suspecting that reorganization would result in diminution of their influence. A coalition of public interest groups opposed the measure for fear the new House Energy Committee would be dominated by the aggressive energy-producing firms. Regional rivalries also were involved. "My fear," explained California Democrat Phillip Burton, "is that, over the long term, members of the producing states are likely to get on the energy committee, as members of the agriculture districts get on the agriculture committees." In the end, self-interest was the winner. "A majority of members of existing

Table 3-1 Congressional Committees with Energy Policy Jurisdiction, 96th Congress, 1979-1980

Committee Jurisdiction	Energy Subcommittees
HOUSE OF REPRESENTATIVES	
Agriculture. Agriculture and forestry in general; rural electrification.	Conservation and Credit; Forests.
Appropriations. Appropriates funds for energy agencies and departments.	Energy and Water Development; Interior; Transportation.
Banking, Finance and Urban Affairs. Energy conservation measures in housing.	Housing and Community Development.
Budget. Studies effect of legislation and taxes on the budget.	
Education and Labor. Coal mining health and safety.	Health and Safety.
Government Operations. Oversight of Energy Department, Nuclear Regulatory Commission, Interior Department.	Environment, Energy and Natural Resources.
Interior and Insular Affairs. Mineral land laws, resources on public lands, mining and leasing programs; environmental impact of energy production and conservation; pipelines; radiological safety, security, and waste disposal; commercial nuclear facilities; forest reserves; Indian affairs.	Energy and the Environment; Mines and Mining; National Parks and Insular Affairs; Water and Power Resources.
Interstate and Foreign Commerce. Public utilities; plant siting; labeling of appliances for energy consumption; gas rationing; oil and gas pricing; civilian petroleum reserves; federal power administrations; pipelines; commercial nuclear facilities; inland waterways; environmental affairs.	Energy and Power; Health and the Environment; Transportation and Commerce.
Merchant Marine and Fisheries. Deepwater ports; ocean dumping; U.S. Coast Guard.	Coast Guard and Navigation; Oceanography.
Public Works and Transportation. Energy conservation related to surface transportation; coal slurry and oil pipelines; Tennessee Valley Authority; deepwater ports.	Surface Transportation; Water Resources.
Science and Technology. Energy R&D, including energy and natural resources, personnel, equipment, and facilities; National Science Foundation; National Aeronautics and Space Administration; Environmental Protection Agency R&D programs.	Energy Development and Applications; Energy Research and Production; Science, Research and Technology; Transportation, Aviation and Communications.

Select Committee on Outer Continental Shelf. Leasing and development of the Outer Continental Shelf (expired June 30, 1980).

Small Business. Energy allocation and marketing, and energy R&D contracts relating to small business.

Ways and Means. Taxes, tariffs, and trade measures relating to energy.

Energy, Environment, Safety and Research.

SENATE

Agriculture, Nutrition and Forestry. Forestry and forest reserves; rural electrification development; natural resource conservation issues.

Agricultural Credit and Rural Electrification; Environment, Soil Conservation and Forestry.

Appropriations. Appropriates funds for energy agencies and departments.

Energy and Water Development; HUD-Independent Agencies; Interior and Related Agencies. Housing and Urban Affairs.

Banking, Housing and Urban Affairs. Energy conservation measures in housing.

Budget. Studies effect of legislation and taxes on the budget.

Commerce, Science and Transportation. Deepwater ports; surface transportation R&D; and agencies with science responsibilities.

Energy and Natural Resources. Energy policy, regulation, and conservation; R&D; speed limits and labeling of appliances; commercial development of nuclear energy; oil and gas production, pricing, and distribution; deepwater ports; hydroelectric power; coal production, and mineral conservation; naval petroleum reserves; mineral leasing; federal power administrations; fuel allocation; forest reserves; conservation fund.

Environment and Public Works. Tennessee Valley Authority; environmental regulation and control of commercial nuclear power; deepwater ports; radiological safety, security, and waste disposal; public parks and recreation areas.

Finance. Taxes, tariffs, and trade measures relating to energy.

Consumer; Science, Technology and Space; Surface Transportation. Energy Conservation and Supply; Energy R&D; Energy Regulation; Energy Resources and Materials Production; Parks, Recreation, and Renewable Resources. Environmental Pollution; Nuclear Regulation; Resource Protection; Transportation; Water Resources. Energy and Foundations; International Trade. Energy, Nuclear Proliferation and Federal Service.

Governmental Affairs. Investigates energy issues; nuclear licensing procedures and waste and spent fuel policy; physical security at nuclear installations.

Labor and Human Resources. Coal mining health and safety.

energy committees were more concerned with protecting their jurisdictional turf than in improving the way the House deals with energy legislation," lamented Representative Patterson.[19]

Five Hundred and Thirty-Five Ambassadors

The fragmentation of power in energy matters throughout Congress is not just a matter of formally divided committee authority. Almost six hundred geographical units—the states and congressional districts in addition to thousands of counties and urban areas in these districts—constitute a vast constellation of divergent parochial interests with powerful influence in the legislative process. Constituents regard their senators and representatives as ambassadors to Washington from the home jurisdiction, as delegates of local interests on whose behalf the member of Congress must be both energetic provider and protector.

As providers, they are expected to acquire skills in the practice of pork barrel politics, the capturing of federal goods and services for the local constituency. As guardians, they must also demonstrate a convincing vigilance in protecting and promoting local interests in legislation. Members' tenure in Washington likely depends as much, if not more, on their ability to fulfill these needs as on their record with national issues. Thus, representatives and senators must fashion a national energy policy within a vortex of competing political pressures and powers: national interests versus parochial interests, and commitments to political party or congressional leaders versus loyalty to local power centers.

The constant intrusion of parochialism upon congressional deliberations more than multiplies the interests whose power must be recognized in building the energy policy agenda. It weakens congressional sensitivity to national needs and priorities in energy affairs and frequently leads members of Congress to hold national policies captive to local interests. Consider, for instance, some major reasons why the House of Representatives rejected the Carter administration's 1979 request for standby authority to impose national gasoline rationing in a fuel emergency:

—The 43 California delegates, regarding cars to be as "essential as food" in their state, objected to any major constraint on highway travel there.

—States due to receive less fuel under the rationing plan objected to the deficit.

—Western and rural states rejected the national allocation of gasoline on an equal basis for all cars because their motorists must drive greater distances than more urban commuters.

—Rural legislators asserted that urbanites could use mass transportation facilities not available in rural areas; consequently, farm families should receive more generous gas allocations than urban ones.[20]

In the end, the interests of vastly divergent constituencies and their claims on Congress, invigorated by periodic elections, gravely inhibit the search for a national consensus on energy policy.

THE IMMENSE BOOTY: THE IMPACT OF ABUNDANCE

The fragmentation of power within government institutions is but one historical inheritance that continues to affect U.S. energy policy. The American experience with its mineral resources has shaped in obvious and subtle ways the manner in which citizens and public officials relate to energy problems. Americans began their national experience with an endowment of natural resources as extravagant as Providence has ever lavished upon a modern nation. For almost two centuries, Americans have been in their own view (and the world's) a "people of plenty." Those who saw the Mississippi Valley when virgin forests climbed to the horizon from both river banks might have sensed no exaggeration when Alexis de Tocqueville marked it as "the most magnificent dwelling place prepared by God for man's abode." Millions of immigrants were lured to the United States by a hundred versions of a ditty sung by pioneers moving toward the unclaimed abundance that was then the West:

> Come along, come along, make no delay,
> Come from every nation, come from every way,
> Our lands are broad enough, don't be alarmed,
> For Uncle Sam is rich enough to give us all a farm.[21]

This natural inheritance in its bountiful variation—what de Tocqueville called "Fortune's immense booty to the Americans"—has affected American culture beyond merely providing the resources from which an enormously productive modern economy could be fashioned. It has strongly influenced, if it did not form, much of the American political vision. Abundance has affected how public officials and citizens define many political problems, what means they consider appropriate for resolving policy issues, and what achievements they believe possible from public management.

This psychology of abundance, particularly its political manifestation, influenced past governmental attitudes toward energy management. Today, such thinking often collides with the imperatives of managing energy as a scarce resource. It is the subtle tyranny of unspoken assumptions. Images and metaphors of abundance, drawn from American history, continue to govern public policy even though that abundance has vanished.

U.S. energy use, as reflected in the nation's growth planning, has especially been affected by the psychology of abundance. With few exceptions, American public officials traditionally have accepted rapid economic growth as desirable, even essential, to civic vitality. "Historically, public opinion has favored development almost irrespective of the cost to the environment," notes a major survey of state and local land law. "Our laws and institutions, many of which evolved during a time when growth was a national ideal, reflect a pro-development bias."[22] Federal policy differed little. "We accepted development as something that occurred naturally," observes a report by the President's Council on Environmental Quality. "The major concerns of government agencies were to see that development was well nourished with infrastructure and that it did not upset the fiscal viability of the community."[23] Economist John Kenneth Galbraith has observed the nation's "preoccupation with production." To Americans, he concluded, "it continued to measure the quality and progress of our civilization."[24]

Visions of continual, even unlimited, economic growth fed on abundant, cheap energy supplies. Policies and programs encouraging growth seldom were formulated with serious attention to their effects on energy reserves or their energy efficiency. Thus, crucial growth sectors of the U.S. economy—including the automobile industry, suburban land development, and highway planning—have been based on highly wasteful, inefficient modes of energy use. Today, continued economic growth requires a better matching of growth targets with limited energy resources, with greater concern for the utilization of efficient forms of power generation. In short, growth planning can no longer assume the unlimited availability of cheap energy.

Yet U.S. government institutions are slow to abandon the psychology of abundance in economic planning. A recent report of the U.S. General Accounting Office (GAO) notes that none of the states with the nation's highest growth rates "had programs specifically aimed at the energy implications of population and industry shifts." In the late 1970s, observed GAO, eight of the nation's largest states still seemed to be shaping their destinies as if no energy crisis had occurred:

> None of the states visited considered energy to be a factor inhibiting future economic and industrial development. Officials in several states said that it was the Federal Government's responsibility to ensure that their states received the energy supplies they need.[25]

The federal government has recently initiated a variety of measures to restrain energy consumption and to make economic policy more sensitive to energy constraints. But the energy implications of most federal economic policy remain unexamined. A case in point is federal tax policy relating to land use. In keeping with traditional federal commitments to economic development, this policy generally favors the rapid construction and sale of single-family dwellings. "The incentive is to build, depreciate, sell, and then build again."[26] Homeowners receive a tax deduction for their mortgage interest; renters receive no such concession. Tax depreciation allowances favor investment in new dwellings rather than the renovation of older ones.

In many other ways, developers and families have powerful incentives to proliferate the single-family subdivisions synonymous with American suburbia. The renovation of older houses to make them more energy efficient, as we have seen, could be as productive to energy efficiency as the building of new energy-conserving structures. In a larger perspective, most federal tax policy affecting consumer spending has been predicated upon growth assumptions now ripe for critical reappraisal in a time of energy resource limits.

PUBLIC OPINION

Energy problems cast U.S. public officials adrift upon a fitful political sea, seeking certain tides of public opinion and finding none. Since the early 1970s, the public mood has been a volatile mixture of several dominant sentiments: confusion over the reality of an energy crisis, deep suspicion about contradictory versions of energy problems and solutions as promoted by the government and energy companies, disagreement over the appropriate energy policy responses, and anger over the burden and sacrifice imposed by energy resource limits. There is no stable, coherent public consensus on most aspects of national energy issues: the voice of the people is nothing more than a confused babble.

This public mood affects energy policy in profound ways. It has encouraged a protracted debate over the proper priorities and policy options for management of the nation's energy resources. Lacking a clear cue from the public, government officials are likely to be cautious about reaching decisions, tolerant of the many competing interests claiming a voice in policy, and insecure about their own policy commitments. Moreover, in the absence of forceful, consistent public demands for policy innovation, incremental solutions tend to dominate in energy policymaking. The public's pervasive distrust of corporate and governmental energy information has weakened the capacity of government to rally public support for crucial national energy policies. A brief explanation of the character of this opinion climate illuminates some reasons for its longevity and its likely persistence.

Is There an Energy Crisis?

One aspect of the American energy dilemma is virtually certain. Most competent studies suggest that the United States, like the rest of the world, faces an energy crisis in the sense that a disastrous shortfall of energy resources likely will occur within a decade or two unless new energy production and energy conservation policies are introduced immediately. The alternative is a potentially catastrophic, chronic disruption of U.S. and world energy supplies.

Millions of Americans do not accept the reality of a national energy shortage serious enough to be called a crisis, but the public has indeed grown more aware of the nation's serious problems with energy availability. In 1979, for instance, 22 percent of a national sample spontaneously listed energy as one of the nation's most important problems; in a similar poll taken seven years earlier, no one had mentioned energy.[27] But most citizens apparently are not convinced that a genuine, chronic energy shortage exists. And the number of believers fluctuates widely. One poll reported in May 1977 that 40 percent of the public believed the crisis was "real," but only 29 percent did by early 1979.[28] By November 1979, more than half the respondents in another national poll asserted that the energy crisis "was fabricated."[29]

A certain degree of skepticism might be attributed to ignorance about basic energy facts. As late as mid-1977, for example, about half of the citizens sampled in one poll were not aware that the United States was importing a significant share of its petroleum consumption.[30] But even policymakers, presumably informed and sophisticated about energy matters, often are confused or skeptical about the existence of an actual crisis. In mid-1979, members of Congress from both political parties had requested that President Carter present convincing evidence of an energy crisis in order to justify the decontrol of petroleum prices. "I come up empty-handed," complained Kentucky Representative Romano L. Mazzoli, "I don't know the answers. I don't know if we're being conned."[31]

This broadly shared uncertainty about the existence of an energy crisis results from a number of factors including conflicting governmental data on energy, a distrust of public officials and agencies, and suspicion laced with resentment about the role of the energy-producing companies in the nation's energy problem.

The Data Circus

One might wonder if public confusion about the U.S energy condition results because citizens do not follow the news or because they do. Much controversy arises from the muddle of conflicting information that emanates from government. This confusion relates to details in estimates of energy supply, distribution, and pricing rather than broad conclusions about domestic energy conditions. But gross data contradictions do occur. Even when the mistakes or inconsistencies are the inevitable result of difficulties in obtaining adequate data, as often happens, the effect is to suggest widespread government ignorance, incompetence, and even deliberate deception.

Practically no area of energy management has been immune to disputes over the accuracy of government energy data. The federal government offered something for everyone in its many versions of the estimated U.S. shortfall of imported petroleum caused by the Iranian crisis in early 1979. The Department of Energy estimated the shortage was at least 500,000 barrels, and perhaps as much as 800,000 barrels, of crude oil daily. The Congressional Research Service, however, contended that the shortage did not exceed even 80,000 barrels daily. And the General Accounting Office estimated the Iranian government was cutting back U.S. oil supplies by 10 to 15 percent, when the actual figure was approximately 4 percent.[32]

One of the Carter administration's most embarrassing incidents was the apparent disappearance of a natural gas shortage that had been repeatedly invoked by the president to justify deregulating the price of interstate natural gas at considerable consumer expense. In his first national energy message in April 1977, the president had informed his television audience that the United States was "now running out of gas and oil" and "cannot substantially increase domestic production."[33] One month after Congress approved national gas deregulation, however, the nation's natural gas reserves somehow magnificently recovered. Secretary of Energy James R. Schlesinger announced in January 1979 that "the United States now has an extraordinary surplus of natural gas. For the next six or seven years at least . . . the Government will shift its energy policy to emphasize consumption of gas."[34]

Public utilities had been warned by Washington in 1977 to begin switching their boilers from natural gas to coal in anticipation of the gas shortage. But by mid-1979, Washington was urging the utilities to consider retaining natural gas instead of switching to coal. This sort of confusion will likely persist through the rest of the decade. Even when the causes are innocent, what people suspect about a problem is as powerful as what they know as fact, and the appearance of governmental performance is as important as the reality of its actions. Continuing conflicts in governmental energy information breed public distrust of such data.

Skepticism About Government

Public distrust of government data feeds on a broader public cynicism toward government and public officials. The character of this disaffection is suggested by a Gallup poll taken in late 1977 when the United States was enduring a natural gas shortage that had threatened to become a crisis. "If a sudden new energy problem were to come up," respondents were asked, "and differing reasons for its cause were given by business, by environmentalists, and by the government, which of these groups would you be most likely to believe?" Approximately half of the respondents expressed confidence in the environmentalists, about a quarter voiced confidence in business, but less than a third said they would believe their government. Less than a quarter of the youngest respondents trusted their public officials.[35] Such citizen distrust of U.S public officials and institutions has been so pervasive since the mid-1960s that it has become a contagion.

The extent of this skepticism is suggested in Table 3-2 that traces the expression of citizen trust "in the people running this country" during the period 1966 to 1979. Significantly, most major private institutions cited in the poll fared better in public esteem that did *any* level of government. This data implies an entrenched, long-term public malaise, and not a transient public distemper that will vanish with better news.

Unfortunately, federal agencies sometimes have been caught in the kind of blatant juggling of energy data that sustains this mood— a reminder of the constant temptation in government to manipulate data to some partisan advantage. In early 1980, for instance, one

Table 3-2   Percentage of Respondents Expressing "A Great Deal of Confidence" in U.S. Institutions and Leaders, 1966 to 1979

Institution	1966	1971	1973	1975	1977	1978	1979
TV news	25%	—	41%	35%	30%	35%	37%
Medicine	73	61%	57	43	55	42	30
Military	62	27	40	24	31	29	29
Press	29	18	30	26	19	23	28
Organized religion	41	27	36	32	34	34	20
Major companies	55	27	29	19	23	22	18
Congress	42	19	29	13	15	10	18
Executive branch	41	23	19	13	23	14	17
Organized labor	22	14	20	14	15	15	10

SOURCE: *Public Opinion*, October/November 1979. Adapted from surveys by Louis Harris and Associates.

congressional committee discovered that Treasury Department officials, anxious not to "embarrass" President Carter, deliberately hid a staff study that contradicted the president's explanation for 1979 crude oil shortages.[36] Such behavior is bipartisan, however; similar antics can be uncovered in most recent administrations.

Tainted Images

The nation's major energy producers have inherited a measure of public distrust and hostility toward their role in energy affairs that is no less intense than public dissatisfaction with government performance. Polls throughout the 1970s and early 1980s consistently revealed that many Americans—often almost two-thirds of those sampled—believed that energy producers were creating and sustaining energy shortages to inflate their profits, or were deliberately obstructing solutions to energy problems, or were providing deceptive data to conceal the true state of U.S. and world energy production levels. Often confused about the nature of energy problems, a large number of Americans was almost certain to hold the energy producers guilty of complicity in major energy emergencies, even when they could not understand the technicalities involved. This general lack of public credibility in industry explanations for energy problems has further diminished public belief that an actual crisis even exists.

Recent events have nourished these public animosities toward energy producers. Major petroleum company profits—traditionally among the most robust in American industry—soared throughout the 1970s until they seemed to many Americans and their political leaders a bloated testimony to the energy industry's economic exploitation of the average consumer. Industry profits had become unprecedented by the late 1970s. In the third quarter of 1979, Exxon's net income had climbed 118 percent compared to the same period in 1978, Gulf Oil had risen by 97 percent, Conoco by 134 percent, and Amoco by 49 percent.[37] Although petroleum industry spokesmen asserted that such profits were necessary to underwrite increasingly expensive exploration for new oil, these figures have been continually disputed by industry critics. One widely publicized study suggested that the nation's five largest oil companies had reinvested only about 50 percent of their available capital in 1978.[38] Most of the reasons given by the energy industry in defense of its economic behavior since 1973 have been sharply and consistently challenged by critics.

The credibility of the petroleum industry in particular has been diminished by repeated governmental revelations or accusations of deliberate price gouging, manipulation of data, mismanagement of energy reserves, and other actions calculated to sustain energy shortages and to increase profits.

The following incidents are representative:

—Twenty major multinational petroleum companies were charged by the Federal Energy Administration with overcharging the public for petroleum products by $336 million between October 1973 and May 1975.

—A House committee staff report asserted that the major oil producers overcharged American consumers by nearly $2 billion between 1974 and 1978.

—The General Accounting Office reported that American oil companies aggravated the spring 1979 petroleum shortage by cutting production of crude oil in the United States during the previous winter, while oil imports from Iran were disrupted.

—A civil trial in Canada revealed that Exxon Corporation occasionally backdated agreements in order to pass on more of its costs to the consumer, disguised increases in company profit margins, and knowingly gave out inaccurate information to consumers, resulting in higher prices.[39]

Many Americans regard such incidents as proof of a petroleum industry scheme—if not an energy industry conspiracy—to create, or exploit, an energy crisis to its own selfish advantage.

An Aversion to Extremes

Amid the fluctuation of current public attitudes about energy management, one discernible trend is an aversion to extreme policy responses. Majorities seem to favor public policies positioned in the most moderate sectors of change. When opinion is fragmented among policy options, it is difficult for policymakers to form substantial majorities for any policy. In any case, public opinion rarely coalesces firmly enough to provide policymakers with a clear cue for radical innovation in a major policy area. In particular, the public mood implies:

—Rejection of massive government takeover of the private energy sector as well as a rejection of largely unregulated private sector energy production.

—Preference for control of potentially dangerous energy technologies, but not a moratorium on their development.

—Approval of mandatory conservation measures, but also a desire for accelerated new energy production.

—Acceptance of government actions for moderate increases in the price of scarce energy resources, but not for severe, short-term price increases.

—Tolerance for some compromises in current standards for environmental protection when necessary for energy production, but not a broad rollback of environmental protection measures.

—Acceptance of the principle of energy conservation, but considerable disagreement over which methods should be used to achieve it.

The tendency of public opinion to aggregate within the moderate range of policy options still leaves government with a multitude of complex, and often extremely difficult, energy policy decisions. Nor does moderation preclude sudden, strong shifts of the public mood in response to particular events. However, as public reaction to the 1979 Three Mile Island nuclear accident indicates, public opinion rarely clusters for very long at the extremes of policy preference: in the aftermath of the nation's most publicized nuclear safety crisis, most Americans still favored continued nuclear power development, although with increased safety regulations.

BUREAUCRACY: THE LOBBY WITHIN

The executive branch of the federal government is, in one perspective, a constitutional fiction—an illusion heightened by organizational charts confining the welter of administrative agencies called the bureaucracy within the boundary of presidential authority. Within the executive branch, there are 13 cabinet departments, more than 50 independent agencies, 6 regulatory commissions, and numerous lesser entities. More than 2.7 million individuals divide their loyalties among these institutions. Closely observed, the executive branch dissolves into a mosaic of disparate bureaucratic interests, each a distinct institutional entity, zealous for its own mission, with special agendas and prejudices—all absorbed in an intricate game of alliance and competition with other actors in and outside the administration.

The president's ability to unite these different interests in some common endeavor across this sprawling domain varies from strong to negligible, no matter the particular time period or president. The bureaucracy is a pluralism of institutional interests vigorously active in shaping the policies it will administer. These competing interests represent government's internal lobby, pressing for advantage with the drive, if not always the style, of private pressure groups.

Agencies and Energy Policy

Bureaucratic pluralism affects the formation of energy policy in several important ways. First, public officials in Congress and the executive branch itself rarely formulate major policies without consulting the various energy bureaucracies that have a stake in a particular issue, just as private groups are consulted. Second, agencies often have strong and conflicting preferences for energy management. An agency's viewpoint evolves from many sources, depending on the nature of its general mission, the particular programs entrusted to it, and its interest group clientele. Thus, the Energy Department's Federal Energy Regulatory Commission (FERC)—responsible under the 1935 Federal Power Act for promoting abundant, reliable supplies of electricity—is more congenial to expansive energy production policies than is the Environmental Protection Agency (EPA), whose legislative mandate includes the control of environmental degradation resulting from energy production.

Differing agency viewpoints assure continuing conflict and shifting alliances among agencies at all stages of policy formulation and implementation. When President Carter created the Interagency Review Group on Waste Management to recommend storage procedures for nuclear waste, the participating agencies formed competing coalitions: the Departments of Energy and State on one side favoring underground storage in New Mexico, with EPA and the President's Council on Environmental Quality on the other side arguing against it. Other actors in the policy process—including the president and his staff, members of Congress, and private interests—constantly seek to exploit bureaucratic interests to their own advantage. Bureaucratic agencies consequently are enmeshed in a complex web of alliances, both permanent and temporary, with other actors in the policy process.

Almost all major federal agencies are affected in some way by energy issues and policies. Among those whose authority bears so heavily upon energy policy that they are discussed at length in subsequent chapters are the Department of Energy (including the Federal Energy Regulatory Commission), the Department of the Interior, the Nuclear Regulatory Commission, the Department of Transportation, and the Environmental Protection Agency. But most major energy issues will affect a multitude of bureaucratic interests, and the resolution of such issues consequently requires complex accommodation among them. Table 3-3 identifies the variety of federal agencies with statutory responsibility for the regulation of power, energy, and transportation. Typically, only a few of these agencies will be involved extensively in the resolution of any particular energy issue, but each commonly reviews major energy proposals and can become an activist in energy policy formulation.

Bureaucratic Behavior

Agencies are predictable performers during policy infighting. An agency's behavior is usually many variations on a few grand themes:

Turfing. An agency's "turf" is its legislative authority, programs, budget, and general mission. Agencies zealously protect their turf, which they suspect is constantly imperiled since one agency's turf may look like opportunity to another. Turf fighting is therefore endemic to bureaucracy.

Look Out for the Clientele. An agency's clientele are the organized interests that have a special concern for its programs. Agencies seek cordial, politically productive relations with their clientele. Agencies often anticipate clientele needs, mobilize these interest groups for political action, and educate their clientele on matters affecting them.

Imperialism. Agencies desire not only to survive but to prosper. It is typical of agency behavior to seek expansion of its authority, additional programs, and increased public visibility. Imperialism can arise from noble as well as base intentions, sometimes disguised as "protecting the public interest."

Proxy Wars. Competing clientele groups often mobilize their bureaucratic patrons who, in effect, become proxies for the private group contenders. A common proxy war on the energy front involves policy conflicts between the Department of Energy (responsive to the energy producers) and the Environmental Protection Agency (alert to environmental interests).

Get Help from the Hill. Agencies constantly form alliances, often shifting, with their friends in Congress on Capitol Hill—senators, representatives, committee staffers, and others—and in the White House where they enjoy privileged access. Consequently, major conflicts within bureaucracy seldom end without drawing presidential and congressional sympathizers into the fray.

Waffling. Agencies "waffle" when they make ambiguous, inconsistent, or contradictory decisions while they ponder what they really want to do about a problem. Waffling often indicates genuine confusion within an agency; sometimes it reflects an inability to make a clear decision. But it is often calculated confusion, meant to keep options open and an agency uncommitted on policy issues.

The Power of Inertia. Agencies can exercise their power to shape policy by not implementing certain aspects of a program or by refusing to take initiative to change programs. This power often is wielded in disguise, as passive obstruction of policy, when an agency insists it lacks sufficient data to make a decision. Inertia sometimes does arise out of a genuine need to study an issue further. Thus, it is often difficult to determine when inertia is a demonstration of responsibility or an evasion of it.

Table 3-3   Federal Agencies with Authority for the Regulation of Power, Energy Resources, and Transportation, 1980

Executive Agencies
Civil Aeronautics Board
Environmental Protection Agency
Federal Maritime Commission
Federal Mine Safety and Health Review Commission
Federal Trade Commission
International Development Cooperation Agency
Interstate Commerce Commission
National Aeronautics and Space Administration
National Railroad Passenger Corporation (AMTRAK)
National Science Foundation
National Transportation Safety Board
Nuclear Regulatory Commission
Tennessee Valley Authority
U.S. International Trade Commission
U.S. Railway Association

Executive Departments
Agriculture Department
Commerce Department
  Bureau of the Census
  International Trade Administration
  Maritime Administration
  National Bureau of Standards
  National Oceanic and Atmospheric Administration
Energy Department
  Economic Regulatory Administration
  Federal Energy Regulatory Commission
  Regional Power Administrations

Housing and Urban Development Department
Interior Department
  Bureau of Land Management
  Bureau of Mines
  Office of Surface Mining Reclamation and Enforcement
  U.S. Geological Survey
  Water and Power Resources Administration
Justice Department
  Antitrust Division
  Land and Natural Resources Division
State Department
Treasury Department
Transportation Department
  Federal Aviation Administration
  Federal Highway Administration
  Federal Railroad Administration
  Materials Transportation Bureau
  National Highway Transportation Safety Administration
  St. Lawrence Seaway Development Corporation
  U.S. Coast Guard
  Urban Mass Transportation Administration

Executive Office
Council on Environmental Quality
Domestic Policy Staff
Office of Management and Budget
Office of Science and Technology Policy
Office of the U.S. Trade Representative

SOURCE: *Washington Information Directory 1980-81* (Washington, D.C.: Congressional Quarterly, 1980), chaps. 6, 15, 16.

PUBLIC INTEREST POLITICS

The pluralism of interests within the administrative branch has been accentuated by the continuing expansion of federal programs in response to new social groups acquiring the political power to gain governmental attention. In a broader perspective, this pluralism also is the administrative expression of the vast social, economic, and political diversity of the American people. In any event, the internal arena of policymaking in the federal executive branch is so predictably divided into pluralistic coalitions of interest that this constraint will repeatedly be noted in all the energy policy issues we examine.

In one respect, the current setting of energy policy formulation is quite unlike that of most public policies during recent decades. Since the mid-1960s, an extremely energetic public interest movement has been an increasingly influential participant in the policy process. The movement itself consists of many new, or newly invigorated, private groups espousing a variety of policies loosely characterized as "public interest" programs. These interests have gained governmental access not only through techniques traditional to most private interests but also through the skillful exploitation of newer influence structures created by government itself.

Although these groups share nothing approaching the coherence of an ideology, they do espouse a variety of causes rooted in many common national values. Taken together, these elements—an organizational base, institutionalized linkage with government, and shared values—define the public interest infrastructure of the American political process. This infrastructure is a newly important constraint on the formulation of most public policy, particularly the making of energy policy.

The Public Interest Ethos

One crucial difference between public interest groups and most other private associations is that public interest groups commonly espouse programs whose benefits will be distributed across socioeconomic sectors rather than primarily confined to a relatively narrow social or economic base. Public interest programs, notes Jeffrey Berry, "will not selectively and materially benefit the membership or activists of the organization."[40]

The public interest movement marches under different banners. The most active associations have promoted environmentalism, consumerism, product safety, civil rights, government reform, technology control, and corporate accountability. Many are mass membership organizations such as Common Cause, the Consumer's Union of the

United States, and—one of the largest—Ralph Nader's Public Citizen, a public interest conglomerate that embraces at least eight specialized groups concerned with issues ranging from health research to tax reform. Some public interest groups, like the Union of Concerned Scientists, have organized scientific and technical professionals to prepare highly proficient evaluations of complex technological issues for the government and the public.

Despite rhetoric and good intentions, the public interest mantle has never fit very securely over most groups attempting to wear it. Most such groups are solidly, if not exclusively, middle-class in membership and leftward-leaning in political preference. If the measure of a public interest organization is the extent to which its membership broadly reflects the nation's social composition or its programs articulate majority sentiments, most public interest groups actually represent not *the* public but a particular public—a public nevertheless far larger than that likely to be represented by other types of interest organizations, and one whose interests often do embrace those of the majority of Americans.

The Legal and Structural Base

The public interest movement has become a major force in energy affairs largely because new legislation and institutional arrangements have been created within government to facilitate such group access to policymakers. These arrangements have benefited the public interest movement so selectively that its critics often attack these arrangements in an effort to reduce the movement's leverage in energy politics.

A number of recent comprehensive federal laws have been responsible. The 1966 Freedom of Information Act, as amended in 1974, compelled government agencies to release all but the most sensitive documents to citizens upon their request. Previously, public interest groups could obtain such data, if at all, only through expensive and time-consuming legal action. The 1969 National Environmental Policy Act (NEPA) requires that all federal agencies produce environmental impact statements on any policy, program, or decision with major environmental impact. This policy provides public interest groups with detailed information about important governmental decisions, an early opportunity to prepare to deal with these issues, and public hearings at which to present their views.

During the 1970s, moreover, numerous congressional actions expanded a citizen's standing (or right) to sue the federal government for nonimplementation of new programs. This legislation removed many previously formidable legal obstacles to citizen groups seeking to hasten the implementation of federal programs affecting the environment and energy policy. The 1970 Clean Air Act, for instance, authorizes "any person" to sue a federal agency for failure to enforce the act. In addition, many federal agencies also have been required to expand opportunities for citizen participation in the development of their programs. In fact, some agencies provide financial assistance to public interest groups to enable them to testify on important agency decisions when their participation is considered especially beneficial and the groups otherwise would not be able to participate.

Public Groups and Energy Policy

The federal government, in effect, has come close to accepting as a principle the public's right to participate in the formulation of major administrative policies, an attitude almost unimaginable a few decades ago.[41] Measures to expand public participation have increased incentives and opportunities for public interest groups to enlarge their influence in the administration of energy-related programs. The public interest sector is now an almost inevitable participant in the formulation and implementation of major energy policies. Most of these groups share broad convictions about energy management that are important for energy policymakers.

Environmentalists have been wary of, and often strongly opposed to, national energy programs that stress extremely accelerated new energy production. Instead, environmental organizations generally advocate energy conservation over increased production as their first priority in the nation's search for more energy. Thus, the environmental movement asserts that the federal government should give less attention to developing new nuclear reactors for electric power and more funding for small solar technologies, mass rapid transit facilities, cogeneration systems, and other procedures that conserve existing energy stocks.

Environmentalists also strongly resist any efforts to relax existing environmental standards in order to facilitate new energy production and believe many technical fixes currently proposed for the nation's energy problems will inflict a multitude of malevolent ecological effects. As we will observe in a later chapter, these are major reasons why most environmental organizations have opposed the nation's ambitious new synthetic fuels program. Environmentalists generally fear that the energy crisis might become a potent psychological weapon that will enable opponents to roll back the environmental progress of the last decade—particularly if the public and its officials can be convinced that the nation must choose between adequate energy supplies or existing environmental protection programs. The anti-nuclear movement draws much of its patronage from the clientele of the public interest sector, especially environmentalists. The movement's assault upon the domestic nuclear power industry sometimes has approached the character of a Holy War where no concessions were given to the opposition.

Many public interest groups have attacked the private energy sector on other grounds: in particular, for its alleged manipulation of the energy market, soaring profits, and dealings with the government. A number of public interest groups representing the scientific community have advocated reform of federal administrative procedures in order to assure a slow, exhaustive investigation of the impact from new technologies before federal agencies promote their development. Some public groups enter the policy arena less from concern with particular energy policies than to assure that the proper rules have been observed during the decisionmaking process.

The impact of these various public groups has been important in energy policy. Because public interest groups are now able to intervene when they feel administrative errors have occurred, some government energy bureaucracies are undoubtedly more careful about observing correct procedures and proper laws in implementing policy. "Atmospheric influence" is what Peter Schuck calls this impact of public groups. Many agencies, he notes, "report that the mere existence of public interest groups, the knowledge that officials 'are being watched,' affects their behavior quite apart from any particular action that such groups may take."[42]

Using their newly acquired rights to participate in federal agency deliberations, public interest groups almost routinely have prolonged deliberations for the development of many new energy production projects. These delays, ranging from months to years, have caused rapid increases in the cost of new energy facilities, such as electric power plants. Obstruction of this kind affects not only power generating plants but also the leasing of sites for offshore oil drilling, the leasing of mineral exploration rights on federal lands in the West, approval of power transmission lines, and other energy issues.

The total effect of these delays can be enormous. In late 1978, for instance, 10 major power generating facilities planned, or partially constructed, in New England were delayed by administrative or judicial action by public interest opponents. The response of critics is predictable. They assert that the new arrangements largely cater to the narrow viewpoint of a noisy, disputatious, inflexible minority of zealots who are quite willing to sacrifice the nation's interest in a secure energy future on the altar of their own ideology. The delays, costs, and uncertainties imposed by the new procedures are not, in this view, worth whatever benefits result. These critics usually demand new presidential, congressional, or administrative remedies to facilitate increased energy production.

Defenders of the new participation arrangements contend that prolonged decisions have more accurately revealed the social and environmental costs of proposed energy facilities. The dollar costs incurred by delay in getting energy production underway, the argument continues, often is more than offset by the intangible savings to society in reduced public health and environmental damage. Moreover, many of the delayed or halted projects are in fact so flawed either technically or financially that they deserve their fate.

The public interest sector, in any case, now has so large an organizational base and so many opportunities to influence policy that it cannot be relegated again to obscurity. The public interest sector quite often is the only major countervailing political force to energy production interests in energy policymaking. Interest groups have provided information about energy issues and have promoted greater public awareness of the national energy situation. Activities such as Sun Day 1978 and the huge anti-nuclear protest that thronged the National Mall in Washington in May 1979 (more than 100,000 people were present) were promoted by these groups. These activities, as well as the more numerous if less dramatic examples of public education and propagandizing by the public interest organizations, amount to a kind of technological education for the American public.

CONCLUSION: WHAT POLITICS MEANS TO ENERGY

This chapter has focused on one recurrent question: How does the U.S. political system shape the nation's response to its energy problems? There is both a long and a short answer. The long answer is that the U.S. political system, closely observed, resolves into several different elements that affect energy policy. We have named and discussed some of the most important of these political elements: political style, fragmentation of governmental power, pervasive influence of organized interest groups, inheritance of traditional attitudes about energy management, and behavior of the governmental bureaucracy and public interest organizations. Each factor introduces a set of biases to the decisionmaking process and provides opportunities for some forms of political action and policy formulation while inhibiting others. In brief, the U.S. political structure, like all governmental structures, can be viewed as a set of institutionalized biases, as an expression of values and beliefs to which energy policies usually must conform in some manner.

The less obvious answer to the question posed in this chapter is nevertheless equally important. The nation's political system also shapes energy policy in a manner that reflects two centuries' experience with energy resources that have been drastically altered within the last several decades. It is obvious that the nation's capabilities to resolve its energy problems successfully will depend as much on the capability of its government institutions to make the appropriate responses as on the capacity of the nation's natural and technological resources.

It is by no means inevitable that Americans will readily alter the political context of future energy decisions in an appropriate manner to fit the emerging energy realities. The nation's energy dilemma, in a sense, has become a critical, even dangerous, problem in political engineering. Having observed how the political system affects energy policy, we are in a better position to understand where improvements should—and perhaps must—occur in U.S. energy policy-making. The substance of this chapter is another reminder that the nation's energy difficulties are a test of the nation's political skills and resilience.

NOTES

1. *New York Times,* July 13, 1979.
2. "The Energy Package: What Has Congress Wrought?," *National Journal,* November 4, 1978.
3. *New York Times,* July 8, 1979.
4. *New York Times,* July 16, 1979.
5. Charles Lindblom, "The Science of 'Muddling Through,'" *Public Administration Review* (Spring 1959): 86.
6. Ibid.
7. *New York Times,* November 10, 1979.
8. Graham T. Allison, *Essence of Decision* (Boston: Little, Brown & Co., 1971), p. 163.
9. Ibid., p. 145.
10. Thomas E. Cronin, *The State of the Presidency,* 2nd ed. (Boston: Little, Brown & Co., 1980), pp. 162, 169.
11. *New York Times,* May 22, 1977.
12. *New York Times,* October 9, 1977. See also David H. Davis, *Energy Politics,* 2nd ed. (New York: St. Martin's Press, 1978), chap. 6.
13. *New York Times,* May 16, 1978.
14. Theodore W. Lowi, *The End of Liberalism* (New York: W. W. Norton & Co., 1969), p. 95.
15. Ibid., p. 107.
16. U.S., General Accounting Office, *Use, Cost, Purpose and Makeup of Department of Energy Advisory Commitees,* Report No. EMD-79-17 (Washington, D.C.: U.S. Government Printing Office, February 2, 1979).
17. Quoted in Robert Stobaugh and Daniel Yergin, eds., *Energy Future: Report of the Energy Project at the Harvard Business School* (New York: Random House, 1979), p. 140.
18. See Bruce I. Oppenheimer, "Policy Effects of U.S. House Reform," *Legislative Studies Quarterly,* I (February 1980): 5-29.
19. Congressional Quarterly *Weekly Report,* March 29, 1980, p. 886.
20. *New York Times,* May 7, 1979.

21. Quoted in David M. Potter, *People of Plenty* (Chicago: University of Chicago Press, 1968), p. 80.
22. William K. Reilly, ed., *The Use of Land* (New York: Thomas Y. Crowell, 1973), p. 14.
23. President's Council on Environmental Quality, *Environmental Quality, 1974* (Washington, D.C.: U.S. Government Printing Office, 1974), p. 27.
24. John Kenneth Galbraith, *The Affluent Society* (New York: New American Library, 1958), p. 103.
25. U.S., General Accounting Office, *Better Planning Needed to Deal with Shifting Regional Energy Demand,* Report No. EMD-78-35 (Washington, D.C.: U.S. Government Printing Office, February 22, 1978).
26. President's Council on Environmental Quality, *Environmental Quality,* p. 27.
27. See *The Gallup Poll Index, 1970-80.*
28. *Public Opinion* (May/June, 1979): 32.
29. *New York Times,* November 6, 1979.
30. *New York Times,* June 2, 1977.
31. *New York Times,* May 31, 1979.
32. *New York Times,* March 18, 1979.
33. Executive Office of the President, Energy Policy and Planning Staff, *The National Energy Plan* (Washington, D.C.: U.S. Government Printing Office, 1977), p. 18.
34. *New York Times,* January 10, 1979.
35. *Public Opinion* (May/June 1978): 27.
36. *New York Times,* January 4, 1980.
37. *New York Times,* October 24, 1979.
38. *New York Times,* November 26, 1979.
39. *New York Times,* April 29, 1978; December 11, 1978; September 14, 1979; October 30, 1979.
40. Jeffrey M. Berry, *Lobbying for the People* (Princeton, N.J.: Princeton University Press, 1977), p. 7.
41. See Walter A. Rosenbaum, "Public Involvement as Reform and Ritual," in *Citizen Participation in America,* ed. Stuart Langton (Lexington, Mass.: Lexington Books, 1978), pp. 81-96.
42. Peter H. Schuck, "Public Interest Groups and the Policy Process," *Public Administration Review* (March/April 1977): 138.

4

Private or Public Goods?:
Energy and the Environment

The energy crisis looks much different in Washington than it does in the small western communities of Colstrip, Montana, and Beulah and Zap, North Dakota. In Washington, the energy problem is regarded as an intimidating bundle of acutely complex issues. But in these tiny western communities, mere specks of dust on the maps of Montana and North Dakota, the energy crisis appears extremely simple: the choice is coal or land. Colstrip, Beulah, and Zap are tiny stages upon which has been mounted a national energy drama. They epitomize a dilemma inherent in the shaping of the nation's energy future that is intractable, dangerous, and unavoidable.

The fate of these communities symbolizes the common destiny of numerous other small towns scattered across the western Plains. They are caught in a national conflict between demands for increased energy production and a concern for protection of the environment, which raises a still broader issue: should private or public interests have the greater claim in public energy management? In this chapter we will examine these issues, briefly discussing why private and public interests compete in energy policy and why they pursue different political strategies. The conflict between energy production and environmental protection in two major energy sectors—coal and nuclear power—will then be examined in greater detail. First, we will take a closer look at Colstrip, Beulah, and Zap, where the human, ecological, and economic stakes in energy management are vividly portrayed.

A WESTERN DILEMMA

The communities of Colstrip, Beulah, and Zap lie atop the Fort Union coal formation, 1.5 billion tons of coal within a minable 6,000 feet of the surface containing perhaps 40 percent of the nation's known coal reserves. This coal is low-sulfur coal, which makes it doubly attractive. Near Colstrip, Montana, the Crow Indians have leased 30,000 acres of their reservation, which contains perhaps 1 million tons of coal, to mining companies. A subsidiary of the American Natural Gas Company intends to construct a $1 billion coal gasification facility between Beulah and Zap, North Dakota, which will annually consume 12 million tons of coal from below the surrounding prairie. The nation's current synthetic fuels program, if fully realized, might require the coal and shale mining of 2 million western acres, an area larger than the state of Delaware. A western coal boom could bring to the 6 states on or near the Fort Union formation more than 100 new strip mines, 300,000 new residents, and perhaps several hundred "mine mouth" electric generating plants, synthetic fuels facilities, and allied installations by the mid-1980s.[1]

Less than 3 percent of the U.S. population now inhabits the vast grasslands, ravines, and wooded foothills that constitute most of the western Plains ecosystem. Most of the 100 communities likely first to feel the shock from a new raid on coal—like Zap, Beulah, and Colstrip—are settlements of fewer than 1,500 people. Unprecedented economic growth surely would ride the crest of the boom. Native Indian tribes like the Crow, Northern Cheyenne, and Navajo could potentially reap billions of dollars in mining royalties, improving the lives of people whose average yearly income is below $1,500. The Crow nation alone owns mineral rights to about one-fifth of the minable coal in the western United States.[2]

Other pockets of community and corporate prosperity would flourish throughout the region. Fossil fuel economies, with their highly productive technological infrastructures, would displace agriculture as the principal livelihood in many areas. But this prosperity could turn out to be a malevolent one, so dearly purchased that most of the region's people remain ambivalent, and even hostile, to its prospect. The fear is not simply for the passing of a life style. There is increasing apprehension that mining technology will irreparably gouge the price of prosperity into the soil by transfiguring thousands of prairie acres into an ecological wasteland.

The essence of the ecological issue is surface mining. Western coal must be strip mined, and stripping is an environmental catastrophe unless rigorously controlled. It can disrupt underground and surface waters, create diffuse acid mine drainage, destroy all vegetative cover, create heavy soil erosion and sedimentation of stream beds, and leave unstable spoil banks to menace public health and safety. In Appalachia, where strip mining has been practiced most extensively, it has left thousands of acres a ravaged and unrecoverable waste. Estimates suggest that more than half of the western grasslands overlying coal seams are amenable to stripping, as are 28 percent of the brushlands and 11 percent of the Ponderosa pine forest located over coal deposits.[3]

In an effort to prevent further ecological ruin, in 1977 Congress passed the Surface Mining Control and Reclamation Act that requires all future strip miners to restore stripped land as a condition for obtaining a mining permit. But the capacity of miners to restore western strip-mined land to productivity is uncertain, even with the best technology and good faith. The restorability of the land depends on a delicate, unpredictable interaction between technological resources and a fragile ecosystem that would be slow to regenerate from any level of environmental derangement. If restoration fails, the damage can diffuse from mining sites to affect adjacent agricultural and grazing lands severely. To the people of the western prairie lands, strip mining is a gamble—with their land as the stakes.

From a larger perspective, the development of coal resources poses problems that are common to most future energy production. Claims for environmental protection must be balanced against equally insistent demands for increased energy supplies whenever further development of energy technologies is contemplated, which is a difficult trade-off. It is often impossible to achieve both goals simultaneously— one cannot mine western coal and also preserve an undisturbed prairie ecosystem. There are two sides involved in the coal conflict: one generally seeks private goods from government, and the other seeks public ones. As a result, each side enjoys different advantages and pursues differing political strategies to achieve its policy goals.

THE POLITICS OF PRIVATE AND PUBLIC GOODS

When government plans future energy management, a flow of goods, or benefits, results from its decisions. In economic terms, these benefits are roughly a mixture of public and private goods. A public good, sometimes called a collective good, is a benefit for the whole society, such that "if any person in a group consumes it, it cannot feasibly be withheld from others in the same group."[4] In contrast, private goods can be "rationed so as to prevent other people from enjoying the benefits of the good."[5] If government could simultaneously produce both public and private benefits from energy management, in the quantity demanded, this distinction might be academic. But government usually must choose between competing claims for public or private goods, or decide the proper mix of the two.

Private and Public Energy Goods

In the past, federal energy policy created a generous flow of private goods. The federal oil depletion allowance, for example, which until recently permitted domestic petroleum producers to deduct from their gross income up to 22 percent of the value of their production, conferred an economic privilege on one particular economic sector. So did federal law limiting the insurance liability of nuclear power plants to $560 million as a form of special investment protection for the industry. Of course, beneficiaries of a selective benefit typically insist they will work for the "public interest."

Indeed, the public rhetoric of private energy interests almost always insists that their private gains nevertheless do possess public merit, even when the evidence is meager. The award for audacity in this respect probably should go to Herman Dieckamp, the president of the corporation that owns the Three Mile Island, Pennsylvania, nuclear reactor whose mismanagement caused a potentially calamitous core meltdown in early 1979. Dieckamp asserted that Washington should help pay the utility's $400 million cleanup costs because the incident had been "an important opportunity to add to the nation's nuclear experience."[6]

The most important public goods involved in energy management are benefits such as public health and safety, national defense, environmental protection, lowered utility costs, and other benefits that are very broadly distributed across the whole society. Few interest groups oppose such benefits on principle. Many such groups nonetheless do oppose policies that purport to create public benefits because some private benefit must be sacrificed or because some private interests must bear most of the cost of producing the public good.

Consider the cost to Alaska's citizens resulting from Congress's decision in 1980 to designate over 100 million acres of federal land in that state as permanent wilderness, a decision made to protect the "public interest" in wilderness preservation. Millions of dollars in royalties from mining, grazing, timbering, and mineral exploration will be lost to the state. Similarly, energy conservation may well serve the public good, but petroleum producers generally oppose a 50 cent per gallon federal tax on gasoline because such a tax would force conservation at the fuel pump with a substantial loss of profit to the gasoline industry.

Getting Goods: Different Strategies

Those interests seeking private and public goods from energy policy enjoy different political advantages and usually pursue divergent strategies in their struggles to get issues on the government agenda and policy formulated. As a rule, promoters of private goods in energy policy seek tangible and immediate benefits, the kind that their beneficiaries will understand and support. Moreover, the political reward to public officials who deliver various private goods is often direct and tangible because those who benefit can see and appreciate what was done for them.

The social cost of creating these private benefits frequently is concealed or is so broadly distributed across society that the cost to the individual appears negligible. Thus, the petroleum industry's ability to deduct the millions of dollars it pays to foreign governments in oil royalties from its annual federal income taxes (a concession granted by the federal government in 1951) has saved the petroleum producers billions of dollars in U.S. taxes over several decades. The cost of this arrangement to the average American is some slight but hidden increase in his or her yearly income tax that offsets the lost oil revenues.

The political setting for promoters of public benefits in energy policy is quite different. These benefits often are vague or intangible, so widely distributed or slow to appear that it is difficult to arouse support from an apathetic public. But the cost of providing the public benefits may be very tangible and immediate: those who do pay are aware of when and how much they sacrifice.

For example, clean air is a vague public good for many Americans. Unless one lives in a severely polluted airshed like Los Angeles, the personal gain in having cleaner air may seem remote. But the public utilities who must control their air pollution will add the cost of low-sulfur coal or smokestack scrubbers to their customers' bills. And the price of a pollution emission control for new cars is on the sticker. Furthermore, it may take decades to attain clean air, and the benefits may not be realized until much later. In any event, a citizen might well enjoy the benefits from clean air without doing anything to obtain it—public goods, after all, cannot be denied to anyone.

These circumstances not only complicate the promotion of public goods in energy when compared to private ones; they also suggest somewhat different conditions for their acquisition. Successful attempts to acquire public energy benefits often are crisis-driven. Success depends on the existence of a broad-scale energy problem that convinces otherwise apathetic Americans that government must promote a solution in the form of public goods (environmental protection, greater product safety, and the like). Advocates of public goods also must wage a continuing campaign within government and among the public to convince them both that the benefits will truly outweigh the costs incurred. Such propaganda is especially imperative when recession, inflation, or other economic dislocations force upon citizens a heightened sensitivity to the private cost of public programs. Finally, groups espousing public goods are usually more dependent on a broad membership base, an active membership, and volunteerism to achieve their ends than are promoters of private goods, whose financial resources and ability to buy professional services are usually greater.

Keeping Goods: Policy Implementation and Interpretation

Congress legislates or the president orders an energy policy that causes some public or private benefit to arise from the law. The arena of conflict now shifts to the bureaucracy and the judicial branch, where the policies must be implemented and interpreted and where new opportunities exist to obtain or obstruct such benefits. Policy formulation has, in effect, displaced the political struggle over energy benefits to the implementation stage of the policy process.

How a policy is implemented and interpreted can affect how government creates public and private advantages in energy policy. First, the costs of these policies—who will actually pay for whatever benefits are involved—are often determined in the administration of a program or policy. For example, Congress has delegated to the Environmental Protection Agency the authority to determine which public utilities must scrub their smokestack emissions, which technology must be used, and when controls must be imposed—in essence, the authority to determine who will bear the cost for clean air. Second, interests dissatisfied with administrative judgments on energy policy matters can challenge, and sometimes overturn, such decisions through court action. Third, Congress and the White House often make policy deliberately vague or ambiguous as a means to facilitate policy formulation. In such instances, the bureaucracy or judiciary may largely determine what public or private benefits will actually arise from a policy.

Promoters of public and private energy goods face different political problems during policy administration. Generally, collective benefits from energy policy are very vulnerable to subversion during administrative delivery. Public support for these policies, such as environmental protection, typically fades after an initial surge of enthusiasm. Furthermore, advocates of public goods often are less affluent, organized, and persistent than their opponents. The opponents of such policies, however, are likely to be well financed, skillfully organized, and extremely persistent in pursuing their interests through the administrative process. In fact, an agency charged with regulating some energy sector in the public interest may sometimes be captured by the interests it regulates, which amounts to capture by those interests most hostile to the public benefits the agency is supposed to create or protect. Thus, it is usually more difficult for proponents of public energy goods to protect their interests in the administrative process than it is for those concerned primarily with private benefits.

When federal programs do succeed in creating benefits (whether private or public) for a large social sector, the beneficiaries will become a tenacious constituency eager to protect or enlarge these programs. This is one reason why it is difficult to terminate, or even to curtail significantly, many federal spending programs no matter how temporary they are intended to be. The interest structures organized about such programs are one reason why supposedly short-term federal programs turn out to be long-term, if not immortal, policies.

Thus, from agenda-setting to policy interpretation, the governmental policy process confronts promoters of private and public energy benefits with different political tasks, opportunities, and probabilities of success. These generalities are more sharply etched by examining the problem of reconciling the interests of environmental protection with those that promote increased energy production.

THE ENERGY-ECOLOGY TRADE-OFF

Protection of the environment is a prime example of a public good, one that government alone must usually provide. The U.S. economic system has traditionally treated the nation's air and water resources as free goods that cost nothing to use. The degradation inflicted upon the environment has usually been regarded by economists as an inevitable "externality"—that is, a cost of producing goods and services that is ignored in the price of those products and services. Society pays the environmental "cost" for producing such goods, not those who produce or consume them directly. Neither the producers nor consumers of goods that cause environmental damage can be easily motivated to curtail the degradation voluntarily until a catastrophe threatens. The federal government has come to assume a unique responsibility to restrain the exploitation of the environment while still permitting its reasonable economic use.

A Constant Issue

Almost all forms of future energy development, with the exception of some passive solar technologies, entail an environmental hazard. The unconstrained use of natural gas and petroleum resources implies a worldwide resource exhaustion within the next several generations. Coal and nuclear power, while potentially more abundant, can be ecologically devastating unless environmentally constrained. The issue in such cases is the extent to which environmental protection is to be traded for future energy resource availability. A comparatively new issue in American energy politics, this trade-off is all the more difficult in the case of coal and nuclear power because a satisfactory formula cannot be readily obtained by appeals to economics or science.

It might be supposed that physical or biological scientists could more readily eliminate some possible energy-ecology trade-offs by specifying the levels of environmental degradation tolerable in energy production, which would at least define a range of energy production prohibited as options for public policymakers. But it is difficult, and sometimes impossible, for scientists to specify confidently the ecological consequences of various energy production levels. The Office of Technology Assessment recently evaluated the ecological risks from increased coal utilization and concluded:

> ... [The] very real deficiency in our knowledge of environmental processes makes it difficult to determine whether current plans for coal development could cause unacceptable impacts. Some of the more spectacular impacts that have been attributed to coal development ... represent risks rather than certainties. Scientists disagree sharply on the extent of the risks, greatly increasing the difficulty in developing environmental policies.[7]

Frequently, scientific experts are able to define a range of estimated environmental effects from differing levels of energy production. However, scientists can seldom provide a definitive answer to the question of how much ecological degradation is too much. Indeed, by a perverse logic, the ambiguity about the ecological effects of energy utilization often expands with increased governmental pressure upon science to provide such data. In mid-1979, the Nuclear Regulatory Commission (NRC) decided, under intense pressure from critics of nuclear power, that its previous estimate of risks from a nuclear reactor accident was no longer "reliable" and, in the words of one NRC staffer, "the bottom line just evaporated from the safety issue."[8] Faced in 1978 with disagreements among health officials concerning the public impact of air pollution, the director of the Environmental Protection Agency's Health Effects Research Lab observed, "I am unaware of any single study in pollution epidemiology in which the results could not lead equally qualified, honest individuals to widely different interpretations."[9] And a recent report on radiation by the National Academy of Sciences appears to have produced only confusion:

> A report of the National Academy of Sciences... was almost totally incomprehensible even to people with scientific backgrounds.... The dispute over the meaning of the numbers that had been assembled ran so deep that a rump group on the committee that conducted the study publicly disavowed some of the main majority views, thus exacerbating the very disagreement the study was supposed to have settled.[10]

Many of these problems are inevitable. In one respect, they testify to the responsibility of the scientific enterprise because data must meet rigorous tests of sustained, critical inquiry. Still, limited scientific data often denies government officials a rigorous standard of judgment when weighing the implications of future energy production policies.

A Historic Bias

Balancing production and environmental priorities in energy development is further complicated by the historic bias of American energy policy. The energy-ecology balance has traditionally been a nonissue in American government. Government policy has heavily favored energy development and consumption with scant regard for its environmental impacts until quite recently. Examples of this bias abound. For more than half a century, the U.S. government vigorously promoted the utilization of automobiles with practically no regard to its long-term air quality implications. The U.S. interstate highway system has become an asphalt memorial to governmental patronage of the automobile. Adorning almost 43,000 miles of American earth at a cost of $68 billion, the highway system is largely underwritten by federal gasoline taxes willingly yielded by Congress and the public as a modest price for continental mobility.

The federal government's responsibilities for fossil fuel resources on the public domain have historically been defined in terms of promoting their production and utilization. The 1970 Mining and Minerals Policy Act, for instance, instructs the Department of the Interior to observe the following priorities in its administration of mineral deposits on federal property:

> The development of economically sound and stable domestic mining, minerals, metals, and mineral reclamation industries; [and] the orderly and economic development of domestic mineral resources, reserves and reclamation of minerals to help assure satisfaction of industrial, security, and environmental needs. . . .[11]

Even nuclear safety could yield to technology development. The Atomic Energy Commission's atomic weapons tests in Nevada in the early 1950s were often careless, and sometimes deliberately negligent, of public safety. An internal AEC memorandum at the time acknowledged that issues of radiation contamination from tests "are not satisfactorily answered at present," nor were they for 25 years thereafter. In a vacuum of ecological sensitivity, it was inevitable that energy production should claim such priority in energy policy-making.

The bias of energy policy is evident in the behavior of large federal bureaucracies whose missions were, and continue to be, enhancement of energy production. From its inception in 1848, the Department of the Interior has had primary responsibility for the administrative stewardship of energy resources on the public domain.

Currently, the department's jurisdiction embraces an estimated 548 million acres of federal land containing about 60 percent of western coal reserves and significant (but not yet accurately estimated) quantities of oil, natural gas, and uranium. In the past, the department unreservedly promoted the rapid leasing and sale of vast tracts of public domain for mining. The Interior Department's zeal for mining the federal domain finally convinced Congress to alter the department's statutory responsibilities so that more sensitivity to land conservation might be imposed.

Today, the Interior Department is expected to follow a legislative formula requiring a "balanced use" of public domain between conservation and resource extraction. Nonetheless, the department's long history of mining promotion, its current minerals programs, and its professional staff all strongly incline the agency toward energy production priorities. Its cordial stance toward mining interests, a powerful and articulate segment of its clientele, has earned the department recognition as the major bureaucratic spokesman for "the coal people."

The Department of Energy (DOE) only took two years to establish its credentials as an energy promoter. Created in March 1977, the department brought together more than 60 fragmented federal energy agencies and programs under one administrative roof and inherited a primary mission to encourage energy production, efficiency, and conservation. Most of the department's 18,700 personnel were assembled from other federal bureaucracies with commitments to energy production, regulation, or research, including the Energy Research and Development Administration (ERDA), the Federal Power Commission (FPC), and the Federal Energy Administration (FEA).

The Department of Energy quickly declared a close identification with the energy production sector in a series of skirmishes with the Environmental Protection Agency (EPA). Throughout 1978, DOE vigorously promoted less stringent pollution control standards for new utility and industrial gas smokestacks than those EPA intended to order. Significantly, DOE's position was closely aligned to that of the petroleum and coal producers. In late 1978, DOE again tilted pens with EPA over proposed safety standards for the strategic mineral beryllium, a suspected carcinogen. Former Energy Secretary James Schlesinger warned that EPA's proposed standards would cost a prohibitive $150 million to implement and would threaten national security. The department's credibility was tarnished in this instance by a revelation that the secretary's data had been entirely obtained from two national beryllium producers when other accepted studies suggested the actual costs would be much less.[12]

The department's close attention to the viewpoint of energy-producing and consuming interests is predictable, even responsible, in light of its congressionally mandated mission. Indeed, DOE would be negligent were it not to promote energy utilization with vigor. The Energy Department is only the most recent bureaucratic representation of government's interest in energy production and the Department of the Interior essentially the first. The two agencies bracket two centuries of continuing federal preoccupation with energy production that is not easily blunted by a recent surge of concern for environmental protection and energy conservation.

Many problems in the trade-off between energy production and environmental conservation can be attributed to the tensions generated in the federal government by the coexistence of energy-promoting and environment-protecting institutions and policies. One may continually observe as well the interplay of political influences noted earlier: political style, institutional partisanship, and technological fixation to name a few. The intricate pattern of political interaction among these many factors can be better appreciated by an examination of the energy-environmental trade-offs currently debated in nuclear energy and coal policy.

THE NUCLEAR POWER ISSUE

The 1970s were a darkening decade for nuclear power. Even so, the year 1979 proved especially baleful. In January, the Nuclear Regulatory Commission (NRC) repudiated its previously low estimate of the radiation risk from a nuclear reactor accident, leaving the issue disturbingly unresolved. In March, the nearly disastrous failure of the reactor cooling system at the Three Mile Island, Pennsylvania, nuclear generating plant forced national attention upon the technological liabilities of the industry. In May, an Oklahoma grand jury awarded $10.5 million in damages to the estate of Karen Silkwood, who had claimed severe injury from plutonium contamination in a nuclear fuel processing plant.

Most alarming to the nuclear industry were the legal implications: it appeared that nuclear facilities might henceforth be liable for damages from their operation even when they had met federal safety standards and showed no evidence of negligence. Also in May, the largest anti-nuclear protest rally in U.S. history assembled on the Washington Mall to hear prominent scientists, public officials, and citizens of all political persuasions denounce the continued growth of the nuclear power industry. In August, NRC reported that it had logged more than 2,800 incidents of nuclear power plant violations of commission rules or other incidents threatening public safety during the previous year.[13] So went a year-long public revelation of the industry's most serious problems: technological risks, mounting public uneasiness, economic uncertainties, legal difficulties, and political controversy. It was a year of bad news that climaxed a decade of blighted hope.

The nuclear power industry has been a multibillion dollar technological gamble, not always so recognized by the public nor admitted by its own proponents. Its development has been an effort to create, largely through public financing, a new energy sector whose immediate benefits to selective regional and economic sectors were justified as serving a more long-term, "larger" public good. The public benefits, however speculative, did appear attractive. Once the early technical and economic obstacles were overcome, nuclear power facilities seemed to promise cheap and abundant energy, a new source of continuing technological innovation, and a stimulant to the national economy. "Nuclear reactors now appear to be the cheapest of all sources of energy," proclaimed the director of the Oak Ridge National Laboratories in 1966.[14] To many informed observers, nuclear power still remains a viable, even essential, energy source whose continued development will eventually produce its promised national rewards—if it is permitted to develop. At the moment, however, continued nuclear power development requires a balancing of the technology's largely selective benefits with the public need for environmental safety.

Private Benefits in the Public Name

By 1980, there were 71 operating nuclear power reactors generating between 10 and 14 percent of the nation's electric power. Current estimates suggest that additional nuclear facilities, now licensed or under construction, will raise the total number of operating plants to about 200 within the next 20 years. Estimated U.S. uranium reserves are ample enough to fuel as many as 375 light water reactors (the only type currently in use) for another 30 years.[15] If spent reactor fuel could be treated by reprocessing and plutonium recycling, fuel reserves could be extended by another 10 to 12 years. Moreover, a viable breeder reactor technology, now in the early stages of development, could practically eliminate this fuel supply constraint. Thus, the United States has a proven technology for generating electricity from nuclear reactors, an ample fuel reserve, and the potential to expand significantly its nuclear generating resources well into the next century.

The nation's relatively small nuclear power sector consists of a few facility manufacturers, several hundred public utilities, numerous subcontractors of nuclear equipment and services, nuclear science professionals, and operators of uranium mines and processing facilities. Although nuclear generating plants are distributed across the United States, the Northeast, Southeast, and Midwest are the primary beneficiaries of this power generating capacity. Together, these three regions account for 93 percent of all the existing nuclear power generation.

This concentration of nuclear installations belies the past scarcity of alternative fuels for these populous areas and the desire to reduce the resulting high cost of available utility fuel. It also represents, as Linda Mulligan has noted, the federal government's tendency to treat the nation as an "energy commons" for most major fuels: energy was made available, relatively cheaply, where it was needed with little sensitivity for the possible inequities between the distribution of benefits and costs.[16] This power plant distribution, in any event, makes a few populous regions of the nation heavily dependent upon nuclear power. (See also Figure 2-2, p. 43.)

From its inception, the nuclear power industry has been heavily subsidized by the federal government, both directly and indirectly. It still remains impossible for the nuclear power sector to operate financially without huge infusions of public capital. Since 1945, Washington has spent more than $12.1 billion for funding research and development for nuclear power facilities.[17] Private industry's share in this research and development enterprise, while increasing since the early 1950s, still represents a small portion of the total costs. Additionally, Washington shared with the embryonic industry a monopoly on nuclear fuel, its fuel processing technology and expertise, its accumulated nuclear research, and the necessary patents and licenses without which the industry could not have begun. Washington continues to underwrite a substantial portion of fuel mining, milling, and reprocessing.

The primary constituency for this federal spending continues to be the private electric utility industry. The Edison Electric Institute and the National Association of Electric Companies, two major utility spokesmen, led the coalition that successfully promoted a 1954 amendment to the original Atomic Energy Act (1946), which permitted private utilities to operate commercial nuclear power facilities and prevented the Atomic Energy Commission from doing the same (and thereby becoming a competitor). Approximately 60 percent of the electricity generated by nuclear power is produced by investor-owned companies. A few nuclear plants are publicly owned; indeed, the Tennessee Valley Authority will soon be the largest producer of electric energy from nuclear reactors with seven reactors anticipated to be on line by the late 1980s.

The fuel- and technology-producing sector of the nuclear power industry is more concentrated. Four corporations—General Electric, Westinghouse, Babcock and Wilcox, and Combustion Engineering—have built all the nuclear plants in the United States. Approximately one-half of the nation's uranium reserves and one-quarter of its uranium

milling capacity are owned by petroleum companies; the remaining
reserves and milling capacity are controlled by the federal government
and a few other private industries.[18]

This intermingling of public utility and government ownership
helps to explain the diverse mix of organized groups speaking at
various times for the industry. The Atomic Industrial Forum, the
industry's official trade association, is but one of them. Both the
Edison Electric Institute, a private utility group, and the American
Public Power Association, which represents consumer-owned utilities,
are concerned with nuclear power development. So are the multitude
of state and local governments with an investment in operating or
planned nuclear facilities. The consortium of interests recently pres-
suring the state of California to permit construction of the huge
Sundesert nuclear facility in the southern part of the state included
the Los Angeles Department of Water and Power, the California
Department of Water Resources, and the cities of Anaheim, Riverside,
Burbank, Pasadena, and Glendale. Since public utilities and government agencies participate in nuclear plant consortia, the nuclear
power industry can claim a quasi-public status that, among other
things, strengthens its right to massive public subsidies. The income
from the industry's operation and its aggregate facility ownership
is still predominantly private, however.

Private beneficiaries of the nuclear industry's operations extend
far beyond regional power consumers, facility operators, capital investors, and technology producers. The construction of nuclear generating plants and their auxiliary services, a $10 billion industry
annually, create a large employment market. Nuclear generating plants,
extremely labor intensive in their construction phase, are still cautiously
supported by most labor unions. Most enthusiastic are the construction
and maintenance trades that reap over $5 billion annually from facility
construction.

Communities in the vicinity of nuclear facility construction have
rarely been unreceptive. It is difficult for local leaders to ignore
the prospect of new jobs and economic invigoration from such construction activity, especially if the beneficiaries are underprivileged
or underemployed. One New York state representative found even
the prospect of five nuclear plants located in his district difficult
to oppose:

> We are situated in one of the less prosperous parts of the state. . . .
> Many of our construction workers have been out of work well over
> a year. You can easily imagine the hope that surges through them
> as the Power Authority unfurls its vision of coming prosperity: 189
> carpenters, 403 pipefitters, 321 electricians, 35 cement finishers—
> all employed directly in the construction of only one of the plants.[19]

The fuel recycling technology—mining, processing, reprocessing, and waste disposal—also glitters as gold. The community of Carlsbad, New Mexico, expects 700 temporary jobs and perhaps 350 permanent ones, as well as a very substantial share of the $330 million project budget, if it accepts construction of a pilot project for underground nuclear waste disposal in the nearby Carlsbad Caverns. The flow of private benefits does not stop at water's edge, however. Domestic manufacturers of nuclear reactors assert that the world market for nuclear reactors will be $25 billion between 1979 and 1985. Westinghouse has pointedly reminded U.S. labor unions that American manufacturers could potentially bestow at least $2 billion in orders to the steel industry and generate one million worker-years of labor, if the international nuclear power market could be captured by the domestic industry.

Yet the nuclear power industry is sick. The industry's economic, environmental, and political problems have rapidly compounded into a deep malaise within the last few years. Most of its troubles can be attributed to the environmental hazards implicit in the nuclear technology. Increasingly, persuasive arguments have been made that the "greater" public good demands a constraint upon whatever "lesser" private benefits (to labor, management, utility stockholders, and even local government) might flow from continued industry development. It is an issue admitting no easy solutions.

Public Goods: The Environmental Issue

A virtual moratorium has been imposed on the construction of new U.S. nuclear facilities. By 1980, more than 140 of the 170 new units once anticipated before the end of the century had been deferred or canceled; reactor manufacturers now privately predict that no new orders are likely to be received until the late 1980s. The pervasive pall throughout the industry shows no sign of lifting. The Office of Technology Assessment explains:

> Capital costs and licensing and construction schedules have increased so much and become so uncertain that few utilities can carry the financial burden now, even though they may be confident that nuclear power ultimately will be cheaper than its alternative.[20]

Part of the problem is obviously economic. The nuclear industry's average power production during 1978 was only 67 percent of its total designed output, or rated capacity, compared to a somewhat higher average for coal-fired plants.[21] Second, nuclear power has turned out to be less competitive with alternative utility fuels than had been predicted for many markets. And construction time for new facilities has now stretched to an average of eight to ten years, which strongly discourages capital investors who must pay millions of dollars in interest during the construction phase before any returns materialize.

These problems would probably not hinder continued massive federal subsidies for the industry (it was always understood to require enormous public underwriting, after all) if nuclear power's long-term prospects were brighter. Many of its economic problems are intensified by the growing concern that the environmental risks of nuclear power necessitate stringent constraints upon its future development.

Waste Disposal. Nuclear generating facilities pose three widely recognized environmental problems. First, a safe disposal procedure for radioactive plant waste is not yet available. Secure disposal seemed no formidable obstacle during the early planning stage of nuclear facilities: most of the spent fuel, the major component of the waste, was expected to be reprocessed. However, the current lack of high capacity reprocessing facilities and the continuing debate about the wisdom of their use forces upon government and the nuclear industry a difficult search for an acceptable alternative. The problem grows more ominous with the years.[22]

About 15,000 nuclear fuel assemblies from generating plants are currently held in temporary storage and another 5,000 are stored annually. Depending on their composition, these wastes may remain dangerously radioactive for 100,000 to 300,000 years. In addition, the power plants have produced 50 million cubic feet of radioactive tools, clothing, and worn-out machinery (currently stored in six "low-level" burial sites) and 140 million tons of radioactive tailings from uranium mines (located elsewhere). Underground burial of these wastes in salt beds or in basalt or granite sites has been proposed, and some experimental facilities are now being constructed. Waste transport to outer space or to the sea bottom has also been suggested.

No solutions have quieted the intense scientific debate about waste disposal or have persuaded the federal government to certify a safe procedure. Late in 1978, the Office of Science and Technology Policy reported that "a solution to the problem of waste disposal is still years away."[23] While federal experts debate, the nuclear industry languishes. The state legislature of California, alarmed by the waste disposal issue, mandated in 1976 that no new nuclear facilities be built in that state until Washington declared a safe disposal procedure. The nuclear industry fears such legislation will become a trend.

Threat of Nuclear Accident. Second, a serious nuclear facility accident remains possible. Despite the nuclear power industry's generally good safety record prior to 1979, Pennsylvania's Three Mile Island accident renewed doubt about the safety of nuclear plants and magnified the credibility of industry critics. Government officials and spokesmen for the industry, who the public perceived as asserting that the probability of such an accident was so low as to be negligible, had to confront a major credibility problem of their own.

Revelations of lesser, nevertheless disturbing, technical problems with nuclear facilities had been almost constant before the Three Mile Island emergency as well as afterward. In mid-1979, the Nuclear Regulatory Commission (NRC) reported that 15 nuclear facilities that were experiencing a problem with their coolant water pipes had leaked small amounts of radioactive water. Shortly before the Three Mile Island affair, NRC ordered 5 nuclear facilities temporarily closed because of deficient analysis of their vulnerability to earthquakes. "The order," explained NRC unreassuringly, "did not mean that the Commission considered the plants unsafe but that it was unsure of their safety."[24]

It is the nature of nuclear technology that any ambiguity or uncertainty about its operations assumes ominous implications. There are approximately 20 million Americans living within 30 miles of a currently operating nuclear reactor, the outer limit of immediate public danger from a catastrophic reactor accident; 10 million of these citizens are living within the 20-mile radius considered especially hazardous during an accident. The possibility that so many Americans might be exposed to a potentially dangerous nuclear plant accident is sufficient to make even low probabilities of such danger seem excessive.

Radiation Exposure. Finally, chronic exposure to low-level radiation from nuclear plants is now considered a possible public health hazard. The debate about the magnitude of risk from low-level radiation, long simmering within scientific circles, boiled into public view when the National Academy of Sciences (NAS) released a study in 1979 predicting that exposure to low-level radiation from nuclear power plants could cause an estimated 2,000 deaths in the United States by the end of the century. The NAS panel generally concluded that low-level radiation risks did not merit public concern, but the panel so disagreed over the magnitude of that risk and was so bitterly fragmented among partisans of differing viewpoints that two sets of conclusions were issued.[25] In an era of widespread political cynicism, continuing debate about the credibility of government research, and public reflection on possible nuclear horrors conjured up by the Three Mile Island incident, the panel's impact was ironic. Seeking to quell debate over low-level radiation, the experts only stimulated it.

Thus emerged the private and public benefits involved in the nuclear power issue: continued development of the industry with all its real and alleged benefits weighed against the need for public protection from a potentially lethal technology. Public officials must decide how much of one good is compatible with the other.

The Politics of Reappraisal

With respect to the policymaking cycle, the current nuclear power controversy reveals the underlying dynamics of the politics of reappraisal. Opponents of past nuclear policy have forced national attention upon their demand for radical policy reappraisal in an effort to make policy more responsive to public interests like environmental protection and public health. In this struggle to reformulate national nuclear policy, one can observe an interplay among many of the political factors earlier identified as important in government decisionmaking.

The Public Interest Sector. The public interest sector has been extremely influential in forcing nuclear policy reappraisal onto the public agenda, primarily due to its ability to use the courts effectively and by the recently expanded opportunities for public participation in the administrative process. The organized opposition to further nuclear industry development is led by the Critical Mass Energy Project (a Ralph Nader organization), the Sierra Club, Friends of the Earth, and a number of scientific groups including the Union of Concerned Scientists. These groups have exploited their new opportunities for intervention in regulatory procedures concerning the licensing of nuclear power facilities. Public intervenors have forced frequent delays in the required regulatory review of new and operating nuclear facilities, which critics allege is deliberate obstruction.

Far more substantial injury was inflicted on the nuclear facility under construction at Seabrook, New Hampshire, by opponents using administrative tactics than by the more publicized demonstrations at the site during 1977 through 1979. In response to public intervenor testimony, the Nuclear Regulatory Commission halted plant construction for seven months in 1977 and two additional months in 1978, delays costing the facility's owners $15 million monthly. Opponents of nuclear power development have also used the courts to considerable advantage in forcing governmental reappraisal of nuclear policy. Such activities have helped public interest groups to counter successfully the political advantage enjoyed by private groups promoting nuclear power through their legislative and public relations resources.

The Media. The role of the media in creating and sustaining a public mood congenial to nuclear policy reappraisal is also significant. But the media have also been exploited to advantage by anti-nuclear forces adept at creating incidents which become "news" by virtue of media attention. The nuclear power industry has been extremely slow to launch an ambitious national advertising campaign because it is unaccustomed to being on the defensive. Significantly, only *after* the March 1979 Three Mile Island event did the industry attempt a media campaign of truly national proportions.

The impact of the media in moving public opinion toward greater skepticism of atomic power is suggested in Table 4-1, which compares public attitudes about nuclear facilities both before and after the Three Mile Island incident. But Three Mile Island was only one of many media revelations contributing to this opinion climate. During 1979, the media also reported:

—Residents of Nevada and Utah living in areas affected by fallout from the nuclear weapons tests at the Nevada test site received federal attention after complaining for years about suspiciously high death rates from cancer in their communities.

—A number of U.S. veterans, among more than 250,000 military personnel exposed to radiation from nuclear weapon tests in the 1950s, sued the federal government for damages and medical costs.

—President Eisenhower, concerned that public reaction might inhibit the development of nuclear weapons, had urged the Atomic Energy Commission in 1953 to conceal from the public any significant dangers of radiation poisoning.[26]

Carefully staged anti-nuclear rallies like those at Seabrook, New Hampshire, and Washington, D.C., are typically media events from their initial conception. The extensive media coverage of the nuclear

Table 4-1 Public Support for Nuclear Plant Construction, Before and After the March 1979 Three Mile Island Incident

	Percentage of Respondents Approving	
	1978	*1979*
"Would you favor or oppose the building of more nuclear power plants in the United States?"	57%	47%
	1977	*1979*
"Would you approve if the nuclear plants for generating electricity are built in your community?"	55%	38%

SOURCE: *Public Opinion,* June/July 1979. Adapted from surveys by Louis Harris and Associates, CBS News, and the *New York Times.*

safety issue has not, as supporters of nuclear power feared, produced a severe public backlash against nuclear power development, however. Ballot propositions to prohibit the licensing of additional nuclear power plants were defeated in every state where they were promoted between 1976 and 1980. Rather, media reports have expanded the range of public tolerance for nuclear policies to now include a major reformulation of older developmental approaches.

Incrementalism. Despite the forces moving the government toward policy reformulation, the impact of incrementalism is still apparent in nuclear policy deliberations. The enormous "sunk costs" in existing public and private nuclear research and operations—a cost now estimated at close to $60 billion—deters most policymakers from abandoning existing or planned facilities. We will observe in a later chapter the extent to which enormous public investment in the Clinch River breeder reactor project has made Congress reluctant to terminate the enterprise, an instructive illustration that publicly financed programs often prevail because they have become costly.

Caution in reformulating national policy is also heightened by the many interests with a stake in existing nuclear power policy. The nuclear power industry was largely a creation of the federal government and is now strong enough to defend its fiscal lifeline against attack. Unable to prevent damage to its program, the industry can fight effectively against radical policy reformulation.

One can also observe the tendency of federal officials to move extremely slowly in reformulating nuclear power policy. A number of the technical design deficiencies exposed by the March 1979 Three Mile Island incident had been known and debated between critics and the staff of the Nuclear Regulatory Commission for a decade prior to the accident. The nuclear waste issue had been raised in the early 1970s in public testimony before a number of congressional committees, including the now-extinct Joint Committee on Atomic Energy and the Atomic Energy Commission (whose regulatory and licensing functions were assumed by the Nuclear Regulatory Commission in 1974 when AEC was abolished). Three Mile Island from this perspective was a catalytic political event: the emergency forced the federal government away from its largely incremental style of assessing risks from nuclear power development.

Administrative Infighting. Nuclear power continues to be controversial within the government. The Department of Energy (especially its Federal Energy Regulatory Commission) and the Nuclear Regulatory Commission lead a coalition of other administrative agencies that are generally sympathetic to future promotion and expansion of the domestic nuclear power industry, albeit with significantly different viewpoints on proper regulatory controls. The Carter administration, Environmental Protection Agency, and State Department have been far more critical of the nuclear power enterprise, although not opposed in principle to further industry development.

These opposing administrative alliances broadly defined the "hard" and "soft" sides of the nuclear issue within the Carter administration. The administrative infighting generated by these differing viewpoints over atomic energy largely focuses on the relative priority to be given to health and environmental concerns in comparison to economic and energy objectives in the industry's future. It is a battle unlikely to end soon.

THE COAL ISSUE

Coal lies beneath the American earth in unrivaled abundance, both beckoning and threatening. Between one-third and one-half of the world's known coal reserves are in the United States. From the inception of the energy crisis, federal energy planners have repeatedly looked to coal as a major future resource. A principal strategy of the Nixon and Ford administrations' Project Independence was "coal and conservation." President Carter had proposed in his 1977 National Energy Plan that the nation increase coal use by 66 percent over the next decade. By 1979, the president's strategy was more ambitious: a public investment, perhaps reaching $88 billion, to create a coal-based synthetic fuels industry. By 1980, Washington had acquired the authority to order industry and utilities to convert their boilers from alternative fuels to coal.

But a new raid on coal may purchase energy at a severe ecological price. Environmentally, coal is the dirtiest of all fuels both to produce and consume. Much of its ecological peril is known; more is suspected. The capacity of technological controls to contain these environmental ravages within acceptable limits is often uncertain. Under different guise, the demands for energy production and environmental protection again require reconciliation. Unlike nuclear energy, however, the risks and rewards of coal development are more easily defined.

Private Rewards of Coal Production

Early in the 1940s, natural gas and petroleum began replacing coal as the nation's primary fossil fuel; ever since, coal has been a sick industry. Employment, production, income, and markets steadily shrank until the industry seemed destined to chronically low production by the early 1970s, with its reserves underutilized and its fortune tied to the electric utilities whose demand (approximately 75 percent of all current coal consumption) constituted its sole major market. A new national program of expanding coal combustion could quickly revive the industry, however. For the coal industry especially, an energy crisis could be beneficient.

The private economic benefits of an increase in coal combustion would be felt particularly in Appalachia, the Midwest, and the northern Plains. It would be experienced by miners, communities adjacent to the mines, the owners and managers of coal firms, and holders of leases on existing but unmined coal reserves.[27] The domestic coal industry possesses the technical capacity and accessible reserves to increase production between 30 and 75 percent in the next decade.

Surface mining technology has greatly increased mine productivity through the use of gargantuan equipment and sophisticated new extraction technologies. In 1976, for instance, the 26 million tons of coal produced by 700 miners working the surface mines of Montana would have required 10,000 workers to produce by older techniques in West Virginia. The capacity to produce coal in increasing quantity and the modest capital required to augment existing production facilities attract energy planners to increased future coal production as a solution to the nation's energy dilemma.

Estimates of the economic impact from a coal boom depend upon the demand model used. Assuming a moderate increase in national coal combustion, still below the target set by the Carter administration, the economic impacts would nonetheless be considerable. In Appalachia, increased national coal consumption would draw perhaps 100,000 new individuals to the region's expanding surface and underground mines. The population impact would be far more substantial in the northern Plains or the West. New mines, requiring between 23,000 and 47,000 new workers, would probably appear. A new population wave, sweeping perhaps a half million new residents into the nation's most sparsely populated regions, would follow. One estimate suggests that 11 of the region's counties might grow at a rate exceeding 5 percent yearly for a decade, fast enough to inflict serious social, economic, and governmental dislocations.[28]

Coal-related income would also follow the population wave into the regions. In the West and northern Plains, new miners would probably share between $850 million and $1 billion in annual wages. State governments would receive additional income through coal mining royalties and federal funds available to mitigate the adverse impacts of rapid socioeconomic development. In Montana, North Dakota, and Wyoming, which contain the largest portion of western coal reserves, it is plausible that mining royalties could constitute the states' largest revenue source. No social group would be affected more directly by this boom than the western Indian tribes that own perhaps one-

third of all the recoverable western coal reserves. For these tribes—
including the Navajo, Hopi, Crow, and Southern Ute—mine leases
could yield one-quarter to one-half billion dollars annually in mining
royalties.

Large "mine mouth" electricity generating plants, located immediately adjacent to surface mines, would probably also proliferate
in order to capitalize on the ample coal availability and minimal
transportation costs. Mine mouth facilities are commonly large (sometimes immense), relatively labor intensive, and revenue productive
to owners and government regulators. Together with the satellite services they require, mine mouth electricity generation could constitute
a major secondary industry where strip mining becomes the established
excavation technology.

The corporate distribution of mining profits is likely to be increasingly concentrated over the next few years. Although there are
more than 3,000 individual firms in the coal mining industry, only
15 of these companies account for more than 40 percent of all coal
production.[29] Such consolidation is typical throughout the industry,
particularly a growing concentration of ownership in the hands of
other energy companies. By 1985, these companies are expected to
control about half of the nation's total coal production. Among these
15 largest coal producers, 6 are owned partially or wholly by petroleum
companies: Consolidation Coal (Continental Oil Company), AMAX
(Standard of California), Island Creek Group (Occidental Petroleum),
Arch Mineral (Ashland Oil and Hunt Oil), Old Ben (SOHIO), and
Pittsburgh & Midway (Gulf Oil). Industry concentration will probably
be hastened by new environmental regulations requiring mining companies to restore their mine sites to environmental productivity because
the economic burdens of such restoration will likely drive many small
operations out of business.

A coal boom also promises to revive the nation's moribund railroad
system and perhaps to launch a coal slurry pipeline industry. Railroads
currently transport almost 80 percent of the nation's coal. Having
suffered a continual decline since World War II, the U.S. railroad
system seemed destined to a twilight of increasing technological ob-
solescence by the late 1970s. A new surge of coal combustion is
regarded as "black gold" within the industry, however. President
Carter's 1977 National Energy Plan probably would have increased
coal loadings by 350 percent between 1978 and 1985. Despite formidable
obstacles faced by the railroads in accommodating a new coal boom
(including deteriorated railroad tracks, aging equipment, and the lack
of many feeder tracks to potential new customers), the railroads
regard a national coal boom as their best, and perhaps last, hope
for economic revival.

Coal slurry pipelines, however, could blight the railroads' revival. Coal is transported in these pipelines by water from the mine to consumers. Powdered and mixed with water in equal proportions, this energy resource can be transported thousands of miles. Only one small slurry pipeline is currently in operation in the United States, but eight more are planned in the West where logistics make slurries most attractive. Slurries could theoretically span the United States as readily as oil or gas pipelines, at a cost competitive with railroad transportation for coal and with equal ability to deliver fuel to major consumers. The railroads have fought vigorously to prevent this potential competitor from acquiring the land necessary to challenge railroad domination of the coal transportation industry. Congress and most state legislatures have viewed the prospect of coal slurry pipelines favorably, however, and slurry promoters expect to construct several major pipeline systems within the next decade.

While a future national coal boom is far from a collective good, its potential benefits would be broadly distributed. It would catapult the affected northern Plains and western state economies into a new era of rapidly accelerating economic development. And perhaps it would lift the presently bleak social and economic prospects of the affected Indian tribes to new and promising proportions. It could create a railroad revival, a growth surge among mining companies' incomes, and perhaps a new slurry pipeline industry. Expanded coal production and utilization could possibly loosen the hold of Middle Eastern governments on the U.S. energy lifeline. If it were not for the ecological consequences—the public good of environmental protection—coal would be almost irresistible.

Environmental Impacts and Collective Goods

Coal utilization at all phases poses immediate and continuing ecological hazards. Unregulated, the cumulative environmental impacts of a coal boom could be catastrophic. All sides of the coal debate recognize that the nation must be protected from these dangers. Beyond this limited agreement, however, bitter controversy prevails. How much environmental protection is essential and how much excessive? What mix of coal production and environmental protection is desirable when the quality of ecological controls is uncertain? What is a reasonable economic burden to impose on coal producers and consumers to achieve environmental safety?

Public officials confront these issues at three phases of coal utilization: surface mining, combustion, and atmospheric dissipation of combustion residues. Each phase illuminates the necessary balancing of public safety and economic benefit inherent in coal policy decisions.

Surface Mining. No form of fossil fuel utilization inflicts a more pervasive, immediate, or violent metamorphosis upon the land than surface mining. The evidence is written into the Appalachian hills: thousands of ravaged and sterile acres, contaminated rivers and streams, decapitated mountain tops and slopes scarred by deserted mine highwalls and fouled by abandoned "orphan banks" of mineral wastes.[30]

The nation has been forced to confront this ravage because a coal boom will be a surface mining boom. Surface mining is cheaper, more efficient, and more profitable to coal producers than is underground shaft mining. By the mid-1980s, surface mines will produce half of Appalachia's coal and constitute most western production. The pervasiveness of surface mining is described in Table 4-2, which indicates the proportion of U.S. coal production obtained by this method in the coal-producing states in 1977.

Belatedly recognizing the lesson of Appalachia, Congress passed the 1977 Surface Mining Control and Reclamation Act (SMCRA), requiring all mining companies to restore their mine sites to ecological vitality. The law mandates, among other things, that mining companies demonstrate a capacity to restore the land as a condition for obtaining a mining permit, that mining be inhibited when it threatens prime farming land, and many other rigorous restraints on surface mining.

Yet the capacity of mining companies to restore the land, especially in the West, remains uncertain even with the best equipment, professional guidance, and good will. According to a recent study, "Very little if any land in the Northern Great Plains has been revegetated for sufficient time or with sufficient variety of species to determine the potential for success in establishing a permanent ecosystem that will sustain grazing or higher uses."[31] Rather, the restoration potential of most western lands is "site specific"—that is, it depends on the particular biological and geological character of the land. Western lands are often fragile ecosystems where sparse rainfall and limited natural vegetation offer meager prospects for easy or sustained land restoration. Requirements to restore surface-mined lands are often, at best, a gamble with nature.

The coal mining industry regards SMCRA as an unreasonable regulatory burden that is neither economically nor environmentally justified. The industry believes the legislation lengthens the time required for mine development from the current three to five years to between eight and sixteen years. Moreover, they assert, it imposes severe restoration costs. Small mining companies will be driven from the market, and the cost of mined coal will rise significantly—events that are not compatible with a national effort to increase coal's supply and cost competitiveness. Industry leaders also maintain that

Table 4-2 U.S. Coal* Production by State and Method of Mining, 1977 (In thousand tons)

Region	Underground		Surface		Total
	Tons	Percentage of Total	Tons	Percentage of Total	
Appalachia					
Alabama	6,580	31	14,640	69	21,220
Georgia	0	—	185	100	185
Kentucky, East	41,005	44	51,145	56	92,150
Maryland	260	8	3,030	9	3,290
Ohio	13,925	30	32,280	70	46,205
Pennsylvania	38,365	46	44,860	54	83,225
Tennessee	4,675	45	5,645	55	10,320
Virginia	26,200	69	11,650	31	37,850
West Virginia	74,030	78	21,375	22	95,405
Total	205,040	53	184,810	47	89,850
Midwest					
Arkansas	20	4	550	96	570
Illinois	29,590	55	24,290	45	53,880
Indiana	525	2	27,470	98	27,995
Iowa	0	—	525	100	525
Kansas	0	—	630	100	630
Kentucky, West	23,010	45	27,785	55	50,795
Missouri	0	—	6,625	100	6,625
Oklahoma	0	—	5,345	100	5,345
Texas	0	—	16,765	100	16,765
Total	53,145	23	109,985	67	163,130
West					
Alaska	0	—	665	100	665
Arizona	0	—	11,475	100	11,475
Colorado	4,205	35	7,715	65	11,920
Montana	0	—	29,320	100	29,320
New Mexico	0	—	11,255	100	11,255
North Dakota	0	—	12,165	100	12,165
Utah	9,240	100	0	—	9,240
Washington	0	—	5,055	100	5,055
Wyoming	0	—	44,500	100	44,500
Total	13,445	10	122,150	90	135,595
U.S. Total	271,630	39	416,945	61	688,575

*Bituminous coal and lignite.

SOURCE: U.S. Department of Energy, Energy Information Administration.

restoration of mined lands to the act's standards is often difficult, if not impossible, when high quality restoration could be achieved by less stringent regulations.

The National Coal Association fought tenaciously against SMCRA through every stage of the legislation's development. Typical of this vehemence was the industry's immediate, albeit unsuccessful, lawsuit to prevent the Interior Department from enforcing its final regulations to implement SMCRA the day after the regulations were announced. Joining the suit were more than 100 coal-producing and consuming interests—"Peabody Coal and practically everybody else," observed one lawyer—in a demonstration of the industry's unrelenting determination to be free of the law.

The actual economic impacts of the new restoration requirements remain uncertain. Many small producers will probably be eliminated from the coal market, and coal prices are likely to rise. There is yet no certain evidence that restoration costs will prevent the remaining producers from marketing coal at a quantity and price compatible with increased national coal utilization, however.

Coal Combustion. The most bitter controversy about coal combustion concerns the appropriateness of federal requirements that electric utilities, the nation's primary coal consumers, install "scrubbers" to remove sulfur oxide from their smokestack emissions. Sulfur oxide is a yellow, acrid, highly toxic gas that is released into ambient air by coal combustion. Acute, short-term population exposure to concentrations of sulfur oxide can be fatal; long-term exposure to relatively low sulfur oxide concentrations is now suspected to produce adverse health effects. These health risks together with the gas's known ecological hazards have prompted the federal government to attempt stringent regulation of sulfur oxide emissions in utility smokestacks.

The 1970 Clean Air Act required the Environmental Protection Agency (EPA) to establish national ambient air quality standards for sulfur oxide, to set standards for sulfur oxide emission controls, and to assure that the states implement such controls. Amendments to the act in 1977 required that sulfur oxide emissions be controlled through technological means. Recently, EPA has interpreted these congressional mandates to mean that most new coal-burning utilities must install stack scrubbers and, insofar as feasible, existing coal-burning utilities must retrofit them.

The electric utility industry generally considers scrubbers to be technologically unreliable and economically inefficient. Industry spokesmen assert that most existing scrubbers repeatedly malfunction, creating severe technical problems and threatening constant plant shutdowns when dependable power generation is essential. The Southwest

Plant in Springfield, Illinois, is typical: since its two scrubbers were installed in 1977, one has failed to operate, and the second has achieved only 60 percent reliability.[32] Scrubbers also raise a utility customer's bill by 15 to 20 percent, the argument continues, even in areas where scrubbers are not necessary to assure local compliance with national air quality standards. Most utilities believe alternative techniques for sulfur oxide reduction—low-sulfur coal, high altitude smokestack discharge, or intermittent coal combustion, for instance— would achieve much the same results.

From EPA's perspective, the utilities exaggerate the technical liabilities of scrubbers. New scrubber technologies are now available, suggests EPA, with far greater reliability and economic efficiency than older models which, in any event, the utilities have often been negligent or incompetent in servicing. The Environmental Protection Agency has repeatedly cited several currently operating scrubber systems as proof that the technology can be both reliable and economically efficient. Many of the scrubber problems, EPA maintains, are actually attributable to the utilities' excessive concern to protect shareholder equity by keeping scrubber costs low; poor (but cheap) scrubber systems are often purchased and maintained by inadequately trained employees.

The scrubber debate swirls through a fog of uncertainty because neither side can be secure in its conclusions. The Office of Technology Assessment (OTA) summarized its own evaluation by noting that scrubbers "are a perfectable technology and one that U.S. powerplants can install with reasonable confidence that high levels of reliability can be attained." But OTA also notes, "there remains a critical question of [scrubber] costs" about which existing estimates are "very much in doubt."[33] In addition, alternative control technologies have been inadequately explored: "None of the actors in the regulatory process appears to have analyzed the probable air quality effects of any of these alternatives."[34]

Such ambiguity raises a common policy dilemma: what set of competing claims should be favored when the technical or economic formula yields no clear resolution? Congress and EPA have chosen to define their most important constituency as the general public rather than the utility owners and shareholders. Thus, EPA policy favors control technologies that appear to maximize opportunities to protect public health and environmental quality rather than alternative strategies more sensitive to the economic viewpoint of the utility sector. It is a case of collective goods displacing private ones as a first priority.

The "Greenhouse Effect." The most ominous of environmental issues attending coal combustion has been far more subtle than the danger from sulfur oxide exposure. In recent years, scientists have expressed growing apprehension about the possible "greenhouse effect" produced in the global atmosphere by mounting worldwide fossil fuel combustion. A few years ago this was treated as nothing more than mere speculation. Newer studies indicate that the greenhouse effect is a plausible and possibly calamitous ecological risk whose global proportions will soon become evident unless constraints on fossil fuel burning, and coal combustion in particular, are imposed. The root of the problem lies in the mounting worldwide atmospheric concentration of carbon dioxide from fossil fuel burning. Scientists had earlier speculated that an increasing carbon dioxide concentration might cause greater atmospheric retention of solar energy now radiated back to space. The result might be a gradual warming of the earth's atmosphere—an effect similar to that observed in a common greenhouse—that would have global impacts.

Speculation about this greenhouse effect has gradually increased to a conviction of danger among many environmental scientists. A recent study by the Department of Energy suggests the urgency currently animating discussion of the issue. "It is the sense of the scientific community," notes the study, "that carbon dioxide from unrestrained combustion of fossil fuels is potentially the most important issue facing mankind."[35] Most unsettling was the report's specification of grave environmental disruption for future generations. The report predicted:

—If the world continues to burn carbon-based fuels at the present rate, the amount of atmospheric carbon dioxide will double by the year 2035. This would increase the average world temperature by 2 to 3 degrees and polar icecap temperature by 9 to 12 degrees.

—Melting of the polar icecaps by the greenhouse effect could raise the sea level by 15 feet.

—Rising sea levels could inundate the nation's coastal areas and turn grain-producing regions of the United States into a dust bowl.

—A doubling of the current rate of U.S. coal combustion could produce notable atmospheric effects by 1990.

Like many doomsday forecasts associated with the environment, the apocalyptic tone of these recent reports creates credibility problems for many Americans. However, the growing concern with the carbon dioxide issue among responsible scientists suggests the matter must now be regarded as a major national (and world) issue that merits serious consideration.

Although the carbon dioxide problem has worldwide origins and consequences, the United States has significantly contributed to its gravity and may make an equally important contribution to its solution. Increased U.S. coal combustion will clearly be the most important short-term source of increased atmospheric carbon dioxide, which is not presently treated as a pollutant in the United States. No effective control technology currently exists to rid carbon dioxide from stack gasses, auto emissions, and other sources. Even a massive national development program is unlikely to produce an effective technology within the time considered essential to initiate abatement efforts. Thus, policymakers confront a situation more difficult than resolving trade-offs between public and private benefits derived from surface mining or sulfur oxide diffusion.

The greenhouse effect currently remains a supposition. No technical fix will be available soon to lessen the severity of possible combustion reduction. In short, policymakers must consider justifying a potentially major restraint on future coal combustion to avert a plausible, but still largely speculative, future catastrophe. Moreover, the carbon dioxide problem has global proportions. In effect, the United States would be denying itself the benefits of major new coal utilization with no assurance that other nations, many of them contributors to the problem, would act with similar prudence. Whatever the theoretical advantages of carbon dioxide abatement, the political obstacles to its implementation remain formidable.

The Politics of Implementation

The federal government has declared no official policy on carbon dioxide emissions (the issue had not made the policy agenda in Congress or the White House by 1980), but Washington has declared its commitment to impose some environmental restraints on both surface mining and sulfur oxide emissions. In effect, Washington has mandated a trade-off while largely leaving to administrative agencies the responsibility for defining the terms of that trade-off. The politics of policy implementation will become the critical context in which much of the balancing between public and private benefits in coal combustion will be calculated. The implementation phase highlights many previously described political elements associated with energy policy. Several merit brief mention.

The Bureaucracy. One aspect of policy implementation illuminated by current U.S. coal policy is the substantial influence of the bureaucracy in the policymaking process. The actual balance of environmental and economic benefits from coal utilization for the most part is determined by three federal agencies: the Department of the Interior (DOI), the Environmental Protection Agency (EPA), and the Department of Energy (DOE).

The Department of the Interior exercises vast discretionary authority at two strategic points in the coal utilization cycle: (1) the leasing of federal land for coal exploration or mining; and (2) enforcement of the 1977 Surface Mining Control and Reclamation Act (SMCRA). Approximately 59 percent of all western coal lands are held in public trust by the federal government. Congress has delegated to DOI the authority to determine (within broad statutory guidelines) which coal reserves will be explored and mined, the appropriate rentals and royalties, and what regulatory constraints will govern awards. In the exercise of this stewardship, DOI can interpret its authority in ways that encourage or restrain mine development, that place high or low priorities on ecological considerations in granting leases, and that respond more or less sympathetically to the coal sector's viewpoint.

The department has historically identified with the mining industry, its natural clientele. Critics assert that DOI continues to do so. In 1977, an authoritative private study admonished DOI for a coal lease "giveaway" that allegedly opened federal land to coal exploration at bargain basement prices.[36] The department's previous apathy about imposing required environmental safeguards on mining enterprises prompted a congressional investigating committee to complain in 1976 that the department was behaving "as if the lands were private property."[37] The Carter administration promised to awaken more ecological sensitivity in the department. Environmentalists regard DOI's performance at enforcing recent federal surface mine regulations as the test of its ecological conscience.

Under SMCRA, the Interior Department must assure that states regulate surface mining according to standards mandated by the law and departmental regulations that interpret the law. The act abounds in opportunities for discretionary judgments by the department and the individual states that will largely shape its impact. The department and the states may decide:

—What lands will be considered "unsuitable for stripping" due to severe ecological impacts from surface mining.

—When coal lands on alluvial valley floors west of the hundredth meridian—rich, ecologically sensitive agricultural land—may be mined so that such mining "will not interrupt, discontinue or preclude farming ... nor materially damage the quality or quantity of underground or surface water. . . ."

—When mining can be permitted on "prime farm lands" because the mine operator has demonstrated "the technological ability to restore the area within a reasonable time to equal or superior form of productivity."[38]

To make such determinations is to apportion thousands of acres of American land between energy conservation and development.

The role of the Environmental Protection Agency (EPA) in calculating these balances is clear, although differently expressed. Under the 1970 Clean Air Act, the agency has the authority to grant exceptions and delays in the installation of smokestack scrubbers, to relax or stiffen requirements for specific types of scrubber technology, to ordain when high- or low-sulfur coal can be burned by utilities (thus, to increase or decrease sulfur oxide stack emissions), and even to modify ambient air quality standards for sulfur oxide under certain conditions. The cumulative impact of these discretionary judgments is to soften, maintain, or perhaps increase sulfur oxide emission controls that, in turn, will powerfully influence the rate of future coal combustion.

The Department of Energy (DOE) is rapidly becoming the most aggressive bureaucratic proponent of policies intended to relax environmental standards in the interest of increased coal utilization. The department affects coal policy both directly—by deciding, for example, the conditions under which new coal combustion technologies may be developed—and indirectly—by using its own influence and mobilizing its clientele throughout the energy sector to promote coal production during the bureaucratic infighting inevitable in coal policy development.

The Energy Department has sharply criticized EPA's performance standards for new coal-burning utilities and industries because the standards are allegedly too expensive to enforce. In addition, DOE has vigorously promoted coal slurry pipelines because they will facilitate the rapid, and relatively inexpensive, distribution of western coal. It is hardly a revelation that DOE should be a partisan of increased coal combustion in light of its organizational mission. Its place in implementing coal policy provides additional bureaucratic leverage to the interests more responsive to economic values in current coal policy than to ecological considerations.

Policy Conflict. The implementation of current U.S. coal policy also reveals that policy conflicts often become displaced from one governmental setting to another without a final resolution. Policy conflict is a portable brawl. All the major parties battling over the proper priorities between economic and environmental considerations—private interest groups, state and local governments, Congress, and the White House—have carried the argument into the governmental arena. Losers in earlier struggles to formulate policy know they can still recoup much of their loss by skillful activism during policy implementation. Partisans of formulated policy know how fragile is their triumph: without an aggressive and vigilant presence during implementation, they may win only a paper victory. Coalitions of public and private groups continually attempt to gain leverage in the coal policy implementation process.

The complexity and importance of this continuing struggle is suggested by EPA's 1977 decision to sue the Tennessee Valley Authority (TVA), itself a government corporation, to compel the utility to install stack scrubbers in compliance with the Clean Air Act. The Tennessee Valley Authority, the largest single producer of electricity in the United States, had been supported in its long resistance to coal scrubbers by many major utilities, the National Coal Association, the governments of Tennessee, Kentucky, and West Virginia (which all feared increased electricity costs), and the Department of Energy. Major public interest and environmental groups, the Justice Department, and several other federal regulatory bodies joined the EPA lawsuit. The state congressional delegations generally sided with TVA and the White House with EPA.

In this instance, the federal courts ruled that TVA could not claim immunity from EPA's standards for stationary sources of sulfur oxide. The resolution of this policy conflict has immense bearing on the nation's commitment to controlling the environmental impact of coal utilization. Coal-fired electricity generators operated by TVA produce approximately 2,083,000 tons of sulfur oxide yearly—more than 33 percent of the Southeast's annual sulfur oxide emissions and 16 percent of the national total. It is noteworthy that virtually all the major actors in earlier battles over the formulation of the Clean Air Act and its amendments were represented in some way in the policy's implementation.

Organized Interests. The mix of private and public benefits derived from coal combustion is dependent upon the activism of the organized interests working through administrative and judicial institutions. The Environmental Protection Agency and the Office of Surface Mining in the Interior Department regard public interest groups as a natural constituency. These groups have lobbied to marshall congressional support for agency decisions sympathetic to environmental values. They have repeatedly gone to court to compel federal agencies to enforce strict interpretations of the Clean Air Act and the Surface Mining Control and Reclamation Act. Indeed, it has largely been through the efforts of these organized interests that many crucial administrative decisions affecting surface mine and air quality regulation have been publicly exposed and thereby altered to the advantage of environmentalists.

The mining industry, electric utilities, railroads, and other private groups with a major stake in increased coal combustion have been equally vigorous in promoting their viewpoints within DOI and EPA. Had it not been for the very determined activity of the National Coal Association and the American Mining Congress, the final regulations written by the Office of Surface Mining to interpret the new federal surface mine regulations would have been even more stringent than they actually turned out to be. In short, the implementation of coal policy expresses the existing cleavages of organized interests in a policy arena that is just as important to the eventual policy outcome as the policy development stage.

CONCLUSION

The conflict between environmental protection and energy production in coal or nuclear power development will continue through the 1980s. The conflict illuminates a problem constant in public energy management: the proper mix between these two considerations in the planning of an energy technology. We have observed that energy production is often a private good while environmental protection is a public good and that the costs and benefits associated with these two policies are often quite dissimilar. Thus, the conflict over the relative priorities of energy production and ecological protection in any field of energy technology is, in good part, a struggle between sides competing to create different patterns of costs and benefits from the eventual public policy outcome.

Viewed somewhat differently, the conflict between environmentalists and energy producers is a disagreement over the relative priority to be given to public or private benefits in energy policy. Environmentalists favor greater attention to environmental or public values while producers generally advocate the opposite. In any event, conflict is almost inevitable since it is difficult for the nation to provide enough of *both* energy production and environmental protection to satisfy both sides of the issue.

Promoters of private and public goods often pursue different political strategies and enjoy different political opportunities in their conflicts over energy policies. Generally, the promoters of private benefits from energy production have, until recently, enjoyed the far better advantage and have reaped the greater rewards. Since the 1970s, however, the balance has shifted considerably. Environmental protection is now sufficiently important in energy policy that public officials must confront the need to observe some environmental considerations in almost any energy program. Nevertheless, it is still an open question as to how vigorous this environmental sensitivity will be in the face of chronic energy shortages and the continued dissatisfaction of most energy producers with current environmental policies. In brief, the current mix of concerns for environmental protection and energy production in public policy is likely to remain unstable and constantly under attack from both sides.

One other implicit but significant dimension to this policy conflict is worth noting. It should now be clear that almost all energy policies become environmental policies, and environmental policies in good part become energy policies. It is virtually impossible for public officials to plan the use of future energy resources and technologies without deciding, if only implicitly, the nation's tolerance for environmental degradation. Conversely, government can rarely establish environmental pollution standards without deciding, in the process, what levels of energy production and which energy technologies will be tolerated. The connection between energy management and environmental quality not only undergirds most energy issues; it also explains why their resolution is often so difficult and the struggle to create a coherent national energy policy so bitter.

NOTES

1. Walter A. Rosenbaum, *Coal and Crisis* (New York: Praeger Publishers, 1978), chap. 2; U.S., Congress, Office of Technology Assessment, *The Direct Use of Coal* (Washington, D.C.: U.S. Government Printing Office, 1979), chap. 6.
2. *New York Times,* January 8, 1978.
3. Rosenbaum, *Coal and Crisis,* chap. 8.
4. Mancur Olson, *The Logic of Collective Action* (Cambridge, Mass.: Harvard University Press, 1965), p. 16.
5. D. W. Pearce, *Environmental Economics* (New York: Longman Inc., 1976), p. 20.
6. *New York Times,* November 9, 1979.
7. U.S., Congress, Office of Technology Assessment, *The Direct Use of Coal,* p. 6.
8. *Washington Post,* January 1, 1979.
9. *New York Times,* March 27, 1978.
10. *New York Times,* May 13, 1979.
11. Stephen L. McDonald, *The Leasing of Federal Lands for Fossil Fuels Production* (Baltimore, Md.: Johns Hopkins University Press, 1979), chap. 2.
12. *Washington Post,* September 18, 1978.
13. *New York Times,* April 15, 1978.
14. Robert Stobaugh and Daniel Yergin, eds., *Energy Future: Report of the Energy Project at the Harvard Business School* (New York: Random House, 1979), p. 115.
15. U.S., Congress, Office of Technology Assessment, *Analysis of the Proposed National Energy Plan* (Washington, D.C.: U.S. Government Printing Office, 1977), p. 59.
16. Linda W. Mulligan, "Energy Regionalism in the United States," in *Energy Policy in the United States,* ed. Seymour Warkov (New York: Praeger Publishers, 1978), p. 2.
17. U.S., General Accounting Office, *Nuclear Power Costs and Subsidies,* Report No. EMD-79-52 (Washington, D.C.: U.S. Government Printing Office, June 12, 1979), p. iii.
18. Congressional Quarterly, *Continuing Energy Crisis in America* (Washington, D.C.: Congressional Quarterly Inc., 1975), p. 38.
19. *New York Times,* March 26, 1977.

20. U.S., Congress, Office of Technology Assessment, *Analysis of the Proposed Energy Plan,* p. 52.
21. For a discussion of the capacity issue, see Ford Foundation, Nuclear Energy Policy Study Group, *Nuclear Power Issues and Choices* (Cambridge, Mass.: Ballinger Publishing Co., 1977), pp. 118-121.
22. Ralph Nader and John Abbotts, *The Menace of Atomic Energy,* (New York: W. W. Norton & Co., 1979), chap. 9.
23. *New York Times,* July 12, 1978.
24. *New York Times,* March 14, 1979.
25. *New York Times,* May 13, 1979.
26. *New York Times,* April 19, 1979.
27. Rosenbaum, *Coal and Crisis,* chap. 2.
28. U.S., Congress, Office of Technology Assessment, *The Direct Use of Coal,* pp. 309-310.
29. U.S., General Accounting Office, *The State of Competition in the Coal Industry,* Report No. EMD-78-22 (Washington, D.C.: U.S. Government Printing Office, December 30, 1977).
30. On the impact of surface mining throughout Appalachia, see Harry M. Caudill, *Night Comes to the Cumberlands* (Boston: Little, Brown & Co., 1962); and Harry M. Caudill, *My Land is Dying* (New York: E. P. Dutton, 1973).
31. Northern Great Plains Resources Program, *Effects of Coal Development in the Northern Great Plains* (Denver, Colo.: Northern Great Plains Resources Program Inc., 1975), p. 53.
32. U.S., Congress, Office of Technology Assessment, *The Direct Use of Coal,* p. 169.
33. Ibid., pp. 172, 173.
34. Ibid., p. 173.
35. *New York Times,* June 9, 1979.
36. Rosenbaum, *Coal and Crisis,* p. 15.
37. Ibid.
38. Ibid., p. 59.

5
What's Fair?:
The Distributive Issue

Martin O. is 56 years old, black, and sick. He lives with his disabled wife and three small grandchildren in the deteriorating inner city ghetto of Hartford, Connecticut. In 1979, the family lived on $586 a month, gleaned from social security and medical benefits. The family each month pays $125 in rent, almost $200 in medical bills, and an additional $60 for medicine. Whatever remains of its income is spent on transportation, food, child care, and other necessary items. During 1979, the price of heating oil for the family and the price of gasoline for its aging car both increased by 35 percent. Officials estimate that they needed almost 20 percent more income after taxes to offset the rising cost of energy. The family faces extreme deprivation because it has no savings. Like 25 million other poor Americans, they are economic casualties of the nation's energy crisis. Their condition forces attention on the distributive aspect of public energy management.

The energy crisis has been one of the most economically disruptive events in recent U.S. history. Most Americans have repeatedly been exposed to a now familiar economic shock: a strong surge in domestic energy prices, interrupted occasionally by sharp escalations following price increases imposed by the Organization of Petroleum Exporting Countries (OPEC). Between 1970 and 1979, the price of imported crude oil rose by almost 800 percent a barrel.[1] During this period, gasoline prices increased by 152 percent, home heating oil by 266 percent, and the average residential electric bill by 140 percent. During the single year of 1979, the average American citizen's total energy expenditures soared by 35 percent.[2] Rising energy prices also drove the nation's inflation rate toward unprecedented levels, and few economists would predict when energy prices might stabilize. Rising energy costs, pulling in tow the nation's total cost of living, have become a way of life.

The growth of energy costs highlights one of the most intensely controversial issues associated with the energy crisis—the distributive issue: how should the benefits and burdens from increasing energy prices be distributed across U.S. society? This volatile problem intrudes so continually and disruptively upon all government energy planning that it obstructs and confuses resolution of urgent energy issues. "The distributional question ignited the most visible fight in an effort to formulate a U.S. energy program," noted informed observers in the late 1970s. According to the Harvard Business School study, "So intense and heated has the debate been that it led participants to make exaggerated statements that have discredited their various positions."[3] The distributive issue is actually a bundle of different, yet related, problems.

In this chapter, we will briefly examine these issues: Should the government intervene to alter the impact of energy prices? What is a "fair" distribution of these price impacts across American society? Whose interests should be considered when attempting to determine this fairness? We will then discuss the viewpoints of major social groups concerning the equity of current energy prices and conclude by observing the importance of these issues in two recent major government energy management decisions: the deregulation of natural gas prices and the levying of the windfall profits tax on the petroleum industry.

SOME MAJOR DISTRIBUTIVE PROBLEMS

Unregulated, the energy marketplace has no social conscience. Rising energy prices punish and reward most Americans, but not on an equal basis and often without respect for their ability to endure the consequences. In New York, for example, increased energy costs had forced the average older American's household to spend one-third of its income on energy by 1979, whereas middle-income families were spending only 9.6 percent.[4] At the same time, stockholders in the nation's major petroleum companies reaped record dividends. In short, Americans differ in their ability to pay higher energy prices, in the sacrifices they experience, and in the extent to which they also benefit from increased energy prices.

Should Government Intervene?

Many economists, together with many political conservatives, believe that energy prices should be permitted to rise with little governmental restraint except perhaps for some buffering of the impact upon the poorest Americans. Advocates of such governmental restraint believe that the nation's energy resources in the long run will be best allocated and achieve energy conservation most quickly when the consumer experiences such price escalation directly and swiftly. According to this logic, the market reflects the true replacement cost of energy resources and far more clearly signals the consumer to conserve energy than would governmentally controlled prices. Furthermore, critics of federal price management usually assert that government intervention in the energy marketplace brings with it new regulatory bureaucracies, costly and confusing masses of new regulations to interfere with the efficient production of energy by private corporations, special concessions to undeserving but politically powerful groups, and other social costs.

This economic theory has not been the dominant public philosophy since the days of the Roosevelt administration (1933 to 1945), but critics of government price regulations have always represented a significant and often influential dissenting public whose demand for governmental restraint on energy price management had to be given some recognition in Washington. Opponents of regulation were particularly encouraged by the November 1980 elections. President Reagan, whose road to the White House was paved with promises to reduce federal economic regulations, seemed anxious to work with the new Republican Senate majority to eliminate many federal energy price controls and other restraints on the energy market.

What Are Fair Impacts?

The majority of the public and its officials do expect some kind of government intervention in the marketplace to offset the undesirable social effects of rising energy prices. But how should the market be corrected? U.S. policymakers, like most citizens, have a crude standard for "fair." In the words of the Congressional Budget Office, a fair pricing policy would mean that "the burdens imposed by that policy are related to the ability of individuals to bear those burdens."[5] This deceptively simple formula leads into a thicket of controversies when it is translated into specific policies, however.

Energy Prices. One conflict concerns the proper price for energy itself. Arguments arise over the extent to which energy producers and their financial beneficiaries are imposing a justified or unreasonable cost upon energy consumers. These arguments frequently become extraordinarily complex. Protracted disputes ensue over what profits are reasonable or excessive and what consumer costs are equitable or unjustified. As we will observe in the discussion of federal regulations on the price of domestic crude oil and natural gas, these themes are central to all controversies over U.S. energy policies.

Economic Relief. Another dispute concerns how much relief is appropriate for individuals or families in different economic strata. At what point, for instance, does an American individual or household qualify as sufficiently distressed by high energy prices to merit public assistance or other economic relief? One study suggests that the average American household with a disposable income under $2,000 in the early 1980s had to spend about half of that income for heating fuels, while slightly less impoverished families (with disposable incomes between $2,000 and $5,000) spent only 16 percent of disposable income for the same purpose.[6]

Which of these households merits economic assistance, and how much should be provided? The issue is further complicated because all families in the same economic category are not equally affected by energy prices. In the late 1970s, an American family with $5,000 in disposable income would have spent about 28 percent of that income for energy needs if it lived in the eastern United States, but only half that amount if it lived in the West.[7]

Economic Compensation. Another question focuses on how those who might merit public economic assistance should be compensated. Should there be direct cash subsidies from government and, if so, from which government—federal, state, or local? Should the assistance be through tax concessions? Should it fully compensate for increasing energy prices? Some experts contend that such a strategy does not sufficiently encourage the recipient to conserve energy.

Inevitably, disputes arise over which procedures are most equitable and sensitive to the real burdens imposed by energy prices. Some states, for instance, have attempted to help the poor pay for energy and other necessities by relating assistance levels to changes in the Consumer Price Index (CPI), the federal government's standard measure of living costs for American families. But during the period 1972 to 1979, the average American's gasoline prices rose by 134 percent and the electric bill by 78 percent, while the CPI, based on a composite of different consumer items, increased only 69 percent.[8] Thus, energy needs have claimed a progressively increasing share of assistance under this arrangement while other, perhaps equally urgent, demands have had to be proportionately neglected.

Transfer Payments. An extremely controversial aspect of fairness concerns the source of money to compensate those whom government decides should receive public relief from rising energy prices. Such relief implies a transfer payment from one social sector to another; no matter how it may be disguised, someone has to pay for this economic compensation. Proponents of energy transfer payments generally assert that those who profit unreasonably or excessively from energy price increases or those affluent enough to bear price rises comfortably should provide the revenue for such income transfers—in other words, energy importers, refiners and distributors, stockholders in energy corporations, other financial interests that profit from higher energy prices, and generally the rich.

These economic interests are sure to argue that their profits are neither excessive nor unreasonable. In fact, many energy producers maintain that such profits are the necessary incentive to assure continued exploration and production. And the middle- and upper-class citizens who might provide the tax revenues to underwrite a substantial portion of these transfer payments are likely to resist increased taxes for this purpose. Indeed, many of these Americans are now seeking tax reductions through energy conservation. In 1979, for example, a government tax credit of up to $300 for improving home energy efficiency was claimed on more than 4.5 million federal tax returns. Thus, those who believe in fairness as a principle in energy pricing often become antagonists when allocating the economic cost of producing this fairness.

These controversies illustrate that fairness has no commonly accepted definition among those interests concerned with U.S. energy prices. Fairness becomes whatever policy settlement can be wrested from the multitude of powerful, contentious interests zealous to shape price policy to their own satisfaction. In the end, fair is what government says it is.

The Political Nature of Distributive Policies

In an uncontrolled economic market, energy prices are largely determined by the supply and demand for an energy resource. But if government declares what will be a fair energy pricing policy, political factors become especially important in that decision. A governmentally controlled price responds to public opinion climates, to the political strength of various interests and geographic constituencies, and to the bias of government institutions.

Moreover, any significant increase in energy prices sends virtually all socioeconomic sectors to government demanding action to buffer the impacts upon them, regardless of the ultimate desirability of those impacts. Explains a study by Resources for the Future:

> People do not believe the real cost of energy has risen. They feel cheated when they are forced to pay higher prices ... they resist every loss of welfare related to energy, regardless of its positive impact on society as a whole.[9]

The effect of this group mobilization may be inefficient, sometimes highly undesirable, distortions of energy supply and demand. Thus, gasoline demand may be kept too high by government policies that prevent gasoline prices from increasing at a rate that reflects the true replacement cost of that fuel. The consumer's interest may be served at the expense of national energy conservation.

Finally, public management of energy pricing means that such pricing policies have a strong tendency to become segmented. The policies for individual fuel prices are likely to be inconsistent, reflecting the particular array of political forces associated with different energy sectors. In the past, federal regulation of interstate natural gas responded to consumer interests (especially municipalities and residential homeowners) and not to the interests of natural gas producers and shippers. In contrast, federal petroleum policy was far more indulgent toward petroleum producers. Arrangements like the oil depletion allowance favored a generous profit to domestic petroleum companies while the consumer's interest, although seldom ignored, was never so imperious as in federal natural gas policy.

In summary, the political allocation of economic impacts from rising energy prices—the business of declaring what is fair—will be biased toward those social interests best able to mobilize and impose their definition of economic equity upon government policies.

WHOSE EQUITY COUNTS?

The list of social groups whose interests merit consideration in federal energy pricing is enormous, yet relatively few groups dominate the policy discussion.

The Disadvantaged

The Poor. The majority of the economically disadvantaged incur real, sometimes calamitous, income losses from climbing energy prices. The poor and their spokesmen feel that they suffer grievously and disproportionately from energy price inflation. Leaders of the disadvantaged also perceive any real or alleged slowing of the nation's economic growth as a particular burden for the underprivileged. This perception shifts the political weight of the underprivileged solidly behind programs to subsidize or otherwise eliminate the income losses suffered from increasing energy costs, while at the same time resisting national policies to conserve energy in ways that appear to threaten economic growth.

There is ample evidence that the poor generally must commit a larger share of their income to energy purchases. The middle-income American family spends about 5 percent of its disposable income on utility bills; low-income families spend between 15 and 30 percent of their income for utilities.[10] Generally, the poorest fifth of the U.S. population has spent approximately two to three times the proportion of its income on energy than have families close to the American average income. For the poor, energy expenditure appears to be about 13 to 15 percent of total family income.[11]

Rising energy prices mean a direct and often immediate diversion of income from other needs or a rapid alteration in life style for poor Americans. In 1977, more than 6 in 10 Americans with annual incomes under $8,000 reported a cutback in driving as a result of increasing gasoline prices, while 6 in 10 Americans with incomes exceeding $20,000 yearly reported driving as much as or more than previously.[12]

Senior Citizens. The elderly, who constitute more than one-third of all low-income U.S. households, are especially vulnerable to rising energy costs since their incomes are usually fixed. Explained a Maine welfare official in describing the plight of the low-income elderly in his state to a congressional committee:

> Right here in the Lewiston area, we have a 70-year-old man who is handicapped. He can't read or write. He lives here alone in an apartment. He has to pay his own gas heat. It cost him $525 last winter to pay for his heat, and he paid $77 in electric bills over the same time. His total income was only $259 a month."[13]

In the Northeast, where home heating oil is the most common source of residential heating for the elderly poor, a gallon of the fuel increased 400 percent in price between 1973 and 1979.[14]

Blacks. Organizations representing black Americans have been among the most effective political spokesmen for the disadvantaged in the energy debate. A major black journal recently summarized the prevailing mood of the black community:

> Black people, along with other minorities, and the poor and the elderly, are the principal casualties [of the energy crisis]. And what this means ... is that Black America has been disproportionately affected by America's energy crisis. Even before the crisis, Black America was using less energy and paying more per unit for it.[15]

Like most organizations representing the disadvantaged, the attitude of the National Association for the Advancement of Colored People (NAACP) toward energy supply is influenced by apprehension over economic growth:

> Since the early 1960s, significant gains have been made toward bringing the nation's Black citizens into the mainstream of America's economic life. This has occurred largely during a period of expansion in the

economy which created new opportunities for jobs ... abundant
energy will be necessary if we are to have a chance to meet these
challenges.... Energy supply development [*sic*] has been critically
important to economic growth.[16]

Many blacks suspect that "energy conservation" is a euphemism
for controlling economic growth to their disadvantage, regardless of
the substance of conservation proposals.

The political system tends to be highly sensitive to claims from
the disadvantaged for equity. Among other reasons, a very high proportion of the elderly, blacks, and other underprivileged live in urban
areas in the Northeast, Sunbelt, and far western states that have
relatively large congressional delegations. The dominance of the Democratic party in Congress and in the White House placed in power
the political party that is traditionally more responsive to minorities
and the disadvantaged. The Democrats by far have been the more
sympathetic party to government economic regulation.

The Middle Class

The American majority is the middle class. Encompassing blue-
collar workers, white-collar occupations, the professions, and a substantial portion of the business community, the vast expanse of social
territory populated by the middle class is also enormous in its energy
consumption. Almost half of middle-income U.S. households have
central air conditioning, and about two-fifths own at least two automobiles. Most possess an automatic washing machine, and 7 in 10
middle-class homes have an automatic dishwasher—an abundance
of appliances far exceeding their incidence among the less affluent.[17]

Compared to the poor, the middle class generally spends a substantially lower proportion of its income on energy, has more opportunities to practice energy conservation and other restraints on
energy use, and enjoys more options in responding to higher energy
prices. Since per capita energy use rises with social status, the more
prosperous American is a more obvious (and some would say more
reasonable) target for government efforts to encourage energy conservation than are the less advantaged.

In the interest of the energy consumer, past federal energy policy
often regulated the market price of energy to keep it relatively low,
an approach that benefited all Americans but especially the more
prosperous who consumed more energy. During most of the 1970s,
for instance, federal controls on domestic petroleum kept the price
of domestic oil about 35 percent below the price of imported oil,
shielding the American consumer from higher world prices. In 1978,
lifting these controls would have added about $12 billion to the
cost of petroleum products.[18] Federal policy insisted that natural gas

sold to consumers on the interstate market be sold at a "just and reasonable" price, eventually driving its price far below that on the unregulated intrastate market. From this perspective, government regulation of energy markets has quite often been advantageous to the American middle class.

This traditional pricing policy is important to an understanding of the responses of the middle class to the debate over the distributive impacts of current energy prices. Labor unions and public interest, consumer, and taxpayer groups have been the most visible and articulate representatives of middle-class viewpoints in the pricing controversy. Like most spokesmen for a middle-class constituency, these groups have tenaciously fought to retain existing energy policies when they restrain energy prices to levels favorable to consumers. In this respect, they have a vested interest in guarding such policies against radical reassessment or termination. When energy prices are decontrolled, noted a recent Ford Foundation study, the resulting income transfers affect primarily the non-poor:

> It is a transfer from consumers generally, some of whom are poor, toward stockholders [in energy companies] not all of whom are rich— some stockholders being pension funds, university endowments, and non-wealthy individuals. Since the non-poor consumers spend more on petroleum products than poor consumers, the larger burden of this transfer in dollar terms is from the non-poor to the comparatively well to do.[19]

State and Regional Interests

The states and regional spokesmen are drawn into the energy price debate in coalition with various producer and consumer groups for several reasons: states and regions may be major energy producers, major energy consumers, or highly susceptible to short-term energy price fluctuations. These circumstances make the states and regions acutely sensitive to major changes in energy prices and quick to assert that they also have a stake in fair federal energy pricing policies.

Energy production is highly concentrated among the states. About 65 percent of the nation's oil and gas is produced from three states (Louisiana, Texas, and Oklahoma), and most uranium has been mined in New Mexico, Colorado, and Utah. Increased coal utilization will add several western states (primarily North Dakota, Wyoming, Montana, and New Mexico) to the present five states that are major coal producers. Altogether, less than one-fourth of the 50 states produce almost two-thirds of the nation's total energy resources.[20]

This energy production provides to these states a substantial portion of their tax revenues, creates a large employment market, and stimulates their economies in many other ways. Political leaders from oil- and gas-producing states strongly identify with the energy producer's desire to remove virtually all federal restraints on energy prices. They understand former Texas Governor Dolph Briscoe's remark that natural gas price controls are "a cocked gun aimed at Texas." Political spokesmen for the coal states, aware of the vast reserves within their jurisdiction, are often zealous to encourage increased national coal consumption.

Several regions of the United States, particularly the Northeast and Southeast, contain many states high in energy consumption but low in energy production. Most northeastern states depend on coal, imported petroleum, and nuclear power for their energy supply. The cost of living and working in the Northeast, like the cost of doing business, is very responsive to short-term alterations in energy prices. A rise in the cost of heating oil is felt with particular acuteness, as are changes in the price of petroleum for electric power generation (about 60 percent of New England's electricity is generated from petroleum). More than half of the 15 southern states producing little, if any, energy feel a competitive disadvantage with other states that are capable of producing cheaper energy by minimizing import costs.

States that produce energy frequently assail the energy-consuming states for allegedly enjoying an unfair advantage under controlled prices. "The Northeast states," claimed a senior vice-president of Continental Oil, "have been buying natural gas at less than replacement value while at the same time they have erected environmental and other barriers preventing development of their own energy resources."[21] Rising energy prices and diverse energy needs have intensified regionalism into a major source of conflict in energy policy. Its implications will be examined more closely in the final chapter.

Energy Producers

The nation's energy producers have been highly predictable and very selective in their attitude toward government intervention in the energy market. Rarely does the energy sector speak with greater unanimity than when discussing energy pricing. Led by the petroleum and natural gas producers who dominate the energy sector in output, wealth, corporate size, and political muscle, energy producers generally advocate government deregulation of domestic petroleum and natural gas prices as long as market prices yield reasonable profits. But energy corporations have often favored government price supports, subsidies, or other economic incentives to encourage the marketing of fuels like coal, synthetic gas, petroleum, and other energy sources they deem as contributing significantly to the nation's energy needs.

The energy sector's aversion to government involvement has never extended to federal, state, or local tax concessions that enhance corporate profits, although no energy sector equals the petroleum industry's dazzling performance in turning federal tax concessions to its advantage. In recent years the petroleum industry has admitted the need for modest tax increases to underwrite transfer payments to the most disadvantaged by the energy crisis. But the industry's concept of fairness still remains markedly less than the tax increases demanded by consumer groups.

Petroleum and natural gas producers have asserted that their large profit increases serve the national, as well as corporate, interest in several ways. First, profits are an incentive to the increasingly expensive search for new domestic energy reserves, and the discovery of new energy reserves will benefit the nation economically and politically. Oil company leaders have recently suggested that rapid decontrol of domestic petroleum, leading to new exploration, would probably add between .2 and 1.5 million barrels per day of new crude oil to the nation's production, perhaps for a decade.

Second, the industry asserts that unregulated petroleum and natural gas prices will reflect the true replacement cost of new energy and will therefore signal to consumers that the terms of energy consumption have drastically changed. These increasing market prices will quickly dampen the nation's demand for new energy and introduce conservation effectively. The industry asserts this market mechanism will control energy demand while leaving the consumer with the maximum freedom to choose the best individual strategy for conservation, an economically efficient procedure according to traditional economic theory.

In response to their critics' charges of "obscene" profits, the petroleum corporations have asserted that current profits are a reasonable offset to many previous years of sharply reduced profits and that much of this profit is reinvested in new oil exploration. Such arguments usually turn on extraordinarily complex and conflicting interpretations of the companies' actual profits, their real rate of reinvestment, and other matters so arcane as to bewilder the average citizen and most public officials.

The nation's major petroleum producers, exploiting their powerful economic and political position to unrivaled advantage among energy companies, in the past were assured a sympathetic government attitude toward energy pricing. Current debate over the distributive impacts of energy pricing is complicated and embittered by controversy over the industry's privileged economic position. The petroleum industry exhibits one of the highest concentrations of corporate wealth, market control, and government influence among any U.S. economic sector.

Although there are more than 300 oil companies in the United States, the largest—the so-called majors—dominate the industry and exert their power most effectively in national politics. Among the majors, five companies rank among the eight largest corporations in the country: Standard Oil (California), Exxon, Texaco, Gulf, and Mobil. These giants, members of a still vaster international oil cartel, accounted for more than one-fifth of total U.S. capital investment in the late 1970s.[22] Control over domestic oil production and a large portion of other energy production is concentrated among these five companies who collectively constitute the majors together with several other oil corporations. A few figures are suggestive.[23] By the late 1970s, the 20 largest petroleum corporations controlled:

—About 94 percent of domestic petroleum reserves.
—Approximately 70 percent of crude oil production.
—Almost 86 percent of domestic refining capacity.

The majors also have a substantial economic interest in other energy sectors. In the late 1970s, they controlled:

—Approximately 72 percent of national gas production.
—About 13 percent of domestic coal reserves.
—Approximately 20 percent of domestic coal production capacity.
—More than 50 percent of uranium reserves.
—About 25 percent of uranium milling capacity.[24]

The powerful political position secured on this economic foundation has enabled the petroleum industry to obtain many tax concessions from government. The industry's political success is due in good part to the work of the American Petroleum Institute (API). With headquarters in Washington, D.C., this industry trade association has more than 450 staff members and an annual budget approaching $20 million. Representatives of API are among the most experienced and effective of all Washington lobbyists. Critics have asserted that these past political privileges, some not wholly eliminated, have exempted the companies from paying their fair share of taxes and now make unreasonable any demands for uncontrolled petroleum prices, which would amount to another reign of economic privilege. The most controversial of these earlier tax privileges were the percentage depletion, the tax deduction for intangible drilling expenses, and the foreign tax credit that collectively saved the U.S. petroleum industry billions of dollars in taxes.

The percentage depletion, as originally enacted by Congress in 1926, permitted domestic oil and gas producers to deduct from their taxable income as much as 27.5 percent of the gross revenue from their wells, as long as this deduction did not exceed half of the producer's net income before the deduction. Moreover, the companies could continue the deduction as long as the property yielded income. The federal government has permitted all U.S. extraction industries to use a depletion allowance since 1913 when the federal income tax was enacted. The allowance was based on the assumption that minerals, oil, and gas owned by a company are capital assets that become depleted as they are extracted from the ground. It is a principle of the federal income tax to avoid taxing capital as if it were income, and the depletion allowance was designed to prevent this situation in the extraction industries. The petroleum producers' allowance has been far more generous than that permitted other extraction industries, however. Although Congress reduced this allowance to 22 percent in 1969, studies have indicated that the percentage depletion still enabled many oil and gas companies to recover from 10 to 20 times the cost of a producing well over its lifetime.

The intangible drilling expense allowed a domestic petroleum producer the unusual privilege of immediately deducting from taxes practically the entire cost of wages, salaries, fuel, machines, tool rentals, and other intangible expenses incurred in developing a well. This concession, together with percentage depletion, represented a tax loss to the federal government of $2.35 billion in 1972.[25] The foreign tax credit allowed U.S. petroleum companies operating internationally to use the taxes paid to one foreign country as a direct offset against taxes owed in the United States on a dollar-for-dollar basis. In the early 1970s, this policy enabled domestic producers to reduce their U.S. taxes by approximately 75 percent.[26]

Critics of the petroleum industry, after decades of bitter struggle, in 1975 finally persuaded Congress to repeal the percentage depletion allowance for the majors, reduce the value of the foreign tax credit, and curtail the deductions permitted as intangible drilling expenses. But the effect of earlier privilege still taints all current arguments over a fair price policy. The industry's critics act as if the petroleum producers have yet to pay back to the nation the full value of the "unfair" tax advantages they enjoyed for almost 50 years.

PETROLEUM PRICES: DECONTROL AND WINDFALL PROFITS

The most important recent controversy over petroleum prices swirled about two intertwined issues: decontrolling the price of domestic crude oil and taxing so-called windfall profits to the oil companies. The two issues reveal two aspects of the policy cycle: the decontrol of petroleum prices involved the termination of an existing public policy, and the windfall profits tax required developing a substantially new policy. These two interdependent issues also illustrate how energy policies interact.

The Oil Price Controversy

Until the early 1970s, the price of crude oil produced or sold domestically was not formally regulated by the federal government. Since the mid-1930s, however, Congress had condoned an interstate agreement (the Compact to Conserve Oil and Gas) that permitted 20 states to regulate oil production in their jurisdictions. These controls were largely exercised to limit production, which was defended as a conservation measure. Its more important effect for the oil producers, however, was to keep the price of domestic crude oil considerably higher than it would otherwise be in an uncontrolled, competitive market. In short, this policy was a backdoor variety of price control. It illustrates the domestic petroleum industry's historic tendency to seek government regulation when it worked to industry advantage. Explains David Davis:

> Economists describe the oil companies' eagerness for governmental regulation as a flight from the market. Business seeks to be governed less by economic laws and more by political laws. Rather than establish price and quantity by supply and demand, they prefer to establish it by legislative and administrative decision making.[27]

This arrangement provoked no great public controversy because the price of crude oil and most of crude oil's distilled products was still relatively low. One gallon of U.S. gasoline, for instance, averaged about 35 cents in 1970; both the consumer interest and company profits were served. In the late 1950s, the petroleum industry once again asked and received from Washington. At that time, imported oil was cheaper than domestic crude, and U.S. producers feared a tide of cheap foreign oil would soon undercut domestic crude oil prices. With congressional collaboration, the Eisenhower administration created quotas on imported crude oil that effectively protected the domestic oil producers from the worst vexation of foreign competition. Economically insulated behind a barrier of federal, state, and local laws, U.S. oil producers and consumers functioned in a sheltered petroleum market, free from the shock of short-term changes in the price or volume of foreign oil.

The underpinnings of this *entente cordiale* between government, oil companies, and consumers gradually faltered in the 1970s. In 1971, the Nixon administration for the first time directly regulated domestic crude oil prices as part of comprehensive wage and price controls intended to counter the effects of mounting national inflation. This first regulated price of domestic crude oil was approximately $4 per barrel, but in 1973 the price of foreign oil rose sharply in response to the growing power of the Organization of Petroleum Exporting Countries (OPEC) cartel.

Congress, alarmed by the soaring domestic petroleum prices and anxious to protect the economy from sudden price increases, passed the Emergency Petroleum Allocation Act that continued the Nixon controls on all crude oil marketed in the United States. The legislation set one price for "old" oil (from domestic wells producing before 1973) and a much higher price for "new" oil (from domestic wells brought into production after 1973); the price of imported oil was not controlled. Domestic oil companies were permitted to use a complex formula for combining the cost of the controlled new and old domestic oil with the uncontrolled imported oil to arrive at a grand average for all their oil sold in the country. Nevertheless, this new average kept the price of crude oil sold in the United States considerably below the cost of imported oil.

Thus, in 1974 the average domestic price for a barrel of crude oil was $6.87, while the uncontrolled price on the world market was about $10.77. Domestic oil companies were unhappy. The newly regulated prices capped their profits by preventing the companies from passing to their customers the total increase in imported oil costs, at a time when the United States (already importing almost a third of its petroleum) was expected to import much more oil in the future. In 1975, the oil companies persuaded the Ford administration and Congress to modify price regulations modestly. The price of new domestic petroleum was permitted to rise in recognition of the mounting cost of imported oil, but the average price of crude sold in the United States could increase no more than 10 percent per year. The petroleum industry was not appeased. In 1976, the regulated price of crude oil sold in the country was about $8.19 per barrel and the world price $11.51.

The 1975 legislation did hold a glimmer of promise for the oil industry, however. Beginning in 1979, the law allowed the president to set new domestic crude oil prices without following the earlier restrictions that limited price increases to 10 percent annually. And Congress also provided that all price controls mandated in the law might end by 1981—if Congress did not object and if the president were willing to do it. In his first term, Jimmy Carter thus inherited a controversy of mounting bitterness, inflamed by rampant inflation, soaring imported petroleum prices, and accusations between consumers and oil producers about the fairness of existing price controls. He also inherited an opportunity to alter price controls and possibly to eliminate them.

The president, like most economists and oil producers, favored the gradual lifting of controls on domestic crude oil. Proponents of decontrol have argued that rising petroleum prices, reflecting the true replacement cost of existing oil, would slow the increase in domestic demand for petroleum and also decrease national consumption of imported oil. Domestic production from deep wells, marginal reserves, and other previously unpromising sources would also be encouraged because oil companies would have more capital to invest in such risky endeavors. Increased petroleum prices would also make solar and other alternative energy sources more competitive than on the current domestic market where petroleum products were given enormous market advantage by controlled prices. Whatever the short-term disadvantages, proponents assert, decontrol in the long term would be an efficient and effective means of inducing energy conservation.

Opponents of decontrol primarily represent consumer groups, the elderly, and the economically disadvantaged. They have asserted that decontrolled petroleum prices would be heavily regressive, forcing upon the least advantaged Americans the greatest burden and the most sacrifice. Moreover, many individuals will have no choice but to continue using automobiles (they may have no alternative transportation to work, for instance); consequently, critics maintain that the extent of petroleum savings is exaggerated. Opponents also allege that oil companies will actually invest relatively little of their new profits in further petroleum exploration; the companies already have enough venture capital, and limited new reserves cannot be expanded simply because more money is available to explore them. Rather, the critics charge, the petroleum companies will reap from decontrol both enormous profits (primarily for stockholders, corporate officials, and company coffers) and new capital to sink into attractive investments outside the energy sector.

The Windfall Profits Issue

Undoubtedly, the so-called windfall profits resulting from increased petroleum prices is the most divisive issue in the decontrol debate. The disposition of these windfall profits lies at the heart of the distributive conflict over petroleum pricing.

Domestic petroleum companies had enjoyed unprecedented profits during the 1970s. Even before the 1973 Arab oil embargo forced the energy crisis onto the public policy agenda, U.S. oil companies were among the nation's most profitable. Between 1968 and 1972, Robert Engler estimates that seven U.S. companies (Exxon, Texaco, Mobil, Standard of California, Gulf, Standard of Indiana, and Shell) amassed more than $44 billion in profits. "These companies," notes Engler, "managed to pay less than $2 billion in United States income taxes during the same period," an effective tax rate of 5 percent on earnings.[28]

The rapid increases in petroleum prices after 1973 created massive windfalls of profits for the industry because prices rose much more steeply than the cost of producing oil. One reliable estimate suggests that between March 1973 and January 1974 petroleum price rises should have caused about a 38 percent jump in the cost of refined petroleum products, but the actual cost increase was 127 percent.[29] How much of this post-embargo price rise was attributable to the OPEC countries and how much to the petroleum industry's desire to squeeze its consumers was fiercely debated. Domestic petroleum prices have been debated ever since for the same reason.

About the only undisputed fact in the petroleum price controversy has been the petroleum industry's soaring profits since the 1973 embargo. By the second quarter of 1979, the average among the majors was a 68.9 percent increase over profits in the previous year's second quarter. Domestic oil company earnings, in comparison with the previous year, included an increase of 809 percent for Ashland Oil, 105 percent for Texaco, 65 percent for Gulf, and 20 percent for Exxon. Critics regarded this explosive growth in profits as excessive if not unethical. The profits also reinforced a suspicion among many Americans that petroleum shortages had been engineered by the oil industry for its own advantage. Although the petroleum companies maintained that their income was reasonable in spite of their escalating profits, they were unable to convince either the White House or a majority of Congress that price decontrols should be eliminated.

The president and most other federal officials recognized that decontrol of petroleum prices, however sensible for energy conservation, could be justified publicly only if associated with a tax on the resulting windfall profits, a tax capturing much of these profits for other purposes. Thus, the federal government would intervene directly in the energy market to drive up the price of petroleum products and to create an allocation of the resulting profits different than would otherwise have occurred. In effect, Washington would impose a politically derived formula for distributive equity in oil company profits. Publicly, the oil companies continued to insist upon decontrol without a windfall tax; privately, most industry leaders were resigned to a stiff tax.

The Solution: Equity by Politics

After more than a year's debate, in 1980 Congress produced a bill gradually decontrolling domestic petroleum prices and concurrently imposing a tax on windfall profits. The bill, a compromise between President Carter's original proposal and different versions enacted in the House and Senate, created complex tax formulas expected to produce about $227.3 billion in new federal funds during the 1980s. Added to existing industry taxes, the new federal assessment appeared to be the largest ever levied against a single U.S. industry. According to the formula enacted in the new law, the tax revenues expected during the 1980s would be divided as follows:

—$56.8 billion (25 percent of the tax) to assist the poor with increased energy costs. About $3.15 billion would be paid in 1981, with half of the balance going to welfare recipients.
—$136.4 billion (60 percent) to provide tax reductions for business and personal income.
—$34.1 billion (15 percent) for energy development and mass transportation programs.[30]

The legislation, however, still left Congress to specify how the funds for tax cuts, energy development, and mass transportation would be divided among the numerous competing interests in each major area.

The tax bill was greeted with no great enthusiasm by most of the interests involved in the oil price controversy. Although the oil companies were left with approximately 22 percent of the windfall profits expected during the 1980s—a total profit figure exceeding $221 billion—industry spokesmen felt the tax excessively depleted the capital they anticipated necessary for new energy exploration in the 1980s. Spokesmen for the disadvantaged complained that the middle class, businesses, and oil companies were the true winners in the battle, while the poor would receive an allocation insufficient to cover their true costs from energy price inflation. Labor and consumer groups protested that the oil companies were permitted to retain too much of their windfall profits. The contending sides continued to disagree over what allocation of windfall profits was truly equitable. Nonetheless, the politically derived formula for distributing the profits was significantly different from what the market would have achieved in the absence of government intervention.

Oil Pricing and the Policy Cycle

Several aspects of the policy cycle are highlighted by the battle to decontrol oil prices, especially the politics of policy termination. In this instance, the result was unusual for termination battles because the opponents of an existing policy won. This is not surprising since existing policies customarily develop a strong private group constituency, a major bureaucratic guardian, friends in Congress, and other political support structures.

The end of oil price controls was hastened in good part by events largely out of the control of the policy opponents themselves. They were able to capitalize on the growing awareness that petroleum needed to be conserved and had been unrealistically cheap. Opponents were also able to exploit public officials' alarm over growing dependence on imported oil with all the economic and security risks it implied. It is difficult to imagine decontrol so quickly achieved without these external events. It is also apparent that outside circumstances powerfully assisted the drive to impose higher taxes on oil company profits. The nation's petroleum industry had successfully fought significant tax increases for many decades. Its resistance was robbed of its political force by the public revelation of mounting corporate profits in the wake of the OPEC price increases. Circumstances were congenial to policy innovation.

The decontrol of oil prices was also abetted by the recent creation of the Department of Energy (DOE). The department, a strong proponent of price decontrol, had been active in the debate since its formation in 1977. While other federal energy agencies had in the past favored oil price decontrols, the organization of many into a single large cabinet-level department greatly enlarged their collective influence. This internal lobbying within the government significantly changed the balance of bureaucratic forces favoring and opposing decontrol.

Public opinion created both constraints and opportunities in the policy formulation stage. Oil price decontrol without a windfall profits tax would have been politically unthinkable in the climate of the late 1970s. From the outset of the price control debate, the gods of political feasibility had to be served: whatever they may have wished privately, public officials were forced to consider decontrol and the tax as a package. In the same vein, the widely recognized hardships imposed upon the poor by energy price inflation made some provision for their relief in the windfall tax plan almost inevitable. Public opinion, moreover, had accomplished for a brief moment what few other political forces had been able to do in the United States: it threw the huge oil production sector on the political defensive and for the first time opened the industry's profits to public appropriation in significant amount.

DECONTROLLING NATURAL GAS PRICES

The oil price controversy was only one battle waged in the late 1970s over the domestic price of the nation's major fuels. Natural gas, the country's second most important energy source, was also embroiled in a bitter debate over its federally controlled price. Washington's decision to decontrol this price ended decades of conflict. As in the oil price debate, distributive issues were the focus of the gas controversy.

The natural gas issue vitally affects most Americans. More than half of the nation's residential dwellings are heated by this clean, efficient fossil fuel. The price controversy involves a debate over the best way to prolong the availability of declining natural gas reserves. Not only are distributive issues involved, but in this instance the controversy illuminates the difficulty (if not the impossibility) of resolving them by econometric models or scientific expertise. Federal natural gas pricing policy is a particularly obvious case of substituting political judgments for economic factors. The controversy also suggests the importance of administrative and judicial actions in shaping the substance of natural gas policy, a reminder that implementation and assessment remain crucial phases in the policymaking process.

The Origins of Controversy

Natural gas has been utilized as fuel in the United States for almost a century, but only after World War II did it become a major domestic energy source. The development of new pipeline technologies, permitting long distance transport of the gas, initiated a growth surge for the industry continuing well into the 1970s. In 1945, natural gas represented scarcely 4 percent of the nation's energy use; by 1975, this figure had climbed to 25 percent. The industry had expanded into a complex, interdependent network of 6,000 natural gas producers (half of these were part of integrated companies that extract, transport, and sell natural gas), major pipelines, and about 1,500 local distributors. Natural gas is used primarily by industry and households: approximately 48 percent of production is used for industrial production and 34 percent for home heating and cooling.

Natural gas producers and distributors are public utilities and are subject to state and federal regulation. Until the 1940s, most pipelines that operated solely within one state were regulated by state utility commissions. After 1945, pipelines rapidly spread across state borders and came under federal regulation as a form of interstate commerce. In the late 1970s, about two-thirds of all gas produced in the United States was federally regulated and the remainder was controlled by the states, a distinction of crucial importance to the natural gas pricing controversy.

Congress sowed the seeds for the controversy it would reap within a few decades when it passed the Natural Gas Act in 1938. Anxious to protect natural gas customers (who included major city utilities as well as individual residences) from price gouging, arbitrary service charges, and other undesirable monopolistic practices, Congress created through the act the Federal Power Commission (FPC) and ordered it to set a "just and reasonable" price for gas sold to customers by the pipelines. Congress assured contention over this regulation by providing no clear guidelines for defining such a price; FPC and the pipelines were soon caught in a continuing controversy over the price issue. Moreover, the price of intrastate gas—gas produced, transported, and sold entirely within one state—was excluded from federal regulation.

The natural gas pricing controversy was further intensified in 1945 when the Supreme Court ruled in a historic case *(Phillips Petroleum Co. v. Wisconsin)* that FPC had the authority to regulate the price of gas charged by the producer to the pipeline—the wellhead price—because this regulation was essential to assure a "just and reasonable" pipeline price. But the Court provided no clear criteria for setting this wellhead price; again, FPC was left to make an administrative determination of a fair pricing policy. By the mid-1950s, the substance of federal natural gas pricing policy had been shaped by the original 1938 congressional legislation, by FPC's subsequent interpretations of that act under authority delegated to it by Congress, and by many federal court cases of which *Phillips v. Wisconsin* was the most important. This combination of policy formulation, implementation, and assessment produced the two most controversial aspects of federal natural gas pricing: the existence of two different natural gas pricing systems and disagreement over how a "just and reasonable" price for federally regulated gas should be calculated.

Two Natural Gas Markets

Between 1940 and the late 1970s, the U.S. natural gas market consisted of two different segments, the "two tier" system so roundly criticized by the natural gas industry. One segment of the market consisted of the natural gas shipped and sold in interstate commerce and regulated by the Federal Power Commission (FPC). (In 1977, FPC was reorganized as the Federal Energy Regulatory Commission (FERC), an independent agency within the newly created Department of Energy.) The other segment of the market involved the gas produced, transported, and distributed solely within a single state and regulated by state utility commissions, primarily in Appalachia and the Southwest. Until the mid-1960s, natural gas was abundant and cheap; the wellhead price, most important of all regulated prices, did not vary greatly between the two markets.

Natural gas reserves began a slow but continual decline in the mid-1960s; newly discovered reserves failed to match new demand

and the wellhead price on the two markets began a major trans-
formation. By the mid-1970s, the markets were strikingly different.
In 1975, the price per thousand cubic feet of natural gas averaged
34 cents on the federally regulated interstate market, but 140 cents
on the state markets.[31] This wide price differential, which resulted
in a difference in customer costs and company profits in the two
markets, was largely due to differing federal and state philosophies
about the nature of a reasonable wellhead price.

What Is a Reasonable Price?

State utility commissions for the most part let the open market
set wellhead prices for natural gas within their jurisdictions. Price
was set by what producers and consumers thought the gas was worth.
After the mid-1960s, declining reserves and the explosive rise of crude
oil prices were principally responsible for driving this wellhead price
sharply upward. Especially potent was the surge of crude oil prices
since the price of natural gas, as the major alternative to petroleum,
increased with these inflated petroleum prices. Thus, in the largely
unregulated intrastate market, natural gas was liberated from the
cost of production as the primary basis for assessing its value. Crude
oil prices, marching relentlessly upward throughout the 1970s, pulled
natural gas prices in tow.

In contrast, the Federal Power Commission had attempted to
determine a "just and reasonable" wellhead price for most of the
nation's gas in its jurisdiction by considering the cost of producing
it. This alone assured that federally regulated prices would be substantially lower than those on the intrastate market and vulnerable
to criticism by gas producers denied the much higher income available
on the other market. The commission's approach, controversial as
it was, might have been more defensible if it were possible to determine
the actual cost of producing natural gas. Notes a recent study at
the Harvard Business School:

> In theory, one can determine the precise production cost of gas.
> In reality, no one can do much more than guess. Specialists have
> even disagreed on whether costs of production have really been rising
> or falling.[32]

The result was interminable and inconclusive wrangling among
experts and the public about the real or acceptable production figures.
Defenders and critics of FPC regulation assaulted each other with
conflicting data, interpretations of data, and extrapolations from data
that left certain only the continuing employment of economists to
fuel the controversy with further analysis. Characteristic of the difficulty
in fixing a reliable production cost for natural gas was one problem,

worth describing to suggest the depth of disagreement. The Harvard study explains:

> Different estimates do not necessarily reflect different "real" costs; they reflect, instead, the differences in the analytic techniques used. As a result, studies placed in evidence before the FPC have shown differences in estimated average unit costs of 500 percent or more for a single company.[33]

This controversy over production costs, together with the two different domestic markets, created intense conflict over natural gas regulation long before the energy crisis emerged in the 1970s. The energy issue, and especially a critical shortage of natural gas between December 1976 and February 1977 that itself almost became a national crisis, forced the deregulation issue to priority on the federal government agenda by the late 1970s.

The Great Battle Begins

During his 1976 presidential election campaign, Jimmy Carter had promised to work for the deregulation of prices on newly produced natural gas. Accepting the argument that natural gas had been sold too cheaply on the interstate market, Carter believed that rising gas prices would encourage gas conservation by dampening consumer demand while simultaneously providing a profit incentive for gas producers to seek new reserves. But Carter was also opposed to huge windfall profits likely for producers if interstate prices were completely decontrolled. Thus, the president proposed to Congress in his original 1977 energy package a much higher price ceiling for natural gas. He also called for a continuation of federal controls on the interstate market and the introduction of controls on the intrastate market. What emerged from Congress in 1978, however, was a measure so different that only Carter's reluctant recognition that no better bill was politically feasible spared the legislation a presidential veto.

That the bill existed at all seemed miraculous. The bill's history was melodrama. Its tempestuous journey through the legislative process during those final crucial months was a saga of disaster just averted, of bitter controversy occasionally relieved by farce. Majorities essential to passing the measure were always precarious. Congress's enormous difficulty in writing any deregulation bill bespoke how intense, tenacious, and apparently irreconcilable were the conflicts that historically characterized the natural gas issue. In the end, however, political compromise defied history.[34]

One reason for the ferocious congressional battle was the powerful, if curious, coalition against Carter's proposal. Major natural gas and petroleum producers opposed it because the measure did not go far enough in removing federal price controls. Congressional conservatives and representatives of many other major U.S. businesses agreed. Spokesmen for consumers and the poor, in alliance with congressional liberals, disliked the measure because it went too far in decontrolling the industry. At one point, the opposition became a coalition among spokesmen for the U.S. Chamber of Commerce, Amoco Oil, Independent Petroleum Association of America, AFL-CIO, United Auto Workers, Americans for Democratic Action, and consumer groups such as the Energy Action Committee and Consumer Federation of America. Also complicating congressional deliberations was President Carter's vacillating stance on the issue. Candidate Carter had urged gradual price deregulation, but President Carter's 1977 National Energy Plan called for continued price controls. In March 1978, after he had sent to Congress his proposals for continued price regulation, Carter did advocate the gradual phasing out of controls.

So many economic groups claimed a right to representation in the formulation of a pricing policy that creating congressional majorities at critical phases of policy formulation was extremely difficult. This was particularly evident in the meetings of the conference committee writing the final decontrol bill between January and October 1978. A committee leader ended one 13-hour marathon meeting at 3:30 a.m. by assuring reporters that the opposing sides had "been able to merge our differences for the first time in 30 years." That compromise evaporated within a week. Three weeks later another apparent compromise bill failed when the committee members, according to an observer, "disagreed about what they had agreed upon." Two later conference committee compromises faltered when a key member each time switched his position on the "final measure."[35] The tortuous path of price deregulation through Congress finally ended in October 1978, when the exhausted conference committee sent to the full Congress a compromise measure that it could accept.

The Industry Viewpoint

The natural gas industry speaks with unanimity on the deregulation issue. The industry's principal lobbying organizations—the American Gas Association, representing both producers and pipelines, and the Interstate Natural Gas Association of America, speaking mainly for pipelines—have urged the immediate decontrol of prices on all interstate gas, particularly the wellhead price. This viewpoint is shared by most members of Congress from gas-producing states, especially Louisiana Democratic Senators Russell B. Long and J. Bennett Johnston and Texas Senators Republican John Tower and Democrat Lloyd Bentsen. Senator Long, chairman of the powerful Finance Committee during the 1978 debate over price controls, led the opposition to President Carter's partial price deregulation. In the House, Louisiana Democrat Joe D. Waggonner and Texas Democrats Charles Wilson and Bob Eckhardt were forceful advocates of the industry's position on the conference committee that drafted the eventual compromise measure.

Producers of natural gas have long asserted that the federally regulated wellhead price is insufficient. It has encouraged producers to withhold gas from sale on the interstate market (or to sell only on the more profitable intrastate market), and it has restricted gas exploration at a time when the nation needs new energy reserves. The artificially low price of natural gas on the interstate market has also encouraged too much demand for the product that should be conserved.

The nation's 25 major gas pipeline companies, being wholly dependent on gas production for their economic survival, have worked vigorously with producers. The companies have also asserted that the rising supply in the interstate system might actually lower consumer gas costs by spreading the pipelines' fixed costs over a much larger volume of gas transported. Even if the deregulation of wellhead prices should increase consumer costs for natural gas, argues the natural gas industry, these rising costs would only reflect the true replacement cost of natural gas. Moreover, the alternative to increasing prices—the rapid constriction of natural gas production—would be an even less acceptable situation to consumers. The industry points out that this would especially hurt the northeastern and midwestern states that depend almost entirely on interstate gas for their supplies. In short, natural gas has been underpriced and overconsumed, which creates an economic subsidy to the consumer that the nation can no longer afford.

The Consumer Viewpoint

Consumer groups, representing primarily residential and commercial users of natural gas, have generally opposed the deregulation of natural gas prices on the interstate market. Congressional spokesmen for consumer groups have habitually treated such deregulation as economic exploitation of the average citizen. South Dakota Democratic Senator James Abourezk, a leader in the 1978 battle against the legislation, claimed that deregulation was a "rip-off" and "rape of the American consumer" whose sole beneficiaries would be "titans of the oil and gas industry, whose lust for profits has been unmatched in the annals of American business."[36] Led by Abourezk in the Senate and Michigan Democrat John D. Dingell in the House, congressional champions of consumer interests almost succeeded in scuttling the legislation. (A 15-hour filibuster organized in the Senate by Abourezk in October 1978 might have killed the bill if President Carter had not intervened on behalf of the legislation.)

The Consumer Federation of America, a coalition of 34 unions, farm groups, and power cooperatives, was among the earliest critics of President Carter's original deregulation proposal. In their view, the measure was "regressive" and a "bonanza for major oil and energy corporations." The Energy Action Committee, another public interest group speaking for consumers, has indicted deregulation on grounds that summarize most consumer organization viewpoints:

—Natural gas producers were already enjoying high profits on the interstate market since they were guaranteed 18 percent return above costs by the Federal Energy Regulatory Commission. Anything more is an unjustified windfall profit.

—Gas supply is better increased by controlling the current end use of the fuel differently. Industries and utilities should not be permitted to use natural gas in boilers.

—The federal government should regulate both gas markets to remove the price discrimination against interstate producers and pipelines.

—Since residential and commercial customers who account for the largest portion of natural gas consumption are unable to conserve much gas even if prices rise, there will be relatively little conservation incentive in deregulation.

—Producers want the value of natural gas measured by the cost of petroleum, which would only guarantee further windfall profits to the industry.[37]

Deregulation At Last

The new legislation, extraordinarily complex even for recent federal energy bills, was a patchwork of provisions betraying the complicated congressional bargaining required to enact it. Essentially, the measure permitted the price of natural gas discovered after the bill's enactment to rise about 10 percent yearly on the interstate market until price controls would be entirely lifted in 1985. Special provisions were included to make industrial users absorb a very large share of the initial rise in prices. Gradually, residential and commercial customers would bear a greater burden of the price increases. Price controls were also extended for the first time to the intrastate market until 1985, when they would be lifted and the two market prices would be alike.

Opponents of deregulation were particularly angered that the president had scarcely signed the new legislation when the "gas bubble" of 1978 was discovered. Late in 1978, Department of Energy officials announced that there had appeared an unexpected gas glut that would produce a large surplus on the consumer market for several years. The Carter administration asserted the glut was actually a bubble that did not substantially change the nation's long-range natural gas condition. The natural gas industry, having argued for a decade that gas reserves were steadily dwindling, sought to rescue its own faltering credibility by assuring the government and gas consumers that the market had not drastically altered. "We think this has misleading implications," argued an industry spokesman. "We want to dispel the view that somehow this available gas supply came up overnight."[38]

Nevertheless, many critics of deregulation and many members of Congress who had accepted the need to stimulate new gas production were confused or angered. Defenders of deregulation asserted that the gas bubble was the result of short-term, unanticipated forces such as a sudden, extensive consumer cutback in demand in anticipation of lower supply. The president was nevertheless embarrassed by the unwelcome bubble, especially because it worked to the considerable advantage of the natural gas industry. The availability of more natural gas than anticipated enabled the industry to once again promote new hookups. Between 1978 and 1980, demand for natural gas climbed far more quickly than the industry had predicted without the bubble. The surplus, equal to about 12 percent of the nation's annual natural gas consumption, permitted the industry to service more than 1.5 million new customers in 1979.

CONCLUSION: FAIR IS A FIGHTING WORD

The battles over crude oil and natural gas prices illustrate the general theme of this chapter: all energy policies create economic winners and losers. This is why the distributive issue, the controversy that concerns which arrangement of winners and losers is acceptable, remains a salient issue in the making of any energy policy. Moreover, solutions are rarely permanent. The losers in these energy battles, or those thinking they have lost, will surely launch additional assaults on the policy in an effort to modify radically or terminate entirely the current settlement.

This chapter also emphasizes that a variety of political factors are introduced alongside the economic ones when government intervenes in the economic marketplace to create a "fair" distribution of economic impacts from an energy policy outcome. A governmental solution to the distributive aspect of any energy policy may depend as much on the state of public opinion, the relative legislative strength of the interests involved, or the electoral implications of various options as on good economic logic or the weight of economic evidence. While the mix of political factors shaping a governmental decision may vary from one distributive issue to another, the public policy solution is likely to be quite different from what the economic marketplace might achieve without government intervention.

We have also observed in the policy struggles of this chapter a phase of the policy cycle that is often ignored: policy termination. With both crude oil and natural gas, the creation of a new federal pricing policy required the termination of a traditional, well-entrenched federal approach to energy price management. However, the termination of these traditional gas and oil pricing policies required a combination of congenial events unlikely to grace the efforts of most interests seeking to overturn other public policies. The narrative is at once a lesson and a warning: we have learned both how policies can be terminated and how infrequently that opportunity arises.

Finally, this chapter emphasizes how politically contentious and impermanent is any definition of fairness in governmental approaches to distributive issues. The nation's major economic interests will rarely share a common definition of what is fair, even when they agree (or seem to agree) on what principles should determine such fairness in federal policies. Distributive policies, in the end, tend to become whatever compromises can produce a congressional majority or whatever policies best reconcile the claims of competing interests on the president or Congress. In short, fairness is a negotiated concept when applied to government's economic policies. And a negotiated settlement, no matter what the cost, is unlikely to endure. Government is forever redefining "fair."

NOTES

1. U.S., General Accounting Office, *The Economic and Energy Effects of Alternative Oil Import Policies* (Washington, D.C.: U.S. Government Printing Office, 1979), p. 1.
2. Figures cited are based on the Consumer Price Index, as reported in *The Economic Report of the President, 1980*, Executive Office of the President (Washington, D.C.: U.S. Government Printing Office, 1980).
3. Robert Stobaugh and Daniel Yergin, eds., *Energy Future: Report of the Energy Project at the Harvard Business School* (New York: Random House, 1979), p. 217.
4. U.S., Congress, House of Representatives, Select Committee on Aging, Subcommittee on Retirement Income and Employment, *Energy and the Elderly: Hearings, October 5, 1979,* 96th Cong., 1st sess., pp. 16-17.
5. U.S., Congressional Budget Office, *President Carter's Energy Proposals: A Perspective* (Washington, D.C.: U.S. Government Printing Office, 1977), p. 116.
6. U.S. Congress, Office of Technology Assessment, *Residential Energy Con-*

servation, Volume I (Washington, D.C.: U.S. Government Printing Office, 1979), chap. 4.

7. U.S., Department of Energy, Office of Energy Research, Satellite System Project Division, *Energy Implications of an Aging Population* (Washington, D.C.: U.S. Government Printing Office, August 1980), p. 51.

8. Office of Technology Assessment, *Residential Energy Conservation,* p. 77.

9. Sam H. Schurr, et al., *Energy in America's Future* (Baltimore: Johns Hopkins University Press, 1979), p. 461.

10. Office of Technology Assessment, *Residential Energy Conservation,* p. 77.

11. The Ford Foundation, Energy Policy Project, *A Time to Choose* (Cambridge, Mass.: Ballinger Publishing Co., 1974), p. 118.

12. *New York Times,* April 29, 1977.

13. Select Committee on Aging, *Energy and the Elderly,* pp. 10-11.

14. Ibid., p. 16.

15. Lerone Bennett Jr., "Black America and 'The Energy Siege,'" *Ebony* (October 1979): 31-32.

16. Ibid., p. 42.

17. Eunice S. Grier, "Energy Consumption in American Households," in *Energy and the Community,* eds. Raymond J. Burby III and A. Fleming Bell (Cambridge, Mass.: Ballinger Publishing Co., 1978), p. 10.

18. Congressional Quarterly, *Energy Policy* (Washington, D.C.: Congressional Quarterly Inc., 1979), p. 55.

19. Hans H. Landsberg, ed., *Energy: The Next Twenty Years* (Cambridge, Mass.: Ballinger Publishing Co., 1979), p. 197.

20. Edward J. Mitchell, ed., *Energy: Regional Goals and the National Interest* (Washington, D.C.: American Enterprise Institute, 1976), p. 3.

21. *New York Times,* April 27, 1977.

22. Robert Engler, *The Brotherhood of Oil* (Chicago: University of Chicago Press, 1977), chap. 3.

23. Ibid., p. 18ff.

24. Stobaugh and Yergin, *Energy Future,* chaps. 2, 4; John M. Blair, *The Control of Oil* (New York: Pantheon Books, 1976), chap. 7; U.S., Congress, Office of Technology Assessment, *The Direct Use of Coal* (Washington, D.C.: U.S. Government Printing Office, 1979), chap. 4.

25. Blair, *The Control of Oil,* p. 189ff.

26. Ibid.

27. David H. Davis, *Energy Politics,* 2nd ed. (New York: St. Martin's Press, 1978), p. 61.

28. Engler, *The Brotherhood of Oil,* p. 54.

29. Congressional Quarterly, *Continuing Energy Crisis in America* (Washington, D.C.: Congressional Quarterly Inc., 1975).

30. *New York Times,* March 2, 1980.

31. Stobaugh and Yergin, *Energy Future,* p. 63.

32. Ibid., p. 65.

33. Ibid.

34. The tribulations in passing the natural gas deregulation measure are well described in Congressional Quarterly, *Energy Policy,* pp. 9-28.

35. Ibid., pp. 13-17.

36. Ibid., p. 20-21.

37. *New York Times,* April 19, 1977.

38. *Washington Post,* November 3, 1978.

6

The Billion Dollar Candle: Energy R&D

The United States entered the 1980s committed to the most expensive technological gamble in its history. In 1980, Congress passed the first legislation authorizing the federal government to underwrite a national synthetic fuels program and providing an initial budget of $20 billion. Compared to other of America's ambitious technology productions, this new program seemed born out of season. Its promotion had been unglamorous and unexciting, nothing to stir the public imagination in the grand manner of moon landings and nuclear power. It was also a risky and extremely formidable business, about which clung a hint of desperation. It seemed appropriate that Arkansas Representative William Alexander should compare the program to an act of embattled faith: "It is better for Americans to light at least one candle and to stop cursing the darkness."

Congress's one candle was a $20 billion appropriation to start a synfuels program, a down payment on an effort whose ultimate cost could overshadow the nation's most expensive past technology programs. Produced from shale oil, tar sands, coal, and organic wastes (such as municipal garbage), synfuels can be made to closely resemble natural gas, petroleum, or products distilled from petroleum such as gasoline. The greatest attraction of these synfuels is their origin in plentiful energy resources that would substitute for the nation's scarcer reserves of crude oil and natural gas.

The synfuels program first surfaced on the policy agenda in July 1979, when President Carter urged the nation to invest $88 billion to encourage private industry to develop new hydrocarbon technologies. This huge investment, raised through taxes on oil company windfall profits, would be administered through a private corporation chartered and financed by the U.S. government, but free to exercise independent judgment on the most prudent investment of its capital. The new company, eventually called the U.S. Synthetic Fuels Corporation, was to be the nation's wealthiest business with assets over twice those of Exxon, then the nation's richest corporation. This new corporation's task would be to create a technology capable of producing the equivalent of 2.5 million barrels of oil daily by 1990, an achievement estimated to cost between $200 and $400 billion (experts could be no more precise). By comparison, the Apollo moon program had cost $25 billion and the entire domestic nuclear power program between $15 and $17 billion by 1980.

Congress responded with legislation firmly committing the federal government to a synthetic fuels program that differed from the White House version primarily in the pace of its initial development. Aware of the enormous uncertainties associated with the technology, Congress preferred the more cautious, yet still lavish, $20 billion initial investment. The Synthetic Fuels Corporation was created and authorized to guarantee fuel purchases, to provide direct loans or price supports, and to offer other incentives for private industry to develop and operate synfuels plants; as a last resort, the federal government was authorized to build and operate such installations itself.

The synfuels program is currently the costliest illustration of the federal government's continuing effort to encourage the development of important scientific research through its own efforts and by collaboration with other public or private institutions.[1] Since World War II, federal spending on research, development, and demonstration of scientific discoveries—"federal RD&D"—has exceeded one-half trillion dollars. A very substantial portion of this federal spending has been allocated for the development of military and civilian energy technologies deemed essential to national security. The modern era of technology development began with the Manhattan Project that produced the first atomic bomb in the early 1940s. A multitude of other energy technologies, including the domestic nuclear power industry, laser beams, and solar energy conversion techniques, was subsequently hastened to development by federal investment. Since the early 1970s, an increasingly large share of all federal RD&D (hereafter referred to as "R&D") spent on energy research has gone to the exploration of new energy production technologies, including not only synthetic fuels technologies but also advanced nuclear fission and fusion, solar generating systems, geothermal power, and other unconventional procedures.

The synthetic fuels program provokes much controversy typical of most other federal programs to develop energy technologies since World War II. In this chapter, we will examine these recurrent issues and their relevance to the nation's most ambitious and expensive current energy programs: nuclear power and synthetic fuels. First, we will discuss why public financing is necessary for the development of energy technologies. This issue involves the relative merits of government spending compared with a *laissez faire* approach that leaves most of the responsibility to the private sector. Technology programs commonly entail expenditures of many millions, or even billions, of public dollars. Economists generally disagree over which arrangement assures the most productive and least wasteful use of such capital. Scientists often argue over which arrangement favors the better quality research. And partisans of various energy systems disagree over the value of developing a technology at all.

Second, we will look at the arguments about the appropriate roles for business and government in a federally assisted technology program. Government and business often approach collaboration with differing ideas about their respective responsibilities for program leadership, design, and implementation. This is no mere second-order problem as compared to the issue of public financing itself. A program's character and its success are influenced as much by the manner in which the participants are organized to implement it as by the decision to fund the program with federal money.

Finally, we will examine how the development of an energy technology is affected by political considerations when government assumes a primary management role. We will note how federal energy programs simultaneously create a scientific, economic, and political structure that is instrumental in shaping the policy outcome. We will discuss the political logic that often dictates governmental decisions about which technologies to promote. We will observe that when the federal government sows millions of dollars in technology development, it always reaps a new set of public and private interests with an investment in the program—the "stake holders"—who create a complex mosaic of political alliances and conflicts over the program. As Hugh Heclo has observed, "New policies create new politics."[2] In federal energy R&D, however, new programs create new politics that operate according to rules typical of government involvement in all types of research and development.

THE GROWTH OF ENERGY R&D

The federal government first assumed direct and total responsibility for the development of a major national technology with the Manhattan Project. Following World War II, the Eisenhower administration's Atoms for Peace program in the early 1950s committed the government to a major role in developing a domestic nuclear power industry.

Federal patronage of energy research was further expanded when
the Soviet Union proclaimed its advanced scientific competence in
1957 with the launching of Sputnik, the world's first space satellite.
This event shocked the United States into recognizing that it was
now engaged in technological competition with the Russians. A succession of space activities in the 1960s, crowned by the Apollo moon
landing in 1969, pressed federal energy technology development at
a fevered pace. Washington continued to maintain, and even enlarge,
its involvement in energy research after the moon landing program
was phased out.

The current synfuels program is part of the nonmilitary portion
of the federal government's energy R&D budget. Until recently, this
nonmilitary spending for energy research represented a modest share
of the nation's total energy research expenditures. Between 1945 and
1969, federal spending on all civilian energy activities represented
less than 10 perent of all domestic R&D funds, almost all of which
went to the nuclear power program; in 1969, nuclear technology claimed
93 percent of all federal energy R&D.[3] The 1973 Arab oil embargo
rearranged the federal government's energy research priorities, and
civilian energy research became a major spending program. In the
decade before 1973, civilian energy research expenditures grew at
a real annual rate of barely 4 percent; during the next two years,
the budget swelled by at least 50 percent yearly to the end of the
1970s.[4]

During the 1970s, energy became the fastest growing category
of federal R&D. By 1980, energy R&D was second only to defense
spending, which accounted for half of the total federal research budget.
This rich infusion of federal dollars into peaceful energy research
rapidly enlarged the federal presence in all facets of this activity
until by 1980 half of the nation's nonmilitary energy research was
federally financed.

Table 6-1 describes the allocation of federal energy R&D between
fiscal 1974 and 1980. Throughout the 1970s, nuclear technology's share
of the budget steadily decreased, while the fossil fuel program and
solar technologies gained in importance. In 1970, the fossil fuel program
was practically nonexistent. Appropriations for the program increased
a thousandfold between 1973 and 1978. With the massive public
funding expected for synfuels in the 1980s, it seems probable that
the synthetic fuels program will soon displace nuclear energy as the
federal government's most heavily supported type of energy research.
Solar technologies, ascending even more spectacularly to importance
from a modest $93 million appropriation in 1976 to approximately
$597 million in 1980, now also claim a significant share of the same
budget.

Table 6-1 Federal Budget Obligations for Energy R&D by Major Categories (In million dollars)

Category	Fiscal Year						
	1974	1975	1976	1977	1978	1979	1980*
Nuclear	1,034 (80%)	1,193 (65%)	753 (59%)	2,095 (68%)	1,378 (54%)	1,452 (43%)	1,401 (41%)
Fossil	110 (9)	435 (24)	323 (25)	503 (16)	684 (27)	826 (25)	796 (23)
Solar	45 (3)	102 (6)	93 (7)	275 (9)	368 (14)	456 (14)	597 (17)
Geothermal	—	20 (1)	31 (2)	52 (2)	106 (4)	136 (4)	111 (3)
Conservation	105 (8)	86 (5)	66 (5)	139 (5)	31 (1)	504 (15)	555 (16)
Total	1,294	1,836	1,266	3,064	2,567	3,374	3,460

*Estimated in *Intersociety Preliminary Analysis of R&D in the FY 1980 Budget*, American Association for the Advancement of Science, 1979.

SOURCE: Office of Mangement and Budget.

THE POLITICS OF R&D

The generous scale of federal energy spending means that energy programs have been transformed into vast, complex institutions linking government with the private sector and the nation's research centers. The importance of these spending increases far transcends the economic or scientific impact the avalanche of federal dollars may have upon its recipients. As energy R&D becomes institutionalized, programs become infused with the values and decisionmaking styles of the political process. Energy R&D becomes a public policy process grounded in many of the political realities associated with public policymaking in general. This political nature of energy research and development, and synfuels development particularly, produces much of the controversy over the wisdom of public funding for energy research and the proper roles of business and government.

If good politics were good economics, disputes over government funding of scientific activity would be less frequent. And if good politics could also be good science, controversies would be rarer still. There are sound scientific and economic reasons why it may be useful, even essential, that the federal government sponsor or conduct scientific research. Disputes over government participation arise because public management often creates undesired consequences or because public officials cannot achieve the original, and justifiable, goals of their activity. It almost seems that the major problem with public management of scientific research is that it has to be achieved through government.

Why Public Funding?

There are several reasons why it may benefit the nation to invest public money in energy research and technology development.[5] Private business may fail to invest in basic research leading to desirable new discoveries because the investment, usually heaviest during the early stages of a technology's development, often must be made with no assurance that the results will be profitable, or even useful, to the company. This is one reason why many firms have been slow to invest in research on decentralized solar technologies like solar space heating and small photovoltaic cells. Another reason for public investment is that a portion of energy research and technology development needs to be created for a public purpose that will not motivate private institutions to undertake the work. The need to protect the vital national interest of national security by decreasing U.S. dependence on imported oil is a compelling reason for public funding of the synthetic fuels program, but not necessarily a persuasive reason for Exxon or General Motors to sink billions of dollars into the undertaking.

Yet another rationale for federal R&D energy spending is to provide private business or research institutions with information in order to convince them to initiate their own research that will benefit the public at large. Once a new technology or a new research program has demonstrated its value, it will be adopted by the private sector. The federal government's heavy subsidization of the first nuclear power plant at Shippingsport, Pennsylvania, was justified on this basis.

Sometimes government R&D can be justified as a last resort for developing a potentially valuable technology when the cost of proving it commercially is too great for private firms to undertake. This same logic leads to suggestions that government should guarantee to purchase products created through new technologies—in effect, to create the first market—to stimulate the technologies' development. Environmentalist and 1980 presidential candidate Barry Commoner has urged the federal government to guarantee to purchase photovoltaic cells in quantities sufficient to provide a profit to the manufacturer. In time, Commoner believes, this guaranteed market will reduce the cell's unit cost and assure its commercial competitiveness.[6]

None of these arguments goes unchallenged. Energy R&D programs are often criticized because a particular private firm desiring federal assistance is allegedly seeking excessive profits by reducing its own investment in its work through federal subsidies. Critics of federal energy R&D sometimes assert that government ought to respect more the wisdom of the economic marketplace: when private promoters of an energy project cannot raise the capital for the undertaking, perhaps the project's economic prospects are indeed too dismal to justify public support. Critics note that Washington is far more talented at making bad investments than at terminating projects. Too often, the federal government continues to invest millions, even billions, of dollars in unproductive research because political pressures prevent an end to the support. Nevertheless, such criticism is rarely sufficient to convince public officials to cancel such research when R&D programs have strong public appeal (cancer research) or strong official support (the Atoms for Peace program).

Patterns of Private Assistance

The federal government has numerous options for its cooperation with private firms in energy research and technology development. Different arrangements result in varying apportionments of responsibility for program funding and management, as well as different shares of the risk involved. Controversy over energy R&D revolves around which level of responsibility and risk is appropriate for government. The most common arrangements are described below.

Government Development and Demonstration of a Technology with Sale or Lease to Private Firms. Under these circumstances, the government absorbs most of the initial costs and risks associated with creating a technology and proving its commercial possibilities. Public agencies may conduct the actual scientific research associated with a technology's development or may finance most of the cost of development in the private sector. During World War II, for instance, the federal government constructed synthetic rubber plants and financed much of their operation until the end of the war when the plants and equipment were sold to private industry. Under the Atoms for Peace program, the patents and licenses that were necessary so that private utilities could operate technologies owned by the government were sold or rented to the utilities.

Creation of a Public or Semipublic Corporation. The federal government may authorize the formation of a corporation, financed wholly or partially by public funds, to make money available to the private sector for technology development or basic scientific research. This arrangement is presumed to encourage less political interference in funding decisions with a consequent improvement in the economic judgment of the corporation's officials. A semipublic corporation may sell stock and distribute profits, as does a wholly private company, which may lure private capital to help underwrite the research and development of a technology. The U.S. Synthetic Fuels Corporation is a semipublic corporation whose operating capital is largely provided by Washington, but whose management is relatively independent of federal control.

Public Funding for Some or All of the Private Costs in the Early Stages. The initial phases of a technology's development— the theoretical studies through the creation of the first operational prototype—are often expensive and hardly attractive commercially. Substantial public funding during these exploratory stages may not only dissipate a company's reluctance to enter the field, but it may also promote the technology to the point where the firm will invest heavily in the remaining development phases. The Department of Energy, for example, is currently providing all the funds for a number of preliminary studies on the feasibility of generating electricity by nuclear fusion.

Public and Private Cost-sharing in a Consortium. The federal government may form a corporation, or consortium, with private firms to create or promote an energy technology. In this case, cost-sharing begins at the outset of the enterprise. Arrangements are included for the sharing of any profits among participants. This approach essentially treats government as merely another partner in the undertaking. A consortium involving the government and several hundred private firms is currently underwriting the cost of developing the first large-scale liquid metal fast breeder reactor in Oak Ridge, Tennessee.

Federal Cost-sharing of Basic Research. Many private firms are engaged in research more concerned with the accumulation of new scientific knowledge than with the immediate creation of a technology. Much medical research conducted by colleges, universities, or pharmaceutical companies falls into this category, as does research in more theoretical fields like mathematics or astronomy. In these instances, government may subsidize the works partially or wholly in hope of hastening a breakthrough, encouraging exploration of new fields, or improving the health, safety, or welfare of the public. Furthermore, basic science research may lead to important but unanticipated new technologies.

Government Purchase Agreements, Price Supports, or Other Market Incentives. Federal agencies often encourage both basic research and technology development by guaranteeing to provide an early market for products created by new technologies or by assuring private firms a minimum price for a product sufficient to provide a profit incentive for its development.

Of course, these strategies can be used in various combinations. The U.S. Synthetic Fuels Corporation, a semipublic corporation, will distribute federal R&D funds to private firms and may also negotiate purchase guarantees, loan guarantees, or price supports with the synfuels producers.

Collaboration between the government and private business has been a mixed success. Generally, corporations involved in federal R&D prefer arrangements providing a strong profit incentive with flexibility in program management and objectives. Funding agencies often insist on constraints against excessive profits and elaborate program arrangements to assure substantial compliance with funding goals. These differing priorities breed tension and controversy in federal research programs, especially if the programs conspicuously fail.

The Political Logic of Energy R&D

Early in 1978, the Department of Energy (DOE) held a press conference to announce its recommendation to Congress that the federal government spend between $20 and $40 billion on synthetic fuels before 1990. A synthetic fuels technology seemed rather exotic to many of the assembled journalists. Why, asked several, did DOE recommend such heavy funding for the program? A department official explained: synfuels would capitalize on the huge U.S. coal and shale oil reserves and would decrease petroleum imports, and the technology had already been used successfully elsewhere. He also added, "It is quite evident that Congress hungers for this sort of thing."[7]

This offhand remark, which opens a window on the politics of energy R&D, is a reminder that governmental decisions about the management of energy technologies are powerfully influenced by political logic and the values of government institutions. Energy R&D programs are simultaneously economic, scientific, and political enterprises where the values associated with each area frequently compete for influence in program design.

Porkbarreling. Aside from other considerations, officials often treat R&D programs as one more kind of distributive good to be valued because such projects stimulate economies, create or strengthen electoral support, or appeal to important publics. In the words of William Ophuls, economic growth is "the secular religion of American society," and elected officials are expected to act as the clergy.[8] A public official who evaluates any form of government spending with keen sensitivity to its economic impacts caters to a public preoccupation with economic well-being. Ophuls explains:

> People want jobs, economic opportunities, and a growing economy. Indeed, to the extent that the system has had a guiding policy at all, it has been precisely to satisfy the rising expectations of its citizens.[9]

The U.S. electoral system, based on geographic representation, readily turns an elected official's preoccupation with public programs into a narrow concentration upon the specific impacts for the home constituency. In this manner, energy R&D can be directly associated with the electoral fortunes of policymakers—if not in fact, then certainly in their fancy. Elected officials are forever alert to opportunities for building political alliances with any groups whose favor may be exchanged for electoral assistance in the political arena. Such thinking disposes officials to treat R&D programs as a medium of political exchange with groups for whom they are important. In return for sponsorship or approval of R&D projects, elected officials improve their political base.

As a result, officials maintain a special regard for large spending and big projects in R&D, the sort of programs with high visibility and impact. The political nature of the R&D process offers incentives for federal agencies seeking congressional or White House favor to sponsor such projects. Writes Edward Tufte about federal economic policy in general:

> There is a bias toward politics with immediate, highly visible bene-
> fits—the myopic politics for myopic voters. Special interests induce
> coalition building politicians to impose small costs on the many
> to achieve large benefits for the few.[10]

Big spending and glamorous projects also create a large pool of potential benefits amenable to broad distribution among public officials and agencies eager to serve their own constituencies; the more interests that can somehow be dealt in for a project, the less opposition it will face. This psychology is especially responsive to technology development, particularly the high technology of nuclear energy and fossil fuel synthesis. Furthermore, segments of the scientific community promote the view that high technology is economic therapy.[11]

Wide Dispersion of Projects. A second consequence of public R&D management is a tendency to disperse projects geographically. This is hardly surprising, given the general inclination of government officials to expand the pool of R&D resources as a means of co-opting program opponents. Quite often, the result is that new programs or projects are created or located less with regard to their scientific or economic merit than to their political effect. Federal R&D programs were exposed to this kind of pressure early and quite successfully. Don K. Price notes that the massive federal involvement in R&D programs following World War II created "all kinds of patronage" for the academic and scientific community. "Political pressure produced automatic formulas to distribute widely the early funding for agriculture and public works research."[12] When project grants were dispensed to only a few universities, the others complained, and regional associations and political spokesmen had to be placated. Observes Price:

> To accommodate the various states and regions which had no uni-
> versities qualified to compete for project grants, programs of financial
> support had to be invented to create new centers of excellence,
> able to compete on an equal basis.[13]

Formation of Constituencies. A third significant impact of energy R&D is the creation of an economically dependent coalition of public and private interests that will organize, if necessary, to perpetuate or expand a program. The Atomic Industrial Forum, representing the nuclear power industry, did not initially lobby for the Atoms for Peace program: it organized to protect, promote, and perpetuate it. The coalition supporting an R&D program usually turns out to have several distinct elements: the bureaucratic agencies administering the program, the geographic areas economically affected by the program, the professional groups working in the program, and other groups and governmental units that ideologically support it.

This constituency formation imposes predictable constraints on future programs. First, major changes must be negotiated on a political as well as a substantive basis. Questions of energy program priorities, funding levels, and duration are generally settled with as much concern for who is affected as for what is done.[14] Moreover, dependent constituencies are often budget expansionists as well as policy conservatives: they can more readily agree on continuing existing programs at increased funding levels than they can agree on substantive policy changes.

Finally, in administering an energy R&D program, the responsible agencies become quite adept at minimizing political and scientific criticism. The federal government has a very large infrastructure of technocratic agencies responsible for multibillion dollar R&D activities: the Department of Defense, National Aeronautics and Space Administration, Department of Energy, National Science Foundation, and National Institutes of Health among them. These agencies seek to co-opt the scientific community and potential technology users into the program, thereby diminishing possibly damaging criticism. As Henry Lambright observes, these agencies may also seek to co-opt White House support by identifying a technology program not with a particular president but with a continuing White House interest such as national prestige, defense, or foreign policy. And the agencies may repackage a program to suit changing national priorities.

Thus, notes Lambright, the National Aeronautics and Space Administration sought to keep the space program relevant by emphasizing first its contribution to national prestige (which suited the Kennedy and Johnson administrations) and by later focusing on its potential energy implications (which will keep it attractive in the 1980s).[15] The bureaucratic bulwark surrounding an R&D program is often constructed with the open or tacit approval of the White House or members of Congress whose own political fortunes may be tied in some manner to a program's success.

Tolerance for Bad Economics. A fourth important consequence of energy R&D is a governmental tolerance for bad economics; excessive cost overruns and continuation of economically unproductive energy activities are frequent. Some federal R&D programs do make economic sense, and many are prudently managed. Much of R&D, especially basic scientific research, is not intended to have any immediate economic payoff. However, programs that are supposed to be disciplined by economic constraints often are not. Cost overruns exceeding the originally estimated expenditures by several hundred percent are not uncommon. Programs with cheerless economic prospects may none-theless survive even though productivity may have been called a program principle.

Government is likely to tolerate such situations for several reasons. Cost overruns may be accepted because national prestige, political careers, presidential ambitions, bureaucratic fortunes, or public opinion is invested in making the program work; and cost is subordinated to results. The Apollo program doubtless would have continued to receive funding in the face of colossal cost overruns if necessary.

Sometimes the federal government feels compelled to bail out private concerns that are unable to produce economically or sci-entifically desirable results from federal R&D simply because the alternative would be even less desirable: failure of the company, massive unemployment, or dangerous technological problems. The fed-eral government had agreed in 1966, for example, to purchase much of the nuclear fuel produced from a commercial reprocessing plant in West Valley, New York, as an incentive for the plant's construction. When the plant failed and the company went bankrupt, immense quantities of dangerous nuclear wastes at the site had to be removed. At a cost exceeding $1 billion, the Department of Energy reluctantly agreed to share the responsibility for the cleanup with the state.[16] Sometimes economically unpromising programs continue through fed-eral R&D because researchers or sponsors bear no economic penalties for the results. A private corporation might be far quicker to forsake a project whose lack of profitability became apparent.

Volatility of Federal Support. A final significant attribute of federal R&D is the uncertain character of federal program sponsorship. Washington can be too quick, as well as too slow, to terminate programs. The government may be too willing to scramble funding priorities or to introduce new programs. This volatility (critics call it "unpredictability") is caused by several factors: sensitivity of policymakers to shifting public moods, sudden emergence of new na-tional issues, or an unexpected turn in international affairs, as well as other unanticipated incidents. Such volatility can mean a lack of continued funding to programs requiring long nurture, as well as a rush into new research that will yield quick results when critical, prudent evaluation of a program is necessary. Program sponsors and constituencies can be induced to oversell a program or alter its character undesirably in order to maintain its political attractiveness.

PEACEFUL ATOMS AND POLITICIZED R&D

The U.S. experience with the development of peaceful nuclear power illustrates how the political logic in federal energy R&D applies to a specific program. The experience with this program, and particularly with the Clinch River situation, depicts some of the unfortunate aspects in governmental involvement in energy technology development. Nonetheless, the experience is instructive not only as a contribution to understanding publicly funded energy development, but also as a portent of ways in which the current synfuels program might be affected by federal sponsorship.

The creation of nuclear-generated electricity represents the nation's first, longest, and most expensive experience in public development of peaceful technologies. It has been a success in at least two respects: the program produced a commercially acceptable nuclear reactor capable of producing electricity, and it created the nuclear power industry now generating an important share of U.S. electric power (about 12 percent in the early 1980s). Many of the nuclear power industry's problems can be attributed to the manner of its political management.

The Atoms for Peace Program

Peaceful atomic power began as a White House vision born of political expediency, as an enterprise far more seductive for Washington than for the private utility industry. First proposed to the United Nations by President Eisenhower in December 1953, the Atoms for Peace program was initiated for two primary reasons: (1) to present the world with an image of U.S. atomic power development free of its menacing military implications; and (2) to assure that the worldwide spread of nuclear materials, then just beginning, would be controlled by the United States.[17]

Government and Business Collaboration. With a heavy political investment in the successful promotion of the peaceful atom, the White House relied on the Atomic Energy Commission (AEC) and the congressional Joint Committee on Atomic Energy (JCAE) to persuade the private utilities to collaborate in the work. The industry was not enthusiastic about joining a peaceful nuclear power program. Henry Lambright explains:

> There were no pressing economic or scientific reasons for doing so. The reality that the AEC had to overcome was the fact that the economic market, for which the atom had been freed, did not need (or want) the product that the AEC and the nation were promoting.[18]

To secure private industry cooperation, Washington brandished a carrot and a stick. The most important stick was the prospect of publicly managed nuclear power. As a result of Washington's threat to proceed with a public nuclear power program, the private firms reluctantly agreed to accept the enormous unknown responsibilities for nuclear power development rather than face the competition. Thus, the 1946 Atomic Energy Act was amended to preclude the Atomic Energy Commission's operation of nuclear installations and to promote instead private nuclear power development, a gesture whose symbolism was considerably more appealing than were the realities it implied for private corporations. The carrot offered by the government was the assurance of massive federal R&D funds to assist the private utilities in developing a nuclear technology, a waiver on initial costs of expensive nuclear fuel, and other federal concessions.

Promotion Versus Regulation. As the program unfolded, the primary two government advocates—the Atomic Energy Commission, the bureaucratic steward of the program, and the Joint Committee on Atomic Energy, the congressional watchdog—were consumed by an increasing zeal for promoting peaceful nuclear power at the sacrifice of prudent regulation. The committee was supposed to review critically the work of AEC, to force restraint on the program when necessary, and to bring crucial issues to public attention. Instead of exercising responsible congressional oversight, the committee became promoter, defender, and savior of the nuclear program. Notes Peter Metzger:

> The Joint Committee itself originated many of the ideas (for the program) from the start and directed the AEC to develop the appropriate technology and sell it to the public. With the role of promoter reversed, the public had nowhere to go in order to reject an idea but to its author, an unlikely place for a fair hearing.[19]

The joint committee was now the initiator, and AEC often the agent, for program developments. The commission was no more successful in its assigned role than was the committee. The 1954 amendments to the Atomic Energy Act assigned to AEC the impossible task of simultaneously promoting and regulating peaceful nuclear power. The five commissioners and their staffs were most conscious of their national mandate to promote commercial nuclear power, which they did with fierce dedication. Explains Henry Lambright, "Seldom, if ever, had a federal agency pushed harder on a private industry to innovate a new technology."[20] The Atomic Energy Commission became the epitome of a mission-oriented agency. However unintentionally, its benevolence toward commercial nuclear power became bland arrogance toward its critics. In its 1959 annual report, for instance, the commission dismissed with a few sentences the criticism that nuclear plant wastes might prove difficult to manage, concluding that "there is no reason to believe that the proliferation of wastes will become a limiting factor on future development of atomic energy for peaceful purposes."[21]

The commission's regulatory responsibilities were often interpreted as if the agency's mission was public relations. In 1966, for example, the commission unilaterally decided to conceal the unexplained loss of 202 pounds of highly enriched uranium from a Pennsylvania processing plant because the revelation "could lead to sensational and probably inaccurate press reports."[22] So tenacious were the loyalties tying the commission to the nuclear power industry that the 1974 legislation dividing the regulatory and promotional activities of AEC between two new agencies, a move intended to free the industry's regulators from promotional concerns, failed to purge regulation of its industry paternalism. In 1978, the Nuclear Regulatory Commission (NRC), newly created to exercise the regulatory controls of the former AEC, deliberately misled Congress by claiming NRC had no evidence that atomic materials had ever been stolen from AEC when, in fact, it knew of such a theft.[23]

The Atomic Energy Commission at times attempted to administer its program impartially. But with JCAE the commission had become the center of an influential coalition to promote commercial nuclear power that embraced the commercial nuclear power industry, most nuclear science professionals, many major research institutions, and many public officials. NRC Commissioner Peter Bradford remarked in 1978 that, in the end, the government had "gravely overestimated" the promise of nuclear energy:

> As bureaucratic and institutional prestige became committed, one almost rational step at a time, to stated and perceived goals that had little to do with the real national interests, truth and other people's money were the first casualties.[24]

Public Management Impacts. Government promotion of commercial nuclear power might have been more successful if the nuclear power program had not been afflicted with the sort of unpredictability in research priorities that often burdens federal R&D management. At a point crucial to the success of the program, the Atomic Energy Commission decided to switch priorities. In the mid-1960s, Washington changed its primary goal from perfecting the light water reactor (then just beginning to be used in the first generation of nuclear power plants) to emphasize instead the more fuel-efficient breeder reactor. Private power companies were unexpectedly left to assume the management of the light water reactor facilities and their complex support technology—in effect, to take responsibility for managing an experimental technology with which they had no experience.[25] Many of the industry's later problems with reactor safety and poor economic performance, epitomized by the Three Mile Island accident of March 1979, can be traced to Washington's failure to complete the evaluation and testing of the light water reactors in close partnership with private industry.

What the federal government had accomplished, however, was the creation of a vast, powerful constituency for the commercial nuclear power program. During its expansionist phase that extended through the 1960s, the program tied diverse socioeconomic sectors to program spending and made them partisan enclaves for nuclear power development. In the early 1970s, the Atomic Energy Commission had contracts with 538 corporations and 223 colleges and universities. Private contractors directly employed 125,000 workers across the nation. Union Carbide Corporation, the largest of these contractors, had received in excess of $330 million in AEC funds by the mid-1970s. In coalition with AEC, the Joint Committee on Atomic Energy, and the numerous senators and representatives for whom nuclear projects meant political pork, this private nuclear power sector managed to preserve and extend the program.

That the nuclear program prospered by its attraction as political pork is illustrated in Figure 6-1, which charts the incremental changes in nuclear R&D funding between fiscal 1970 and 1979. Two patterns are evident: (1) funding tended to increase, often quite sharply, during the fiscal years overlapping congressional and presidential elections; and (2) peaks in funding increments corresponded to presidential election years. This pattern, characteristic of federal transfer payments in general, strongly implies that incremental funding decisions were quite sensitive to an electoral calculus. Decisions about program support levels were apparently made, at critical electoral periods, on the basis of political advantage as well as substantive merit.

The Clinch River Saga

The Clinch River battle reveals how political factors shape the character of struggles over program termination. It displays in fine detail the interplay of conflicting political forces generated when business and government disagree over the management of a major R&D project. The battle illustrates the capacity of economic constituencies to organize for the protection of R&D programs, the tendency for political issues to dominate policy choices, the pervasiveness of a bargaining style in conflict resolution, and the high economic costs imposed on project management by political conflicts over program operations.

The New Breeder Technology. In 1970, when the future of commercial nuclear power still seemed benign, Congress authorized the Atomic Energy Commission to join with private industry in building a liquid metal fast breeder nuclear reactor (LMFBR) near Oak Ridge, Tennessee. Known as the Clinch River project (CRP), the program was intended to demonstrate that the LMFBR could be licensed and operated reliably for electric utility needs; as a prototype, it was also expected to supply data about the technological, environ-

Figure 6-1   Incremental Changes in Budget Allocation for Nuclear Research and Development, Fiscal 1970 to 1979

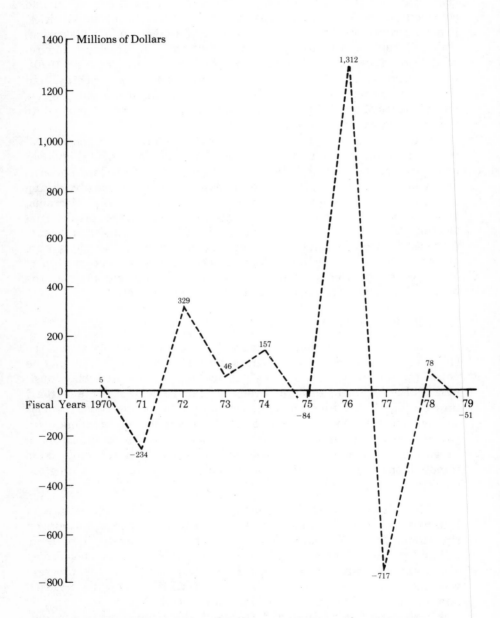

SOURCE: Office of Management and Budget, *The Budget In Brief, 1970-1980.*

mental, and economic aspects of the LMFBR that was considered essential for designing a larger commercial version for electric utilities.[26]

The federal government had decided that the future of commercial nuclear power lay in the breeder technology, and the CRP was conceived on a scale appropriate to great expectations. When complete, the facility was to be a one-third scale reactor generating about 380 megawatts of electricity, sufficient to supply a city of 250,000 people. Expected to cost approximately $667 million, the reactor was to be operational by 1980. It would be a showpiece technology: the most expensive production of the most expensive nuclear R&D program, a demonstration of the breeder's feasibility, and an example of productive collaboration between government and business.

The Nixon administration strongly endorsed the program, especially the major role it assigned to industry. Westinghouse Corporation was designated the prime reactor manufacturer, and a consortium consisting of the Atomic Energy Commission, Commonwealth Edison of Chicago, and the Tennessee Valley Authority was set up to manage the project. More than 753 private and municipal utilities contributed about $257 million to this consortium as part of the basic financing. The Clinch River project had been vigorously endorsed by Tennessee Senator Howard Baker (then Senate minority leader), by most of the other Tennessee congressional delegates, by the Oak Ridge community, and by numerous nuclear scientists.

As a national center of nuclear research, Oak Ridge was a logical site for so complex an enterprise. In fact, however, several years would elapse before most components of the project ever appeared in Oak Ridge. Many essential elements were to be designed and fabricated elsewhere, and much of the basic research would also be conducted far afield of Tennessee. In effect, the Clinch River project was a national undertaking enlisting the talents of public and private institutions across the country. Thus, the CRP began with strong political backing, a broad and diverse national constituency, and substantial funding.

The Carter Administration. The undercurrent of controversy surrounding the Clinch River project finally erupted into national headlines shortly after Jimmy Carter's inauguration in 1977. Critics had always warned that the breeder technology would proliferate nuclear weapons worldwide because its fuels and fission products could be manufactured into an atomic bomb. These materials, opponents cautioned, could fall under the control of other nations or terrorist groups if the United States exported the breeder technology as anticipated. Citing the dangers of nuclear weapons proliferation, President Carter announced in April 1977 that he would recommend to Congress the rapid termination of the Clinch River project. A political struggle over the fate of the project quickly spread across the entire terrain of U.S. commercial nuclear R&D.[27] Partisans of the LMFBR marshalled a counteroffensive in which all the interests with a stake in the project were enlisted.

By the late 1970s, the economic consequences of the project's fate were far more substantial than at its inception. The facility was now estimated to cost at least $2.2 billion and to require funding through 1987. The federal government was spending approximately $12.5 million monthly to pay 350 persons in Oak Ridge and another 5,500 people in 23 additional states working on the facility. Washington had already invested $474 million in the project by early 1978. Conservative estimates suggested it would cost between $150 and $350 million to terminate the project or an additional $1.2 to $1.4 billion to complete it.[28]

The president faced formidable congressional opposition to his project termination bid. In addition to the Senate Minority Leader, Tennessee's Howard Baker, the project's termination was opposed by Democratic Representative Marilyn Lloyd from the Oak Ridge district, a member of the House Science and Technology Committee whose approval was essential for termination. A multitude of senators and representatives from both parties was already angered by an earlier hit list from one of the president's first legislative programs that proposed to terminate 32 water resource projects already authorized by Congress. To many of the legislators, the president was again tampering with porkbarrel projects, something most members of Congress viewed as the political equivalent of defacing a shrine. The multitude of public and private utilities sharing the cost of the Clinch River project, all 741 of them, had their own friends in Congress ready to fight for the liquid metal fast breeder reactor which the nuclear power industry widely regarded as its best, and perhaps last, hope for an economic future. The White House forces were themselves disarrayed. Publicly, the Department of Energy maintained a mildly supportive stance toward Carter's proposal. Privately, DOE was working in Congress to find a compromise to keep the project afloat. Congressional Democrats, despite a nominal commitment to support the president as their national leader, were deeply divided over Carter's leadership and programs.

Carter had requested approximately $33 million to terminate the project, but in November 1977, after many months of prolonged debate, Congress voted $80 million to continue the reactor program for another year. The congressional debate increasingly focused less on the scientific and economic merits of the project than upon its political symbolism. For many senators and representatives, the issue was now national prestige, technological competition, and international security. The ranking minority member of the House Science and Technology Committee, New York Republican John W. Wydler, sounded a common concern during a floor debate when he warned that the project's termination would mean that the United States "won't be in the club anymore." The club, he exhorted, should be irresistible:

> They're going ahead all over the world where they have the capacity to do so, to develop the breeder reactor. We're going to put ourselves out of this ballgame.[29]

Alabama Democrat Walter Flowers, also a committee member, scolded his colleagues for timidity: "We're acting like an ostrich instead of an eagle if we don't go ahead with the Clinch River breeder reactor."[30]

Compromise? President Carter vetoed Congress's appropriation to continue the project. In February 1978, both the House and Senate voted to override the veto, and the LMFBR rose from its budgetary ashes. In early March, the president refused to spend the congressional appropriations designated for the project. Appealing to the U.S. Comptroller General for a ruling on the legality of the president's action, Congress was told that Carter lacked the authority to terminate the CRP in this manner.

At this point, the president and Congress attempted to avoid a dangerous confrontation over their respective constitutional powers by fashioning a compromise. By late 1978, the White House had agreed to propose a new breeder R&D program beginning with design studies for a facility different from the LMFBR but perhaps two or three times the size of the phantom Clinch River facility. The compromise collapsed, however, and all that could be salvaged was an agreement to continue the debate into the next congressional session. The federal government had been spending $13 million monthly on the project throughout 1978. Congress and the president agreed to vote $172.5 million to continue the project through 1979, while the combatants prepared for another round during the 1979 congressional deliberations on the fiscal 1980 budget.

The LMFBR was again left dangling between extinction and reprieve during 1979. The White House continued to try to persuade Congress to cancel the Clinch River facility. Arguments aired fully in earlier committee and floor debates were resurrected by both sides. When the House voted in late July to continue funding for the LMFBR, 110 Democrats broke ranks with the president to vote for the Clinch River program. By attaching the appropriations for the breeder program as a rider to an essential bill to meet the federal payroll, Congress assured that Carter would not veto the Clinch River funds. For the third consecutive year, the president declared his displeasure with the program and vowed to resume the fight in 1980.

But 1980 brought no resolution to the conflict. Instead, the federal government spent approximately $221 million more on the Clinch River facility as it debated how much to appropriate for 1981. President Carter, preoccupied with his reelection campaign and the Iranian hostage crisis, had little time to invest in the breeder controversy. With the election of a new Republican president and Senate majority, Congress and President Carter were disposed in early 1981 to leave the resolution of the Clinch River battle to the incoming administration.

The Consequences of Controversy. As the Clinch River project continued in a limbo between White House antipathy and congressional protection, the consequences of the political struggle over the project's future were obvious. The battle had grossly inflated the project costs and development time. During the many months of each congressional session when the CRP's future was up in the air, project managers had slowed much of the work, postponed scheduled activities, and sometimes suspended planning until the project budget was clarified. By the early 1980s, the project was 10 years behind schedule. The anticipated project cost had swollen from the original $667 million to more than $2.6 billion.

Somewhat perversely, as the sunk costs in the project mounted— the dollars invested, the institutional commitments, the specialized technology already developed, the symbolism attached to the project— it became more important to some participants in the struggle that the project be continued. Summarizing some of these sunk costs, the General Accounting Office noted that federal rejection of the Clinch River facility could well "reduce public confidence" and "inhibit further efforts to commercialize the technology."[31]

As the debate over the breeder technology continued, political considerations increasingly displaced scientific or economic reasons for project decisions. One example was the almost instinctive tendency of the Tennessee congressional delegation and other legislators whose constituents were clientele of the program to protect their political status by defending the project. In another instance, the White House decision to propose a new and highly expensive alternate breeder reactor program was apparently made to create a bargaining chip to use as a trade-off with CRP proponents in exchange for termination of the Clinch River project. Many legislators from both political parties with no substantial political or economic stake in the project nonetheless also voted for the LMFBR to embarrass the president or to register their displeasure at what they perceived to be his cavalier attitude toward congressional prerogatives in the management of R&D programs.

The role of bureaucracy in the struggle was clear and predictable. As so often happens in R&D programs, the sponsoring agency (in this case, the Department of Energy) was primarily a project partisan and collaborator with its clientele in advancing the program. This stance was not necessarily a selfish or irresponsible one. The department, conscious of its mission to promote domestic energy resources and extremely reluctant to endorse measures that might severely inhibit a domestic nuclear power capability, may well have been pursuing what it considered to be the "public interest." Nevertheless, DOE rendered the executive branch a house divided and undermined the president's management of a major federal program. The Clinch River conflict underscores the extraordinary difficulty in terminating large, expensive R&D enterprises when the clientele can mobilize politically to defend them.

SYNFUELS AND R&D POLITICS

It might be argued with some justification that the Clinch River saga represents such an exaggeration of the problems with federal management of research and development that it should not be treated as a typical program. Nonetheless, it raises important issues that should be debated as the nation now contemplates the creation of a synthetic fuels R&D program that could eclipse the scale of the peaceful nuclear power program in its spending and political visibility. In this respect, the national experience with nuclear R&D remains troublesome and, to some, prophetic.

The prospect of a Synfuels Age arouses grave misgivings among some observers who believe that the new program will become the fossil fuel reenactment of the national mistakes with peaceful nuclear technology development. Beyond the inherent technical and economic difficulties with synfuels, critics predict that the new program will be afflicted with the same problems public management created for nuclear R&D. However, one inheritance of the nuclear experience has been the national education in technology development and mismanagement that it provided.

A Different Approach?

Both the government and the public seem in some ways prepared to manage synfuels with greater prudence and more political sophistication than under the earlier commercial nuclear program. Congress today has far more suitable institutional resources and collective experience upon which to draw in evaluating the synfuels program. Conscious of the problems with nuclear power and other technologies, Congress in 1972 created its Office of Technology Assessment (OTA) to provide independent evaluation of the impacts and problems associated with its sponsorship of new technologies. The General Accounting Office (GAO), a congressional watchdog over the executive branch, in the last decade has shown increasing skill and aggressiveness in calling to the legislators' attention real or potential problems (scientific, economic, and political) that are associated with technology programs.

That Congress did learn something from its mistakes with nuclear R&D is further suggested by recent events in its treatment of nuclear and synthetic fuels. The congressional decision in 1974 to divide the regulatory and promotional responsibilities of the former Atomic Energy Commission and in 1977 to abolish the Joint Committee on Atomic Energy indicated congressional recognition of the excesses often characterizing the nuclear power program.

The congressional approach to initiating the synfuels program also bespoke far greater caution, if not skepticism, than did its reception of the commercial nuclear program almost three decades earlier. The enactment of the synfuels program was preceded by a long public debate on its merits during which reservations about the economic, scientific, and political virtues of the enterprise were thoroughly aired in committees and on the floors of both congressional chambers, in sharp contrast to the cloistered and largely uncritical deliberations with which the nuclear technology program was greeted in Congress. Furthermore, the initial $20 billion appropriation for the synfuels program, although generous even by federal R&D standards, was far less than the $88 billion the White House had originally requested. Additional program funding, while authorized in the amount of $68 billion, remained unspecified and dependent on later review of the initial program's success.

The synfuels program has also begun in a very different legal and pressure group setting than did the commercial nuclear R&D program. A number of new federal laws, including potentially stringent regulatory programs, may now impose legal constraints upon the environmental hazards of synfuels development. The Clean Air Act (1970), National Environmental Policy Act (1969), Federal Water Pollution Control Act (1972), and Toxic Substances Control Act (1976)—together with their subsequent amendments—are all directly relevant to the development of synthetic fuels. In several different ways, these measures provide the legal standing and the substantive grounds for citizen groups and government regulators to apply legal restraints on synfuels technologies should they threaten to become ecologically dangerous. Without the will to enforce them, of course, such laws remain little more than paper barriers to synfuels technologies. The Environmental Protection Agency, created in 1970, does possess the statutory mandate to enforce these measures, however. The emergence of the new public interest sector and the increasing aggressiveness of organized scientific professionals, as discussed in earlier chapters, has created an important external pressure on the federal government to implement these regulatory programs. The ability of these legal and institutional constraints to force a continuing, critical appraisal of synthetic fuels development is likely to be tested severely, as many of the circumstances leading to the less desirable aspects of nuclear R&D development are already evident in the synfuels program.

Some Old Problems

The White House and Congress possess strong incentives to build numerous synfuels facilities, generously scattered across the nation, abundant in governmental largesse flowing toward the many public and private constituencies that crave a share of whatever federal public works are currently attainable. In recent years, for instance, the nation's governors have persistently used the energy crisis as an occasion to criticize the White House for too much concern with energy conservation and too little interest in energy production. In 1979, the National Governors' Association urged Washington to speed up energy production, especially nuclear and synfuels development. The western governors, sensitive to the ominous environmental risks to their fragile ecosystems from an uncontrolled coal boom, were nevertheless of two minds with respect to coal use: they desired the rewards of a coal boom, but not its attendant environmental devastation.

Economic Impact. From the perspective of Congress and the White House, a synfuels facility can readily become a political commodity, the more attractive because of its visibility, to be used in bargaining with constituencies desiring economic growth. Commercial-scale coal gasification and liquefaction plants or shale oil conversion facilities may pump billions of dollars into the regions where they are sited. These facilities are highly labor intensive; one expert at the Department of Energy has calculated that the smallest commercial liquefaction facility would require perhaps 2,500 workers during the construction phase and about 725 individuals for its operating staff.[32] Even prototype synfuels facilities translate into heavy employment and spending.

The diverse economic impacts from a synfuels operation are suggested in detail by the proposal of five oil pipelines to build a $1.4 billion coal gasification plant near Beulah, North Dakota. According to preliminary studies, the facility would:

—Require the mining of 9 million tons of coal annually.

—Cause the strip mining of 500 acres of lignite coal beds yearly and about 13,000 acres over 25 years.

—Raise nearby farmland values from $100 to $1,000 an acre.

—Employ about 3,000 workers at peak construction.

—Double the county's population within a decade.

—Create a growth surge in nearby towns within 20 to 30 miles.[33]

Such gargantuan facilities would exceed the size and economic impact of even the largest existing nuclear generating plants.

Environmental Hazards. Like nuclear power, the economic benefits of synfuels development are also freighted with potentially grave environmental risks. Once again, government officials will be forced to strike some balance between the economic benefits and ecological hazards in energy production. Synfuels facilities will vastly intensify national coal consumption and thus hasten the spread of strip mining across the nation's coalfields. A single facility for converting coal into a high-energy natural gas, for instance, would require an estimated 6.6 million tons of coal annually.[34] One of the most common technologies for converting coal into a petroleum fuel would need about 12.5 million tons of coal every year.[35]

Synfuels facilities are also likely to create high resource demands at their sites and to generate a variety of hazardous effluents. Some commercial coal gasification technologies may require up to 1.2 billion gallons of water per hour.[36] An extremely large volume of solid, liquid, and gaseous wastes produced by synfuels facilities may be highly toxic. Apprehension is compounded by ignorance because the nature of these potential toxins is often difficult to predict accurately. The Department of Energy notes in its assessment of the environmental impact from a commercial coal gasification plant:

> An important concern raised by coal gasification processes is the large quantity of solid wastes which will be generated. Currently, little is known about the chemistry or biology of these materials; the toxicity and fate of these solid wastes must be determined. . . . A major concern relating to commercial gasification is exposure of workers and nearby residents to effluents which may contain carcinogenic polycyclic aromatic hydrocarbons (PAH). The potential for acute exposures to carbon monoxide, sulfur oxides, and nitrogen oxides is present also. . . . Quench and clean up waters contain condensed volatile organic and inorganic materials, including regulated and unregulated hazardous agents. . . . Little is known about control of carcinogens that could be regulated . . . or how industry can cope with handling the volumes of liquid waste which might require special handling and disposal.[37]

The department's coal liquefaction assessment describes a nasty chemical cocktail likely to appear as "leachate" from plant solid wastes:

It is highly likely that a number of process residues and waste materials will be found to contain toxic, mutogenic, and carcinogenic materials and [to] pose work force, occupational and ecological risks ... process solid wastes from all sources may contain materials which can be leached from the residue, modified by factors in soil and water in ways which change their bioavailability and toxicity, and which will then pose unexplored [hazards to] environmental health.[38]

Given the large volume, high toxicity, and meager knowledge of these synfuels plant wastes, any strong pressures upon government to subordinate ecological protection to economic benefits in synfuels development pose as severe an environmental danger as did nuclear power development.

Shaky Economics. Federal sponsors of synfuels R&D may be faced with circumstances encouraging them to subsidize heavily synfuels development in the face of highly discouraging economic prospects. In the early days of the commercial nuclear power program, large federal subsidies to the first nuclear generating plants were rationalized as necessary to lure private investors into the field whereupon it was predicted the economics would become more favorable. Commercial nuclear facilities continually failed to establish a strong profit record, however. The industry was nevertheless federally supported and its shaky economics obscured long after the problem should have been faced squarely.

It is by no means clear that commercial synthetic fuels will be economically attractive. Consider the economic circumstances of Canada's major synthetic fuels facility in Alberta. To the uncritical observer, the plant appears to be successful. A consortium of private and public corporations have financed the facility to manufacture petroleum from oil shale. When complete, two plants currently under construction will produce 130,000 barrels of synthetic fuels daily, about 6 percent of Canada's total crude oil production in 1979. When a third plant is finished, the complex might produce as much as a quarter of Canada's total crude oil consumption by the late 1980s. These plants continue to be heavily subsidized, however. Although they produced for the first time a profit of $19 million in 1978, the smallest existing plant still carried a 10-year deficit of $35.3 million.

Furthermore, oil shale conversion, like other synthetic fuels technologies, is highly energy intensive, and any estimate of the energy generated by the plants must take account of the energy also required to produce it. A 260-megawatt electric generating facility was necessary to provide the Canadian facility's own power. The large trucks required to transport shale and waste within the plant get only four miles to each gallon of gasoline. And the four mammoth draglines used for shale mining, each with a bucket capable of carrying 130 tons of material, require enough electricity to light a city of 4,500 people.[39]

Some economists believe that, like the Alberta installation, other synfuels technologies will require such substantial energy sources and governmental economic props that their true value to the nation may not justify these costs. In any event, the U.S. experience with nuclear R&D would suggest that the enormous technical, economic, and political investment to be made in synfuels R&D might well create a strong disinclination among public agencies to admit any economic deficiencies of synfuels or to face them realistically.

In short, the risks to the nation arise not only from the technological or economic gambles inherent in creating a viable synfuels industry but also from the danger that the public and its government will not, or cannot, learn enough from the mistakes in nuclear R&D management to prevent their repetition.

CONCLUSION

This chapter has been an exercise in social accounting. We have explored the benefits and costs of governmental cooperation with business in energy research and development. We have observed that the federal government in the last three decades has become the largest investor and chief promoter of the nation's energy research. This research is primarily a collaborative activity embracing government, private industry, scientific research institutions, and a host of other enterprises. Federal energy research infuses billions of dollars into the U.S. economy each year and thus has become a major source of national economic productivity. Thousands of businesses, both large and small, depend upon this federal support to underwrite their own production, to create a healthy profit profile, and to obtain new investment capital. In short, federal energy R&D sustains a vast and important infrastructure of the U.S. economy.

We have noted, as well, the many sound reasons for federal support of energy R&D. Often government funding is essential to provide the incentives for private companies to conduct research that is vital to the nation but inappropriate, or unsuitable, for government itself to undertake. Moreover, sometimes private business is better able to conduct the research task than is the government. Nonetheless, we have seen that when government assumes a major responsibility for energy research funding or management, social and economic costs often result: unproductive or uneconomical programs may continue, excessive costs or delays may be imposed on energy research and development, and unwise technical decisions may be made.

These and other social costs arise because energy R&D programs develop their own powerful political constituencies that exert pressure on officials to protect programs despite their failures. This situation would be troubling if only because it represents billions of wasted federal dollars. The persistence of potentially dangerous technologies without sufficient public examination and debate adds to this concern. Federal management of R&D creates a constant problem—the necessity of a periodic public accounting to assure that the public benefits of R&D programs outweigh the social costs they impose.

All this would be little more than an exercise in history if it applied only to past energy programs. However, current federal management of domestic nuclear power facilities ignores many of the problems that we have associated with government handling of energy R&D. More importantly, the federal government is about to launch an ambitious synthetic fuels program that is vulnerable to the same mistakes experienced in other areas of federal energy development. In this perspective, the national experience with public management of energy research poses a continuing challenge that becomes more pressing as the nation's need for accelerated energy research expands. Can the United States summon its vast human and material resources, inspire their organization with its undisputed technological genius, and produce new energy technologies both efficiently and responsibly? The social benefits derived from federal energy research must be made to outweigh its costs during the next few decades when the nation most urgently requires a demonstration of competence and responsibility in its energy programs.

NOTES

1. Library of Congress, Congressional Research Service, *Coal Gasification and Liquefaction,* Issue Brief No. IB77105 (Washington, D.C.: U.S. Government Printing Office, 1978).
2. Hugh Heclo, "Issue Networks and the Executive Establishment," in *The New American Political System,* ed. Anthony King (Washington, D.C.: American Enterprise Institute, 1979), p. 102.
3. National Science Foundation, *An Analysis of Federal R&D Funding by Function,* No. 77-326 (Washington, D.C.: National Science Foundation, 1977).
4. John E. Tilton, *U.S. Energy R&D Policy: The Role of Economics* (Washington, D.C.: Resources For The Future, 1974), p. 4.
5. Ibid., chap. 3.
6. Barry Commoner, *The Politics of Energy* (New York: Alfred A. Knopf, 1979), chap. 5.
7. *New York Times,* February 25, 1978.
8. William Ophuls, *Ecology and the Politics of Scarcity* (San Francisco: W. H. Freeman and Co., 1977), p. 190.
9. Ibid.

10. Edward R. Tufte, *Political Control of the Economy* (Princeton, N.J.: Princeton University Press, 1978), p. 143.
11. Willis H. Shapley and Don I. Phillips, eds., *Research and Development in the Federal Budget, FY 1979* (Washington, D.C.: American Association for the Advancement of Science, 1979), p. 78.
12. Don K. Price, "Money and Influence: The Links of Science to Public Policy," *Daedalus* (Summer 1974): 101-102.
13. Ibid.
14. Tilton, *U.S. Energy R&D Policy*, p. 52.
15. W. Henry Lambright, *Governing Science and Technology* (New York: Oxford University Press, 1976), p. 44ff.
16. *New York Times,* December 5, 1978.
17. David H. Davis, *Energy Politics,* 2nd ed. (New York: St. Martin's Press, 1978), p. 180.
18. Lambright, *Governing Science and Technology,* p. 75.
19. Peter Metzger, *The Atomic Establishment* (New York: Simon & Schuster, 1972), p. 20.
20. Lambright, *Governing Science and Technology,* p. 74.
21. *New York Times,* July 9, 1979.
22. *New York Times,* March 24, 1978.
23. *New York Times,* July 9, 1978.
24. Ibid.
25. Robert Stobaugh and Daniel Yergin, eds., *Energy Future: Report of the Energy Project at the Harvard Business School* (New York: Random House, 1979), p. 118.
26. Library of Congress, Congressional Research Service, *Breeder Reactors: The Clinch River Project,* Issue Brief No. IB77088 (Washington, D.C.: U.S. Government Printing Office, 1978).
27. On the Clinch River project battle, see Library of Congress, Congressional Research Service, *Breeder Reactors;* U.S., General Accounting Office, *The Clinch River Breeder Reactor: Should the Congress Continue to Fund It?,* Report No. EMD-79-62 (Washington, D.C.: U.S. Government Printing Office, 1979); and U.S., General Accounting Office, *U.S. Fast Breeder Reactor Program Needs Direction,* Report No. EMD 80-81 (Washington, D.C.: U.S. Government Printing Office, 1980).
28. General Accounting Office, *The Clinch River Breeder Reactor,* p. 18.
29. *New York Times,* September 20, 1977.
30. Ibid.
31. General Accounting Office, *The Clinch River Breeder Reactor,* p. iv.
32. This source was interviewed by the author.
33. *New York Times,* September 2, 1979.
34. U.S., Department of Energy, *Environmental Readiness Document: Coal Gasification* (Washington, D.C.: U.S. Government Printing Office, 1978), p. 9.
35. U.S, Department of Energy, *Environmental Readiness Document: Coal Liquefaction* (Washington, D.C.: U.S. Government Printing Office, 1978), p. D-2.
36. Library of Congress, Congressional Research Service, *Coal Gasification and Liquefaction,* p. 13.
37. U.S., Department of Energy, *Coal Gasification,* pp. 2, 12, 14.
38. U.S., Department of Energy, *Coal Liquefaction,* p. 12.
39. *New York Times,* November 27, 1979.

7

Choices:
Energy Policy in the 1980s

One era of the energy crisis has already passed. The 1970s were a decade of revelation and appraisal. The 1980s, the second era, will be a decade of policy commitments. During the 1970s, the United States was compelled to recognize both its unstable energy economy and the need to reorganize political institutions and public policy to deal with the crisis. It was a decade of agenda-setting: energy issues had to be elevated to continuing salience on the national political agenda.

In retrospect, the energy policies of the 1970s were primarily temporary, and often misguided, efforts to come to terms with the new national energy condition. They were mostly experiments and expedients to buy time while public officials pondered more appropriate responses. Project Independence, which promised the chimera of national independence from imported oil by 1985, now seems little more than an effort to banish the intractable reality of dwindling domestic fuel reserves by an official government proclamation. President Carter's 1977 National Energy Plan was the first effort of a chief executive to portray the true character of the energy crisis to the American people. The plan was more important for its symbolism than for its substance, however, as Congress largely reduced Carter's proposal to incoherence. Except for a handful of measures including the 1978 gradual decontrol of crude oil and natural gas prices, the nation's energy policies during the 1970s were for the most part tentative and conservative.

The 1980s will be different. During this decade, the United States will commit its resources to energy policies destined to shape, perhaps irreversibly and unintentionally, the character of the U.S. energy structure in the next century. The nation will be making these long-term policy commitments not merely by means of legislation, executive orders, or other official declarations of substantive policy. Many energy policies currently being contemplated demand such a massive investment of resources for their implementation that they will acquire an embedded political and economic support structure that will be difficult, if not impossible, to turn aside later. The accretion of enormous social and physical resources about these programs may mean an implicit and irreversible U.S. commitment to new energy programs without full public recognition and debate of their implications. In other words, commitment to such policies may virtually preclude a later recourse to other energy options. Americans must recognize and examine the actual consequences of energy policies and debate these implications fully and openly to assure compatibility with wise energy use and democratic values.

In this final chapter, we will examine five of the issues whose resolution during the 1980s will decisively shape U.S. energy policy well into the next century. First, we will describe how Washington's choice of priorities among different energy technologies will lead the United States down a "hard" energy path or a "soft" energy path with different—and possibly dangerously different—social and economic consequences. The growth of energy regionalism in the United States will also be discussed to help us appreciate the difficulties faced by energy policymakers in reconciling these often conflicting regional interests with the national energy interest. Next we will explain the responsibility of policymakers to protect future generations from possibly dangerous risks from the rapid development of energy technologies. We will then discuss why the United States must look carefully and critically at the relationship between energy use and economic growth in choosing future energy policies. Finally, we will emphasize the need for policies that encourage the increasing ability of citizens and public officials to make informed judgments about the social, economic, and environmental ramifications of energy production— the need for the development of a national talent at technology assessment. Throughout this chapter, we will stress the importance of public involvement in the making of appropriate U.S. energy policy choices in the 1980s.

ENERGY PATHS: HARD AND SOFT OPTIONS

The crucial energy policies of the 1980s will involve some mix of three significantly different approaches to energy management: conservation, "hard" energy options, and "soft" energy options. Energy conservation stresses the more efficient use of existing energy resources: improved home insulation, passive solar technologies, more efficient automobile engine performance, and other techniques intended to prolong the availability of increasingly scarce petroleum and natural gas resources. Conservation can save significant quantities of petroleum and natural gas, but new energy production facilities and technologies will nevertheless be required to meet future national energy demand. The United States is at a juncture between two broad energy options, or alternative strategies, that will lead the country toward different energy futures. The nation must now decide what mix of these strategies it will implement in the 1980s.

Amory Lovins, a U.S. physicist and environmental activist, has suggested in his book *Soft Energy Paths: Toward a Durable Peace* that the alternative energy strategies facing the United States can be called "hard" and "soft" energy paths.[1] Lovins, whose ideas strongly influence current discussions of U.S. energy policy, explains that the "hard" energy path stresses sustained growth of energy production to meet anticipated future demand as projected from past energy consumption. This strategy means a rapid expansion in coal utilization, a new search for increasingly elusive oil and natural gas reserves, and continued growth of the nuclear power industry. Project Independence and the massive new synfuels program are examples of the hard energy path. This path also leads toward the continued growth well into the next century of centralized systems that generate electricity.

In comparison, the "soft" energy path emphasizes more restrained production of energy based on a deliberate effort to moderate future national demand. The soft energy strategy relies on solar and other renewable energies and favors better end use of existing energy sources. The soft energy path points to an energy future where small, decentralized systems form an increasingly large component of the U.S. energy sector.

The distinction between soft and hard energy paths is important if only because these alternatives entail significantly different magnitudes of national investment and differing orders of environmental risk and technical feasibility. But Lovins and other critics of hard energy paths have also extrapolated provocative political implications from economic and technical comparisons between the two paths. They assert that Americans must recognize the political consequences of alternative energy strategies because the two paths entail very different political costs, and risks. Ostensibly, the United States is selecting energy policies; actually, it is choosing different styles of future governance. This assumption of a crucial link between the organization of energy technologies and governmental structures, however speculative, has become the catalyst for a growing debate concerning the social implications of future energy policies.

Some Tough Questions about Hard Energy

Enough has already been said about hard energy options—synfuels technologies, increased coal combustion, and the nuclear power industry—to suggest that their enormous capital costs, environmental hazards, and technical uncertainties are indeed realities. Advocates of these technologies acknowledge such liabilities but remain convinced that their advantages will eventually outweigh their costs.

Less often emphasized is that hard energy strategies rely heavily upon centralized generation of electricity and production of synfuels, both inefficient forms of energy conversion yielding vast quantities of power ill-suited to its end use. Conversion of petroleum, natural gas, and coal to electricity wastes about two-thirds of the fuel potential in the original source; conversion of coal through synfuels technologies wastes at least one-third of coal's energy potential.[2] Uses of electricity including residential heating and cooling, industrial refrigeration, and commercial or industrial electric motor power could be more efficiently supplied by other means. Lovins explains:

> Plainly, we are using premium fuels and electricity for many tasks for which their high energy quality is superfluous, wasteful, and expensive, and a hard path would make this inelegant practice even more common. Where we want only to create temperature differences of tens of degrees, we should meet the need with sources whose potential is tens or hundreds of degrees, not with a flame temperature of thousands or a nuclear reaction temperature equivalent to trillions—like cutting butter with a chainsaw.[3]

In short, huge centralized generating systems are unnecessary to meet a large portion of the energy demand now placed upon them; continued expansion of such systems compounds this inefficiency many times. These systems are especially wasteful when soft energy technologies can provide far more efficient forms of energy conversion to electricity and a more appropriate quality of electricity for many end uses.

Lovins finds the political implications of expanding hard energy technologies the most objectionable. Rapid expansion will place heavy stress upon scarce resources such as labor, technical skills, materials, facility sites, and available capital, the result being "a compulsory diversion from whatever priorities are backed by the weakest constituencies."[4] In practice, this will mean a radical depletion of national resources available for the exploration and invention of more economically and environmentally benign technologies. Americans will be forced to become progressively more dependent upon inefficient energy technologies that will come to assume ever greater importance to national order. Already huge technological, commercial, and industrial institutions will increase in size due to massive infusions of national resources for expanded hard energy production and will acquire the political representation to resist modification of these arrangements. In the end, the development of soft energy technologies will be increasingly difficult as soft path components are "starved into garbled and incoherent fragments."[5] Hard energy technologies will crowd the limited energy policy space so fiercely that the United States will be unable to pursue other energy strategies simultaneously.

Lovins points out that centralized power generation, as the organizing principle of hard energy technologies, tends to create a technological elite whose command of essential public resources is not easily kept accountable to those dependent upon them:

> In an electrical world, your lifeline comes not from an understandable neighborhood technology run by people you know who are at your own social level, but rather from an alien, remote and perhaps humiliatingly uncontrollable technology run by a faraway, bureaucratized, technical elite who have probably never heard of you.

He predicts a divorce of social power from political accountability:

> Decisions about who shall have how much energy at what price also become centralized—a politically dangerous trend because it divides those who use energy from those who supply and regulate it. Those who do not like the decisions can simply be disconnected.

A third potential danger in hard energy strategies is the likelihood that objectionable political, legal, and institutional arrangements will have to be created to protect society from the environmental and political risks of technologies such as nuclear fission and fusion systems. Lovins notes:

> Discouraging nuclear violence and coercion requires some abrogation of civil liberties.... Guarding long-lived wastes against geological or social contingencies implies some form of hierarchical social rigidity or homogeneity to insulate the technological priesthood from social turbulence.[6]

In the end, Lovins speculates, the unique properties of nuclear energy may tempt government officials to subvert democracy in the name of social responsibility:

> Making political decisions about nuclear hazards that are compulsory, remote from social experience, disputed, unknown, or unknowable may tempt governments to bypass democratic decision in favor of an elitist technocracy.[7]

With its imperious demands on social resources and intolerance of alternative energy strategies, Lovins believes the hard energy path will narrow social diversity and freedom of choice by making it impossible for most citizens to choose soft energy systems.

Is Soft Energy an Alternative?

Compared to the bleak predictions for hard energy, the soft energy path has two advantages. Technically, the soft energy strategy advocates more efficient energy conversion and better matching of energy sources to end uses. Politically, the soft path avoids the coercive, centralized institutional structures promoted by hard energy systems. In the lexicon of Lovins and his collaborators, soft energy includes all forms of renewable energy (such as solar, hydropower, biomass, and geothermal), technologies that convert such energy to electricity, and energy conservation techniques. Soft, explains Lovins, is a "textual description, intended to mean not vague, mushy, speculative or ephemeral, but rather flexible, resilient, sustainable and benign."[8]

Solar technologies best illustrate the technical efficiency of soft energy systems. Solar energy systems convert energy to electricity much more efficiently than do hard energy technologies, and a large portion of end uses now served by centrally generated electricity could better utilize solar-generated electricity. Lovins asserts that the path of soft energy requires "a prompt and serious commitment to efficient use of energy" together with the "rapid development of renewable energy sources matched in scale and in energy quality to end use needs"[9] In other words, he calls for the immediate adoption and further development of major conservation measures, especially the increased use of solar techologies.

This matching of energy to its end use implies an increasing substitution of solar heating and cooling systems, electrovoltaic cells, and other forms of solar energy generation to replace centrally generated electricity now used in residential dwellings and industry. Advocates of a soft energy path assert that rapid development of soft energy technologies combined with various energy conservation measures already available to most Americans would greatly reduce the need for additional power plants that burn fossil fuels, nuclear power plants, and synfuels production facilities. Recognizing that several decades may pass before these soft energy technologies will be sufficiently developed to meet national energy demand, Lovins does recommend a short period of increased coal combustion. Coal would be used as a bridge fuel to lead the nation toward a more diversified energy structure, a temporary measure that would rapidly become obsolete as soft energy technologies replace existing central power systems.

From a political perspective, the premier advantage of soft energy technologies is that they "not only tolerate but encourage diverse values and lifestyles."[10] Solar energy systems are highly decentralized, easily controllable by their users, flexible in their uses, and potentially available to almost everyone (assuming unit costs can be reduced through further research and increased production). Individuals maintain the freedom to decide how to use such energy systems and cannot easily be disconnected from their energy lifelines by a remote bureaucracy or a technical breakdown. What is more, solar energy systems do not preclude individuals from using other forms of energy— centralized electricity, for instance—if they so choose. To enthusiasts of the soft energy path, solar energy is the technological antidote to most of the alleged social miseries anticipated from hard energy strategies.

The Meaning for the 1980s

Lovins has as many critics as defenders among those concerned with the nation's energy management—not only the predictable critics representing the nation's electric and nuclear power industries, but also scientists, economists, and other social science professionals. The critics argue less with Lovins's technical analysis of existing U.S. energy conversion—it is no secret that much energy is inefficiently converted to electricity and put to equally wasteful end uses—than with his apocalyptic predictions for U.S. society. Opponents assert that Lovins has postulated an energy future more suitable to science fiction. They note that the dire political consequences anticipated from hard energy are hardly inevitable and cite evidence that shows Lovins's social prophecies to be a tenuous fabric of suppositions, biases, half-truths, misinterpretations, and shaky inferences unsustainable upon critical examination. In the end, the validity of Lovins's social vision must be left to the test of time.

For the present, Lovins is less important for his conclusions than for the issues he raises. These issues provide essential criteria for evaluating any energy policies considered for adoption during the 1980s. First, Lovins's analysis is a forceful reminder that those energy technologies likely to survive and prosper in the next several decades will not necessarily be the most efficient, most socially or physically benign, or most technically elegant; instead they will be those technologies able to create and sustain a supportive political environment. As David Orr has observed, the development of energy technologies is not a Darwinian progression through which the "fittest" systems survive. As he explains it:

> [An] alternative and more accurate approach would place technological change in its social and political context and explain the development and adoption of a technology as a result of social values, a specific set of economic and political payoffs, and its technical feasibility.[11]

This implies that no dependable, self-correcting social mechanism exists in the United States to prevent the nation from sustaining, perhaps at severely mounting cost, increasingly obsolescent and inefficient energy forms. The nation's energy future must be shaped through political action.

Second, Lovins's work should alert those concerned with future energy policy to inquire about the extent to which new energy production arrangements may in fact require or encourage new legal and political contexts for their successful implementation. The compatibility of these arrangements with traditional constitutional and democratic values must be explored. Lovins's tendency to see disagreeable consequences from all hard energy paths should not obscure his insight.

The operation of nuclear power plants has created a number of special political and legal arrangements that illustrate the tendency of public officials to protect a technology deemed "essential." In a singular arrangement never extended to other energy producers, Congress passed the 1957 Price-Anderson Act that created a unique limitation on the insurance liability of nuclear power plants. In an effort to lure a private corporation into constructing a nuclear fuel reprocessing plant in West Valley, New York, that state's government signed an agreement largely releasing the company from any responsibility for its own radioactive wastes. Upon termination of the lease, the state of New York was to assume full responsibility for the "perpetual operation, surveillance, maintenance, replacement and insurance" of the abandoned site, anticipated to be highly radioactive by that time.[12]

The need to protect stored nuclear wastes or other energy-related toxics from sabotage, inadvertent release, or other human acts could easily lead public officials to advocate the abrogation of customary civil or criminal procedures or the subversion of constitutional rights in the name of public safety or national survival. This suggests an uncommon but important standard for evaluating new national investments in energy technologies: Are the legal and political contexts in which these technologies must operate compatible with U.S. political culture and law? If the answer is "no," "maybe," or "yes, but . . .," any evaluation of the technology must make such risks as explicit as possible.

Finally, the soft/hard energy perspective should warn those concerned with U.S. energy policy that energy strategies ought not to force out other future energy systems. The United States should encourage diversity, resilience, and practicality in its energy production, rather than launch crash programs based on hard energy technologies that promise to achieve extravagant results within a short time. Such crash programs have enormous political appeal because they promise high levels of public spending (hence much political pork) and appear to do something quickly and visibly about national problems. These hard energy policies can easily dominate energy planning.

Perversely, crash programs often become most formidable when failure threatens. As the sunk costs invested in a program rise, the potential losses from program failure also increase until the program's "stake holders" are loathe to admit defeat, even when faced with apparently convincing evidence. Indeed, to the extent that policymakers base their future political and economic planning upon the success of a crash program for energy development, they can ill afford its abandonment lest the whole skein of energy planning becomes unraveled.

If this situation seems excessively speculative, consider how closely the present U.S. commitment to synfuels production resembles a crash program. We have already observed that the White House and Congress, in a rare accord on energy matters, agreed in 1980 to appropriate $20 billion to subsidize synfuels development, an unprecedented gamble that the nation's technological reputation remained valid. This huge initial investment is staked upon a quick and massive energy return. The program intends to create by 1987 at least 10 synfuels plants, each capable of producing 50,000 barrels of oil equivalent daily, with a long-term objective of 2 million barrels by 1992 (about one-third of the 1980 U.S. imported oil supply). House Majority Leader James C. Wright Jr. has described the program as a "great stride forward toward making this country energy-independent."[13] The political investments in the synfuels program, like the economic ones, were mounting even before the ink dried on the president's signature on the bill.

Moreover, the synfuels program is committed to production targets considered speculative even by the most optimistic analysts. Failure—perhaps catastrophic failure—is possible. Should the program falter badly, would those interests heavily invested in its success be willing, or even able, to turn the nation's energy strategies in a different direction? Would solar technologies, energy conservation, and other alternative energy approaches, some perhaps only at critical early development stages, continue to prosper in the face of a collapsing synfuels program? More essential than the right answer is to know the right questions about energy policies in the 1980s.

POLITICAL EQUITY AND PUBLIC PARTICIPATION

As government energy policies of the 1980s increasingly involve decisions about which energy technologies to promote and where to site them, the need to expose the full range of social impacts from such decisions grows apace. Government institutions are keenly sensitive to the short-range, tangible economic impacts derived from prospective energy policies. Those interests affected by these policies commonly possess the sufficient resources to assure their viewpoints will be represented within government through lobbying, voting, and other traditional forms of political activism.

Other impacts, just as crucial, may not be as immediately apparent with the affected interests less organized to represent themselves. For example, the ecological devastation inflicted upon the Appalachian hills by strip mining became fully apparent only when decades magnified the environmental toll. Sometimes the true social costs of energy decisions may not be readily calculated because they are not easily rendered in economic terms. Deterioration in air quality over major national parks such as Yosemite and Yellowstone is likely if power generating plants are built in adjacent areas that contain readily accessible coal. The loss of this pristine air would constitute a major social impact for those citizens who live in these areas or use the parks for recreation. As these illustrations suggest, the social impacts of energy decisions can assume such a great diversity of forms and persist for such long periods of time that public officials must actively encourage procedures that promote their recognition to the fullest extent possible.

It is therefore important that the development of future energy policies include a generous measure of public participation to maximize opportunities for consideration of the full range of likely consequences. It is particularly imperative that this citizen involvement extend not only to the processes of agenda-setting, policy formulation, or legitimation, but especially to the stage of policy implementation where the administrative process may otherwise obscure the nature and implications of energy decisions. Activities more suited to the administrative process—such as public hearings, workshops, citizen advisory commissions, and community surveys—should play an increasingly important part in the implementation of new energy programs.

The public should be involved in broad-range energy policy decisions (such as an agency's determination of regulations for the construction of coal-fired generating plants) as well as the application of these general policies in particular cases (such as a decision to permit a power generating plant on a specific site). Indeed, it may only be through public involvement in the "little" decisions that the actual social impacts of broad administrative policies will be recognized. As David Orr remarks, a decision about where to site an energy facility involves important social equities:

The lack of participation conceals a system of winners and losers. The winners are cooled, coiffured, and entertained electrically, while the losers are strip-mined, irradiated, and polluted.[14]

Public involvement should penetrate the administrative process both broadly and deeply.

The federal government has attempted to decentralize energy decisions and to encourage a larger measure of public involvement in making them. Citizens have been invited to become active in the writing of agency regulations for environmental controls on energy production facilities. Decisions about the designation of federal lands for wilderness, national parks, national forests, and other uses that preclude their future development for energy needs are now also open to greater public scrutiny.

Increased public participation in future energy policymaking will be difficult despite its apparent virtues. Public participation is no panacea for resolving all the problems that energy decisions create for social equity. In fact, increased public involvement can actually intensify some of these inequities rather than ameliorate them and sometimes exacerbate conflict among the involved interests. It often works to the advantage of the best organized groups that may be disproportionately drawn from the middle class, the public interest lobbies, or perhaps the business and industrial interests likely to favor relatively unrestrained energy production. Proponents of rapid energy production have criticized such participation in the administrative process on the grounds that it delays the construction of needed energy facilities, imposes enormous additional costs upon government, and often leads to prolonged litigation by environmentalists and others who speak for special interests.

As the federal government moves into new domains of energy management in the 1980s, these issues will be raised with increasing forcefulness. Although the benefits from extensive public involvement in energy policymaking often equal or exceed the costs incurred, it is by no means certain that public participation will foster greater public acceptance of energy decisions. Expanded participation in the administrative process does expose a wider range of viewpoints and information to the government's attention, however. Public involvement also promotes opportunities for those interests affected to identify their stake in energy policy decisions.

The issues involved in public participation in energy policies can be better appreciated by examining two problems of political equity that will be characteristic of energy planning during the 1980s. These problems illuminate the great diversity of social impacts that must be considered in any evaluation of energy policies in this decade.

Energy Regionalism

The organization of the major energy-producing and consuming states into regional blocs has infused new vigor into regional claims upon national energy policy. Reconciling these increasingly aggressive assertions of regional interests with the compelling need for an effective national energy policy is a major task for policymakers in the 1980s.

The West. One especially troublesome set of issues is posed by the concerns of the western and northern Plains states that contain most of the nation's remaining coal, uranium, oil shale, and petroleum reserves. Spokesmen for these energy-producing states insist upon the rapid development of their energy resources but deplore the devastation of the land or the native culture. Most western political leaders have been quite eager to develop their energy resources provided their states keep a healthy share of the mining royalties and also receive fair federal compensation for the social burdens inflicted by an energy boom. A recent governor of New Mexico was fond of saying that his state was "the Saudi Arabia of uranium."

These leaders are particularly aggrieved that most of their energy resources lie within their grasp but outside their control under federal authority. A third of western lands is public domain—approximately 750 million acres of land, excluding Alaska. In the opinion of the western states, the fate of this land and its energy resources ultimately resides in the hands of a remote, impersonal Washington bureaucracy responsible to elected officials who largely represent other regions and interests. Local leaders believe that state-controlled energy resources would permit more ambitious exploration for new resources and do away with "unreasonable" environmental restrictions for energy production on federal lands. Many western state governments have staged a so-called sagebrush rebellion to reclaim jurisdiction over these territories. The Nevada legislature, for instance, declared in 1979 that 49 million acres of land controlled by the U.S. Bureau of Land Management belonged to the state, a move calculated to promote a lawsuit challenging the constitutionality of further U.S. ownership of the western public domain.[15]

As Colorado Governor Richard D. Lamm has said, a "growing feeling of regional paranoia" exists in the West, a suspicion that their land and people will be reduced to an "energy colony" through exploitation by the more populous, politically powerful, energy-hungry Northeast and burgeoning Sunbelt states.[16] "First they steal our water, then they pollute our air, next they strip the whole West for their stupid energy consumption, and now, in return, they give us everybody else's radioactive excrement," complained the mayor of a small North Dakota community situated near a scheduled federal nuclear waste depository.[17] "They"—the water thieves, air polluters, and strip miners—means the economically and politically powerful: the big cities, the East, the power companies, and the Washington bureaucracy.

Such exploitation seems plausible when western state officials contemplate their impoverished national political power.[18] The entire congressional delegation from these western coal states does not equal that from Ohio, the nation's heaviest coal consumer. If a coalition of these energy-hungry states should wield its congressional power to insist on generous access to western energy without adequate safeguards, the West fears a massive geographic displacement of energy development costs from the benefits would result. The city dwellers, suburbanites, easterners, and Sunbelters would get their coveted energy while the farmers, rural dwellers, and other residents of the thinly populated western regions would inherit the social, environmental, and economic penalties of producing it.

What is more, reckless local exploitation of energy resources may be as real a danger as the assumed threat from the West's energy-hungry neighbors. Many inhabitants of the West are extremely protective of their unique quality of life. Those who live by the land fully understand that the threat in unregulated energy development is degraded ground water and contaminated soil. But as western state and local governments become increasingly dependent upon mining royalties, federal assistance for energy development, and other forms of energy-generated income, state and local leaders may find it increasingly difficult to contain energy development within prudent bounds or to resist the demands of the state's energy producers.

The states of Louisiana and Alaska illustrate how energy revenues can readily capture state budgets. Traditionally a large oil and gas producer, Louisiana receives from energy-related taxes 40 percent of its annual budget. Alaska, like a sourdough miner suddenly striking it rich, is flush with tax revenues from the Alaskan oil pipeline. Oil taxes now account for two-thirds of state expenditures.[19] In the wake of this bonanza, Alaska's political leadership has mounted a warlike national campaign to free its enormous wilderness area from federal control. In July 1979, the state bought a full-page advertisement in major national newspapers to declare:

> Alaska has the potential to help eliminate the lines at America's gas stations. We have known energy reserves, or the potential, to heat—and cool—into the next century. . . . We ask only for title to our lands; access to them; the right to manage our fish and wildlife . . . the exclusion of known valuable resources from prohibitive federal systems.[20]

Unless counterbalanced with vigilant protection of the environment, this preoccupation with energy production could easily make

Alaska its own worst enemy. Local political and administrative processes must be opened to the active participation of all "stake holders"
to achieve the delicate balance between western energy production
and resource conservation.

The Northeast and Midwest. Lacking abundant energy reserves,
the energy-dependent states of the Northeast and Midwest fear they
will be forced to pay excessively for their energy, resulting in a
massive outflow of resources and economic stagnation. In 1980 the
Northeast-Midwest Congressional Coalition, representing members of
Congress from 18 states, issued a statement describing the different
regional impacts anticipated from increasing energy consumption and
oil price decontrols. By 1990, the statement noted, the energy-producing
states would enjoy an increase of $127.7 billion from severance taxes
on conventional energy sources.[21] The energy-consuming states favor
increased federal spending within their regions to offset the drain
of their mounting energy expenditures. They also advocate measures
to prevent excessive profits and price gouging among energy producers.

The South and Sunbelt. As the nation's fastest growing regions,
the South and Sunbelt states are equally concerned that their large
demand for future energy be given equal priority in national energy
policy decisions. States like Georgia, North Carolina, and South Carolina—where rapid commercial and industrial development depends
on the secure, expanding availability of electric power—seek assurance
that the fuels and facilities necessary to provide that power will
be available and that a national energy rationing plan, if enacted,
will take full account of their increasing energy demands.

Few states are more skittish about energy prices or availability
than those Sunbelt states whose economies depend heavily on tourism.
Summer travel is a $115 billion business in the United States, and
the brief gasoline shortage of summer 1979 was an economic chill
particularly for the Sunbelt. Indicators of tourist activity for that
summer were down as much as 20 percent. Florida, where tourism
provides one-third of state revenues, considers any threatened disruption of this market an economic emergency. The Arab oil embargo
of winter 1973 cost the Miami area alone more than $600 million
in business and the state $30 million in tax revenues. Tourist-dependent
states are especially concerned that they will suffer disproportionately
from short-term increases in gasoline prices or constrictions on national
gasoline supply. The economic sectionalism of the South has been
epitomized in a battle cry from Georgia Governor George Busbee:

> We are vastly out-numbered, out-organized and out-funded by the
> Northern coalition. We are faced with a situation where well-organized
> groups are generating often self-serving data from which Federal

policy is being derived—at our expense. We cannot afford to sit idly by.[23]

Vigorous energy regionalism introduces a strong tendency to polarize and fragment the political interests from which coalitions must be created to sustain an effective national energy policy. The extreme diversity of these interests—within regions as well as between them—requires expanded procedural arrangements for government decision-making, particularly in the administrative process, that will permit such interests to be recognized.

Who Speaks for our Children?

Energy decisions in the 1980s also must be held accountable to future generations in some formal and explicit manner because these choices involve complex transfers of social impacts across vast periods of time. Decisions about the rate of energy production, for example, involve determinations of how fast to consume rapidly exhaustible resources. In effect, the current generation possesses the almost deific power to deny, deplete drastically, or conserve the energy inheritance of the United States and the rest of the world.

Many of the energy technologies under development or proposed for rapid commercialization may create large volumes of dangerously persistent toxic wastes, radioactive materials, and other process residues that will have to be controlled by future generations. The half-life of some radioactive wastes from nuclear power plants is several hundred thousand years. In many cases, toxics likely to result from synfuels technologies are known or suspected carcinogens or mutagens. The nation's domestic nuclear power program lacked proper recognition of the difficulty in disposing of such wastes. The United States at present has no proven procedures, nor extensive experimental evidence, for safe disposal of synfuels wastes. These energy technologies are being developed and proliferated with the implicit assumption that their hazards will eventually be technically manageable in a manner acceptable to future generations.

Complex experimental technologies can create surprises. It is often difficult, if not impossible, for conscientious scientists and technicians to predict the developmental course of a new technology. Even familiar technologies that are considered manageable can have subtle or sustained low-level detrimental effects whose cumulative impact remains significant but unrecognized for decades. The greenhouse effect from fossil fuel combustion was not identified (in fact, was not even considered plausible enough to merit concern) until after coal combustion technologies had been widely used for decades.

The hazardous environmental effects of fossil fuel recovery, quite apart from damage inflicted by technologies that utilize such fuels, also persist through time. Strip mining is an obvious example. With reclamation techniques barely beyond their experimental stages, it remains an open question whether the pervasive ecological disruption from stripping in Appalachia and the West can be technically controlled. Just as problematical is the government's ability to sustain the will to enforce a rigorous national restoration program. Environmental degradation from fossil fuel recovery that depends upon government regulation for its containment is captive to the public mood and political priorities of a constantly changing electorate. One generation unleashes an environmental menace and vows to keep it at bay, but another may lack the will, or the means, to redeem such a promise.

In effect, advanced energy technologies have changed the meaning of "social risk." An extremely delicate balance must be struck between the calculated risks for future generations and the possibly immense social costs of not developing a technology at all. While many energy technologies now under development or active experimentation (like solar, wind, and geothermal systems) are predictably so benign as to pose relatively few cross-generational risks, others (such as nuclear fusion technologies) pose serious risks as well as potentially immense benefits.

In practical terms, protecting the interests of succeeding generations in energy technology development requires that such interests be identified early and responsibly in governmental deliberations concerning these technologies. The implications for energy policy in the 1980s are profound:

—The long-range effects of a technology's development should be weighed along with other impacts.

—No technology should be developed unless these long-term consequences have been identified.

—The interests of succeeding generations should, if necessary, be given legal standing or other formal status to permit those who represent these interests to intervene administratively in governmental decisions about technology development.

—The long-term impacts of technology development should be calculated on a scale that distinguishes gradients of risk across a broad range of impacts—from dangers to human survival at one extreme to those risks that affect particular institutions, localities, or social groups at the other.

—Technologies in the highest risk categories should be subject to requirements for extraordinary legislative majorities, mandatory frequent program reauthorizations, compulsory scientific certification, and other safeguards.

—The process of risk assessment should require that public participation occur at every significant phase of technology development.

Some critics have suggested that the development of hazardous energy technologies must involve a "social forecasting" to assure that the social effects of technologies are compatible with the values of a democratic society. Among others, Amory Lovins and David Orr have suggested that the United States should develop no technologies that cannot be democratically controlled—in effect, the institutional design for the public management of a technology should prevent a "technological priesthood" that may assume power via technology manipulation or a monopoly of technical information. Others have argued that no energy technologies or production sites should be developed unless a majority of those citizens living and working near the sites have approved them. These proposals for social forecasting are an effort to force decisionmakers to weigh the social and political spillovers from an energy technology on an equal basis with its relatively more easily determined economic and technical implications.

None of these many proposals for greater sensitivity to generational equity in energy decisions is free of difficulties in substance or implementation. How far into the future should this equity extend? How can the possibly conflicting interests of future generations be reconciled with those of the present one? How can decisions be made when many social impacts can only be stated in terms of degrees of risk, or the necessary information can only be obtained long after such decisions must be made? And so forth. Regardless of the difficulties, however, issues of generational risk must now be explicitly introduced into the energy policymaking process.

RETHINKING FUTURE ENERGY DEMAND

Debate over energy policy is often driven by unexamined and unarticulated assumptions. Two persistent notions commonly underlie assertions that U.S. energy production must be expanded extensively. One assumption is that a slackening rate of growth in energy production will drag with it the pace of future economic growth. The other is that future demand for electric power will continue near the historic trend, at an incremental growth rate close to demand during the last several decades. Such rationalizations for an energy production boom merit critical appraisal given the enormous problems inherent in a massive national drive for more energy.

Enough studies are now available to suggest that the relationship between national energy consumption and economic growth is not linear. Energy production does not necessarily predict economic growth.

Data from the Harvard Business School, together with studies from other public and private institutions, indicate that the western industrialized nations have often been able to achieve and sustain relatively high levels of economic growth without necessarily expanding energy production on the same scale.[24] Recent U.S. experience suggests as much. In 1978, the United States consumed only 2 percent more petroleum than the previous year, and energy use increased about 1.9 percent, while the economy expanded by 3.9 percent. The executive director of the Petroleum Industry Research Foundation, himself a leading petroleum economist not likely to argue against the growth of future energy production, nonetheless remarked in 1979, "People were saying this kind of thing [conservation] would lead to stagnation of the economy but it hasn't."[25]

Further evidence that economic growth and energy production do not necessarily march in tandem is suggested by 1979 statistics. Between 1978 and 1979, U.S. energy production actually declined slightly from 78.15 quads (or quadrillion Btu) to 78.02 quads, while the gross national product (GNP) rose by 2.3 percent. In fact, during the 1970s energy consumption grew by 1.9 percent each year, but the average GNP increased by 2.9 percent. By achieving greater technical efficiency in energy use and by substituting labor or capital resources for energy, the United States apparently has been able to keep economic growth significantly ahead of energy consumption.[26]

Prior to the 1970s, it was considered economic gospel that the U.S. demand for electricity would increase approximately 7 percent each year. This figure was commonly used to estimate the nation's future energy demand. The 1970s have refuted this notion of increased demand, however. In 1978, U.S. electric power consumption rose only 2.8 percent; between 1973 and 1978, annual consumption increased an average of barely 3 percent. The nation's utilities nevertheless continued to increase new generating capacity according to expected future demand based on the historic trend. By 1980, the industry had about twice the reserve generating capacity considered adequate as a safety margin.[27] Many utility spokesmen and economists attribute the significant slackening of demand for new electricity to rising energy prices. As many economists had predicted, market forces have been imposing energy conservation upon the American consumer.

These statistics about energy, electricity, and economic growth have important implications for energy planning in the 1980s. The data suggest that energy conservation should not be equated with economic recession or stagnation, as evangelists for expanded energy production have often implied. Uncritically accepted, this reasoning readily provokes a disruptive social polarization over energy policy. Minorities, organized labor, the economically disadvantaged, and others who associate a vigorous economy with social advancement are likely to suspect that policies promising controls on economic growth discriminate against them, in effect if not by intent. In other words, energy conservation can be made to appear the instrument of social prejudice dignified as sound resource management. The president of the Edison Electric Institute, the national association of investor-owned utilities, implied such an attitude when he asserted in 1980 that expansion of electric generating capacity was desirable "in the best interests of the poor and because it would allow greater economic growth."[28] It should now be apparent that the relationship between increased energy use and economic growth can no longer be treated as axiomatic. By implication, energy conservation is not necessarily incompatible with an expanding economy.

Current estimates of future energy demand must be carefully reexamined, particularly if they are derived from econometric models. Such projections may in fact be extrapolations from the historic trend of electric power consumption or predictions based on the assumption that slackening energy production precludes economic growth. It is important to determine, if possible, what assumptions went into the models, although such information is usually less publicized than the model's predictions.

It follows that proposals for new federal energy projects must be critically examined for questionable presumptions of energy consumption patterns. Federal energy agencies are often tempted to accept higher projections of future energy demand that create a more persuasive case for their new projects. One 1978 study of future energy demand in the Northwest, for instance, found that the federal agencies eligible to construct energy projects there had consistently estimated regional energy demands well above the projections determined by private institutions.[29] Rarely is the public sophisticated enough to challenge the assumptions underlying agency forecasts. The longer inaccurate energy growth data remain unchallenged in government planning, the more likely that this data will be reproduced, borrowed, and used to support other government studies.

Inaccurate projections of future energy patterns are not confined to electricity demand or relationships between the GNP and the rate of energy production. Almost *all* extrapolations of energy data from the past to the future should be treated as tentative and revisable on the basis of our present awareness that patterns of energy use can and do change, sometimes suddenly and dramatically. As Amory Lovins remarks, "trends are not destiny." History should not be treated as a sort of blinder on the imagination, as if the future must be forecast by a peculiar logic from past experience. Energy planning has to be free to challenge historic trends, to reject automatic extrapolations from the past to the future, and to examine the premises upon which future world scenarios are constructed.

NEEDED: CONTINUING NATIONAL
TECHNOLOGY ASSESSMENT

It should now be apparent that energy technologies are both cause and solution to national energy problems. No future energy policies can be properly evaluated without careful attention to the environmental, economic, political, and other impacts of existing or proposed energy technologies. The nation's ability to deal both wisely and decisively with its present energy problems presumes a capacity to understand and assess the present and future effects of energy technologies upon all aspects of U.S. society.

Much can be done to strengthen the national capacity for technology assessment. The panoply of federal institutions with responsibility for technology assessment—specifically the science advisory committees to the White House, Office of Technology Assessment, General Accounting Office, and the National Academy of Sciences—should be preserved and strengthened. If possible, their resources and services should be made available to state and local governments. While a variety of different organizations and structures can be created to encourage technology assessment at state and local levels (state colleges and universities could be employed in this task), it is important that the capacity for this technology assessment be developed before the crucial energy issues of the 1980s have been largely resolved.

Public interest groups, particularly scientific organizations and other professional groups with a competence in technology assessment, should also become actively involved in government policymaking. To be sure, significant costs are involved in encouraging this group activism, including delay in formulating crucial policies, increased contention and litigation over many policies, and even the eventual cancellation of some large or prestigious energy projects. Balanced against these losses is the recognition that a growing competence in technology assessment among private interests has often been responsible for uncovering past mistakes in government energy planning, for preventing or revising existing energy plans deemed inadequate, and for providing public officials with a higher quality of substantive information upon which to base energy decisions.

Finally, technology assessment should be included in the curriculum of the nation's schools as a routine part of science education. Such a component would introduce students to the importance of technology assessment, suggest how it can lead to improved national planning, and show where failures of technology assessment have proven costly. The intent of such an education should not be to provoke a continuing suspicion of technology, but instead to help students become individuals capable of responsible judgments about future technology issues. This proposal for a public consciousness-raising about technology and its social meaning should not be an impossible nor even unwelcome task for a nation that prides itself on its scientific genius.

CONCLUSION

The ending of this book takes us back to the beginning. In the first chapter, we noted that the management of the nation's energy problems has increasingly become a governmental responsibility. Indeed, the nation's ability to solve its energy dilemma now depends as much upon the character of its political system as upon the character of its national resources. Energy *politics* matters just as much as economics, technology, population growth, resources, or any other factor in shaping the character of U.S. energy use, currently or in the future.

The issues explored in this chapter highlight this intimate relationship between government and energy management. These issues illustrate that virtually all important energy problems routinely gravitate toward government. The proper priorities between hard and soft energy systems, the balancing of regional energy interests, the protection of future generations from the hazards of energy production, the appropriate rate of future energy growth, the need for technology assessment—inseparable issues in the development of any energy policy—are now governmental problems for the 1980s. The inescapable connection between government, politics, and energy management means that the U.S. capacity to manage its energy problems successfully requires that its governmental and political system as well as its resources be adequate for that task.

"Adequate" means several things. First, resolving energy problems in the 1980s will require that policymakers overcome their biases about energy production inherited from earlier generations of energy abundance. It means that U.S. public officials should avoid the temptation to rely exclusively on a familiar incremental political style. Finally, it means that officials must balance concern for the environment and future generations against private interests and present needs in making energy policy choices. None of this is easily or swiftly accomplished. It remains essential, however, that the U.S. political system exhibit the resiliency and creativity to adapt old institutions and political styles to new emerging energy realities. The energy crisis is a testing of U.S. institutions as well as a testing of its technology and resources.

The intimate connection between energy problems and government is also a reminder that national energy policies must meet the test of political feasibility. We have stressed the technical and political constraints that limit and guide government officials—the "givens" in the governmental setting to which policy must conform. The energy policies likely to be successful in the 1980s—those that address most usefully the issues we have explored in this chapter—will be policies that lie within the capacity of government and the political process to achieve. They will not necessarily be the "best" policies judged by a strict standard of logic, fairness, or technical finesse but those taking account of the potential strengths and limits inherent in the U.S. political process. One can hope that American leaders have the imagination and courage to demand that the nation's political institutions produce the best possible solutions to energy problems given these situational and political constraints. Ultimately, the nation's energy planning must be based upon the hope—perhaps it is a wish—that the policies government can implement are those it needs to implement.

NOTES

1. The most complete statement among Lovins's many descriptions of the alternative energy paths is found in Amory B. Lovins, *Soft Energy Paths: Toward A Durable Peace* (New York: Harper & Row, 1979).
2. Ibid., chap. 2.
3. Ibid., p. 40.
4. Ibid., p. 54.
5. Ibid., p. 59.
6. Ibid., p. 55.
7. Ibid., p. 56.
8. Ibid., p. 38.
9. Ibid., pp. 38-39.
10. Ibid., p. 152.
11. David W. Orr, "U.S. Energy Policy and the Political Economy of Participation," *Journal of Politics*, vol. 41, no. 1 (November 1979): 1053.
12. *New York Times Magazine*, April 10, 1977. See also U.S., General Accounting Office, *Status of Efforts to Clean Up the Shut-down Western New York Nuclear Service Center*, Report No. EMD-80-69 (Washington, D.C.: U.S. Government Printing Office, 1980).
13. *New York Times*, June 17, 1980.
14. Orr, "U.S. Energy Policy and the Political Economy of Participation," p. 1049.
15. *New York Times*, September 2, 1979.
16. *New York Times*, May 2, 1978.
17. *New York Times*, May 10, 1978. On the western regional viewpoint, see U.S., General Accounting Office, *Rocky Mountain Energy Resource*

Development: Status, Potential, and Socioeconomic Issues, Report No. EMD-77-23 (Washington, D.C.: U.S. Government Printing Office, 1977).

18. On the political implications of this regional disparity in political influence, see Walter A. Rosenbaum, *Coal and Crisis* (New York: Praeger Publishers, 1978), chap. 5.
19. *New York Times,* June 24, 1978.
20. *New York Times,* July 2, 1979.
21. *New York Times,* April 20, 1980.
22. *New York Times,* September 19, 1979.
23. *New York Times,* December 18, 1977.
24. On the relationship between energy use and world economic growth, see Mason Willrich, *Energy and World Politics* (New York: The Free Press, 1975), chap. 4; Sam H. Schurr et al., *Energy in America's Future* (Baltimore: Johns Hopkins University Press, 1979), chaps. 3, 4; and Robert Stobaugh and Daniel Yergin, eds., *Energy Future: Report of the Energy Project at the Harvard Business School* (New York: Random House, 1979), chap. 6.
25. *New York Times,* March 4, 1979. On the problems in predicting future energy demand from historic trends, see National Academy of Sciences, Committee on Nuclear and Alternative Energy Systems, *Energy In Transition: 1985-2010* (San Francisco: W. H. Freeman and Co., 1980), chap. 2.
26. *New York Times,* May 18, 1980.
27. *New York Times,* April 6, 1980.
28. Ibid.
29. U.S., General Accounting Office, *Region at the Crossroads: The Pacific Northwest Searches for New Sources of Electric Energy,* Report No. EMD-78-76 (Washington, D.C.: U.S. Government Printing Office, 1978).

Glossary of Energy Acronyms

AEC	Atomic Energy Commission
bbl	Barrel
Btu	British thermal unit
CBO	Congressional Budget Office
CEQ	Council on Environmental Quality
CRP	Clinch River project
DOE	Department of Energy
DOI	Department of the Interior
EIA	Energy Information Administration
EPA	Environmental Protection Agency
ERA	Economic Regulatory Administration
ERDA	Energy Research and Development Administration
FEA	Federal Energy Administration
FERC	Federal Energy Regulatory Commission
FPC	Federal Power Commission
GAO	General Accounting Office
JCAE	Joint Committee on Atomic Energy
LMFBR	Liquid metal fast breeder reactor
NAS	National Academy of Sciences
NEPA	National Environmental Policy Act of 1969
NEP	President Carter's 1977 National Energy Plan
NRC	Nuclear Regulatory Commission
OCS	Outer Continental Shelf

OPEC	Organization of Petroleum Exporting Countries
OTA	Office of Technology Assessment
RD&D	Research, development, and demonstration
R&D	Research and development
SMCRA	Surface Mining Control and Reclamation Act of 1977
TVA	Tennessee Valley Authority

Suggested Readings

Carnesale, Albert, et. al. *Options For U.S. Energy Policy*. San Francisco: Institute For Contemporary Studies, 1977.

Caudill, Harry. *My Land Is Dying*. New York: E. P. Dutton, 1973.

Congressional Quarterly. *Energy Policy*. Washington, D.C.: Congressional Quarterly, 1979.

Davis, David H. *Energy Politics*. 2nd ed. New York: St. Martin's Press, 1978.

Ford Foundation, Nuclear Energy Policy Study Group. *Nuclear Power Issues and Choices*. Cambridge: Ballinger Publishing Co., 1977.

Lambright, W. Henry. *Governing Science And Technology*. New York: Oxford University Press, 1976.

Mitchell, Edward J., ed. *Energy: Regional Goals and The National Interest*. Washington, D.C.: American Enterprise Institute, 1976.

National Academy of Sciences, National Research Council. *Energy In Transition, 1985-2010*. San Francisco: W. H. Freeman and Co., 1980.

Ophuls, William. *Ecology and the Politics of Scarcity*. San Francisco: W. H. Freeman and Co., 1977.

President's Commission on Coal. *Coal Data Book*. Washington, D.C.: U.S. Government Printing Office, 1980.

Schurr, Sam H., et al. *Energy In America's Future*. Baltimore: Johns Hopkins University Press, 1979.

Stobaugh, Robert, and Yergin, Daniel, eds. *Energy Future: Report of the Energy Project at the Harvard Business School*. New York: Random House, 1979.

U.S., Congress, Office of Technology Assessment. *Application of Solar Technology to Today's Energy Needs*. Washington, D.C.: U.S. Government Printing Office, 1978.

———. *The Direct Use of Coal*. Washington, D.C.: U.S. Government Printing Office, 1978.

Index